I0754911

RESTRUNG

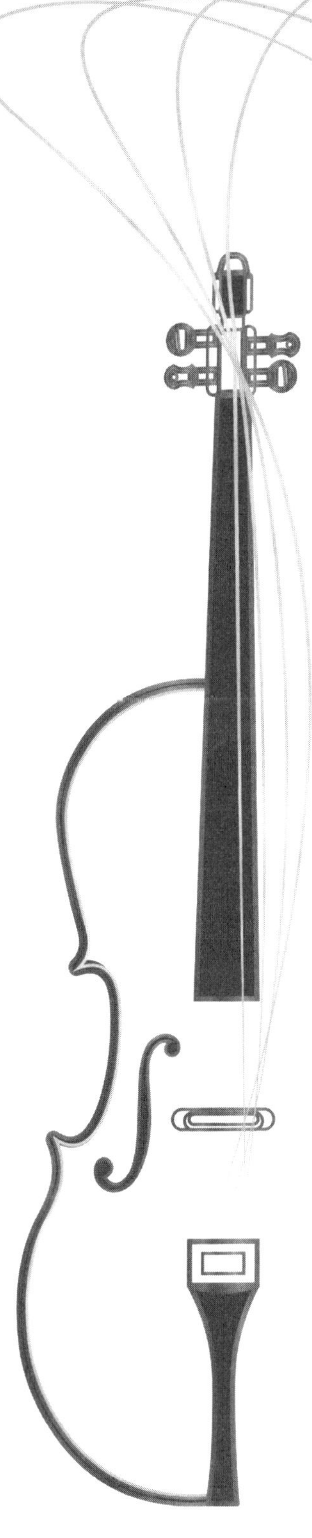

RESTRUNG

A Memoir *of* Music *and* Transformation

VIJAY GUPTA

DA CAPO

New York Boston

Da Capo
Hachette Book Group
1290 Avenue of the Americas
New York, NY 10104
dacapopublishing.com
@dacapopublishing

First Edition: June 2026

Da Capo is an imprint of Grand Central Publishing. The Da Capo name and logo are registered trademarks of Hachette Book Group, Inc.

The publisher is not responsible for websites (or their content) that are not owned by the publisher.

The Hachette Speakers Bureau provides a wide range of authors for speaking events. To find out more, visit hachettespeakersbureau.com or email HachetteSpeakers@hbgusa.com.

Da Capo books may be purchased in bulk for business, educational, or promotional use. For information, please contact your local bookseller or email the Hachette Book Group Special Markets Department at Special.Markets@hbgusa.com.

Interior Illustrations by Vijay Gupta

Print book interior design by Amy Quinn

Library of Congress Cataloging-in-Publication Data

Name: Gupta, Robert Vijay author
Title: Restrung : a memoir of music and transformation / Vijay Gupta.
Description: New York : Da Capo, 2026.
Identifiers: LCCN 2025049574 | ISBN 9780306835964 hardcover | ISBN 9780306835971 trade paperback | ISBN 9780306835988 ebook
Subjects: LCSH: Gupta, Robert Vijay | Violinists—United States—Biography | LCGFT: Autobiographies
Classification: LCC ML418.G95 A3 2026 | DDC 787.2092 [B]—dc23/eng/20260121
LC record available at https://lccn.loc.gov/2025049574

ISBNs: 978-0-306-83596-4 (hardcover); 978-0-306-83598-8 (ebook)

Printed in the United States of America

LSC-C

Printing 1, 2026

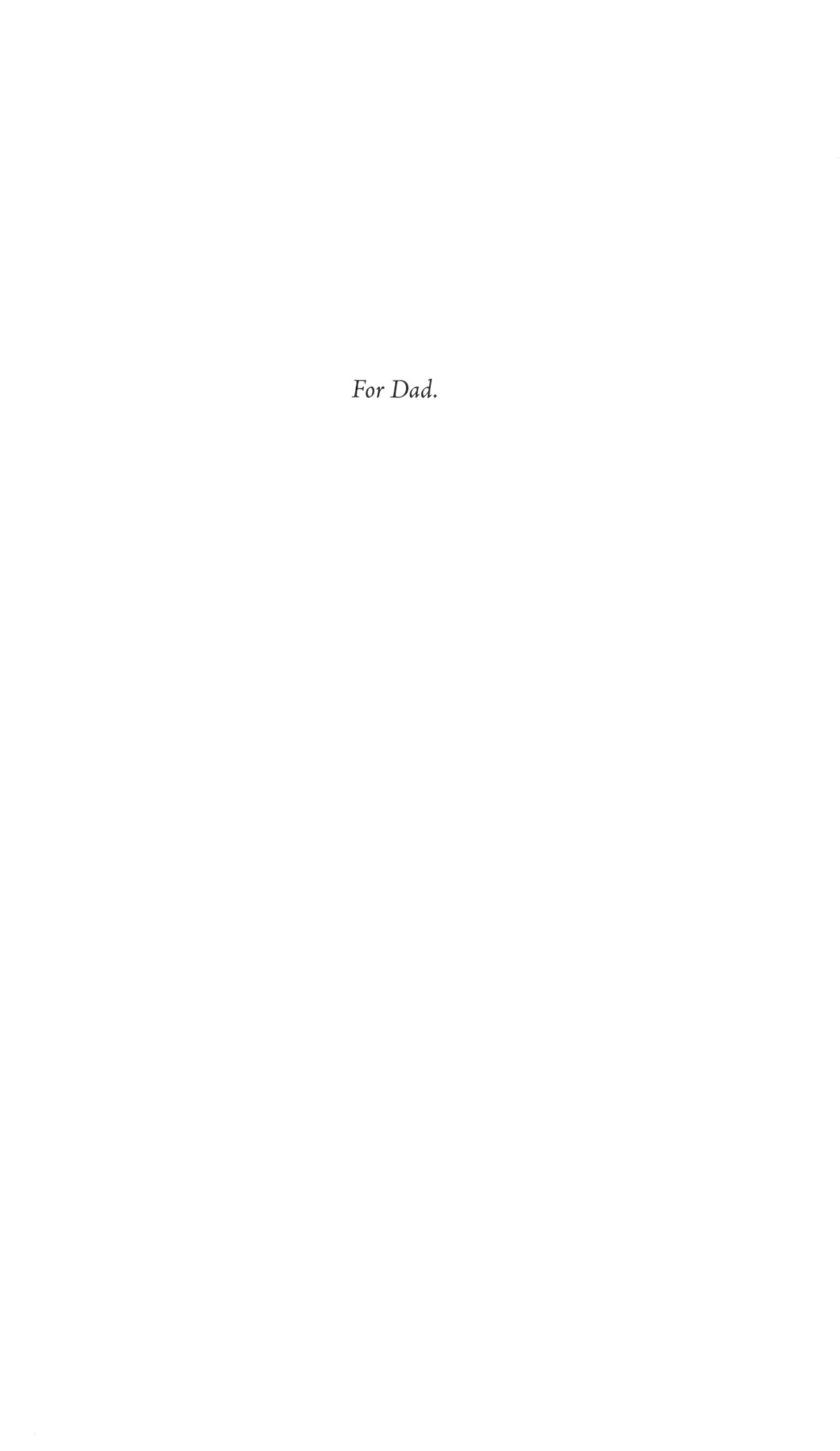
For Dad.

Music fills the infinite between two souls.

—**Rabindranath Tagore**

Memory is particular to each of us, and in the pages that follow, I have tried to tell the story that lives in me. I have changed certain names, descriptions, and dates, and some dialogue has been shaped through recollection.

CONTENTS

FOREWORD

"The Place Where Hope Begins"

Restrung is a rich and often astonishing feast of stories delivered with such vivid precision, such unflinching candor, and such heart that I suspect every reader will find herself shaken and inspired at her core. It takes us into the complexities of family ambition, the challenges of philanthropy, and the pressures that shadow achievement and into exactly the kinds of places—in our culture and inside our hearts—that many of us, all too often, try to avoid. Besides all that, it's crafted by a prodigiously talented young musician, speaker, and hero of social justice who just happens to be an enviably accomplished and nuanced writer.

Yet Hollywood itself might be shy about presenting the story of a boy born to struggling immigrant parents who finds himself playing Carnegie Hall at the age of eight, appearing on *The Oprah Winfrey Show* while still in elementary school, and, by age eleven, making his international debut as a violinist with Zubin Mehta and the Israel Philharmonic. He enters college at twelve, scores a research internship at Harvard's Center for Neurologic Diseases while going through the Yale School of Music, and, having completed his premed courses at seventeen, two years later wins a place as violinist with the world-class Los Angeles Philharmonic. And that's only the beginning of a transfixing and affecting story that questions all our performances—onstage and in life—and unsettles every assumption about how one can "disappear into excellence."

We learn here about Saint Julian and Handel's many trials, about bubonic plague on Skid Row and Bengali customs, all seamlessly woven together, but at its subtle heart *Restrung* begins as an unusually honest tale of the costs of immigration. Vivek Gupta, bearing the namesake "Bulbul," and his wife arrive in the United States from India, and he begins working at baggage claim at John F. Kennedy International Airport while his spouse, who's completed premed studies back home, labors behind a cash register at one of the airport's duty-free stores. They dream of making a better life for their two sons, and soon they succeed beyond every expectation. But as their eldest, Vijay, becomes Robert and Bobby and then Vijay again, he confronts many of the trickiest challenges of "making it" while his parents have to wonder whether they've raised him to become a stranger to them. Before we know it, we're learning more about America, and its archetypal stresses, than we might have ever reckoned with before.

~

I felt blessed the first time I got to meet Vijay. I didn't yet know his name when a friend suggested him as a perfect guest for the onstage conversation series I'd hosted for decades in Santa Barbara. Some of what my friend told me was arresting enough—he was one of the youngest violinists ever to be hired by a major American orchestra, he'd given a celebrated TED Talk, and he'd received a MacArthur genius grant—but nothing prepared me for the articulate, openhearted, and deeply poised soul who opened our conversation with some Bach and then spoke with rare conviction and intelligence about giving up his position within a major orchestra to bring music to prisons, to veterans, to chemotherapy wards, and to the largest population of the unhoused in the land.

We'd been fortunate to host Philip Glass, Meredith Monk, Salman Rushdie, and all kinds of other eminences over the years, but here was someone young, ardent, offering a new set of possibilities before our eyes. To every question Vijay offered a torrent of beautifully eloquent phrases and perceptions, and to every email I sent he would offer an instant and thoughtful heartfelt response. Here was the rare soul who knew the Benedictine monastery where I regularly stay—though he, as I, was born into Hinduism—as well as the even rarer being who could tell me what lies behind the triumphal chords in a Mozart or Bach concerto.

Part of the wonder of *Restrung* is, not surprisingly, that it shows how much music can soothe the savage beast—in each of us, but in society as well, and, most startling, in the musician, too; it's a guidebook to how a physician can heal himself, and how an artist may do the same. Music can never—as we painfully learn—heal the rifts within families or cure all of society's ills or people's troubles. But it offers us an image of something beyond ourselves that's within ourselves, and that, though marked by time, carries us out of time, and soars beyond every division of class or economic circumstance.

I can't remember ever reading descriptions of living within music—and feeling in tune with an audience, dissolving divisions, playing into a "deep listening"—as evocative as the ones I find here. And in the tiny biographies of composers he loves, Vijay reminds us how much of the beauty of their work arose from suffering. Reading of Robert Schumann, for example, I thought initially of convergences with Vijay's life—and then of how much the beloved nineteenth-century musician had in common with some of the shivering souls cast out into our streets.

Hollywood would give us a stirring account, if telling this story, of how the incarcerated are freed by music and the lost are found. Vijay, by contrast, is too seasoned and sophisticated to offer us instant solutions. He comes to see through the limits of speaking "fluent nonprofit," and he learns never to expect too much as he works to protect the dying from the interventions of the "well intentioned." Yes, there's a contrast between philanthropists congratulating themselves on their goodness and the tens of thousands sleeping around Skid Row, but some of the former are strikingly kind, and some of the latter understandably enraged.

Yet, if the first surprise of the book is to show us how many of the gifted souls in a high-level orchestra are wounded or disengaged, even as they can step onto a stage and touch a thousand hearts, the second is to present dozens of professional musicians devoting their rare free time to taking their talents to places that others among us might shun. One essential purpose of *Restrung* is to suggest that it's not just audiences that musicians are working to restore, but themselves.

~

I could cover dozens of pages simply making sense of the world of music, as it comes to us here, and the ways in which it interacts with the world of those forgotten on our streets, who surround us in affluent cities like the one in which I write, two hours from Skid Row. But what gives a whole other dimension to this memoir is the private story, of the often shocking cruelties that can attend the pursuit of the American Dream. Looked at in one way, the story of a little boy, of displaced parents, conquering the worlds of music and the academy in his teens, vindicates all our hopes for the New World and the opportunities it offers; seen behind closed doors, it reveals to us how much high achievement can mean pulling yourself away from your culture and from the people who made you. It can mean finding yourself entwined with them and imprisoned within their hopes, even when none of that is healthy, and it can result in a success that's the polar opposite of fulfillment.

We see here a child who's torn in two directions—to follow his passions and to achieve his parents' dreams—and doesn't know how to become himself without betraying the ones who made him. His story also evolves into one about a boy wonder with a conscience who finds himself leading two lives—at the very least—as he moves through glittering soirees, broken streets, and all the drama that awaits him at home. As a writer myself, I know how hard it is to tell any one of these stories, let alone all of them at once. And how it's even harder to maintain one's balance, and to see, as Vijay writes in one typically discerning moment, how much his parents did for him, as well as to him.

It's this rending human story, delivered with such fearless clarity and intimacy, that makes me think of this book in the context of classic works of literature from Jhumpa Lahiri or Ayad Akhtar. It's very much the story of our times and it chimes with the increasing—and welcome—flood of books telling of the struggles of Black writers to get the better of their circumstances, the torn loyalties of newcomers from Ethiopia or Nigeria, the aspirations of all those crossing the American border from the south. What is the cost of sacrifice, and how can one keep alive the home one has inherited while one's sights are set on a new and seemingly better home? How can one transcend the conditions of one's parents without leaving them behind, and how can one then not get blinded by the spotlight glare of acclaim, especially if it's premised on ignoring the shattered lives outside?

This all comes together in a remarkable scene—one of many—where Vijay describes driving away from the glittering Frank Gehry–designed Disney Hall in downtown Los Angeles and finding himself, after missing a turn, among the more than eleven thousand souls sleeping in tents and rolling themselves along on wheelchairs or stumbling through the center of ragged streets. He's steering a blue Camry, having only recently acquired his driver's license, and his father, who has come to live with him and oversee his son's rise, tries with all his might to keep the two of them away from the desperate faces they see outside. Meanwhile, a Beethoven quartet, one of the last pieces the composer wrote, is playing in all its tenderness from the speakers in their car. The music, the scenes of destitution, the rare status Vijay has somehow achieved, all the fears and parental pressures he has been experiencing, come together with a force that's overpowering. It feels like the harrowing shadow side of the moments of numinous harmony he has evoked when playing certain passages on his violin.

But I don't think many readers will forget the scenes of Vijay trying with all his heart to let himself be transported by the music even as his parents fret that the music will take him away from them. He plays the violin as a little boy in the hope that it can heal the strains at home, he feels tears coming to his eyes as he listens to his little brother sing "Once in Royal David's City" in a Hudson Valley church. But second place will never be enough among "Bengal tigers," and Vijay finds himself at once making good on the fact that his name means "victory" in his parents' tongue and then running away from it entirely.

Few could relate to his extraordinary accomplishments, but everyone can understand his emotions. Some of what he describes here of his parents' actions sounds insupportable; yet some of their sacrifices to make their son great—driving seventy miles each way several times a week—are all but unimaginable. This is the rare story of growing up that can take us unforgettably into an American boy's longing for independence, just as it takes us into his immigrant parents' anxious clinging to accomplishment. "I'd folded myself into obedience so thoroughly," we read at one point, "I forgot it was a performance."

And oh, the descriptions of music here, in which the artist learns to balance surrender with control and to lose himself in what he's making! I have never heard harmonics opened up from within as they are in this book, and by someone who's familiar enough with neurology to know, scientifically, how much music can be medicine for inertia or depression. The scenes in which we read of the performer striking up a conversation with his audience that becomes communion, until the listeners' very stillness "becomes a kind of music, too," carry us up to the heavens even—especially—when set amid scenes of sorrow that sound infernal.

The "slow-burning miracle" of the opening movement of Johannes Brahms's Fourth Symphony sounds "like a secret muttered in half sleep." The undulations in a Schumann quartet are "as if an animal were caught in a maw." This writer feels music so profoundly that we begin to live within the chords—the pauses—he evokes, and, most of all, to come to see that the cries of pain he hears, from amid the audiences and from within the composers he cherishes, are not so very different from his own.

~

I will leave readers to discover for themselves all the surprises that ensue, on Skid Row and out of public view. But let me just end this foreword, already much longer than I intended, by noting that, three years after our first meeting, I flew back into California one January night to introduce a new book of mine to the world, a meditation on silence and transformation and wildfire called *Aflame*. As a taxi guided me back to my family home, inching around mountain turns, I looked up to see that all the lights in our house were out; once I stepped inside, I realized that the landlines were dead, too. Our electric company had turned off all power because high winds threatened to spark flames that could burn down our home, which had been built to replace an earlier house, on the same property, that had burned to the ground years earlier. By the light of a little white lantern, I checked my emails and learned that terrible fires were, at that very moment, scything through many parts of Los Angeles, including the small town where Vijay lives.

Through the jet-lagged night, messages kept flooding in, telling of devastation and chaos. Two weeks later, I was due to be holding an event around *Aflame* in Pasadena, very close to where many were losing not just their livelihoods but their lives. I had already asked Vijay if he would engage me in a public conversation in the century-old bookstore there—Who else knew so much about monasticism, about transcendence, about crossing borders? Now we both sensed that his music, as much as his presence and words, would be the instrument of healing so many were crying out for.

Vijay had been bringing his gift to those in need for years; very few people knew or felt so deeply how much music can do. Surrounded in the bookstore by the rubble the flames had left behind, he began to play for a room of people made tender by all that they and their neighbors had endured. Many were unhoused now and displaced. He shared some Bach with us, and he offered up an arrangement of Leonard Cohen's "Hallelujah" for solo violin. He engaged me in a sparkling, wide-awake discussion, in which we felt that everything was at stake. And as I finished reading the book you have in front of you, I came to see that it, deep down, is a version of the same: a sincere, heart-stopping sharing of world-class strength—and vulnerability—designed to help us all move toward better, truer, deeper versions of ourselves.

—Pico Iyer
Santa Barbara, California
July 2025

PRELUDE

"Jesus on the Main Line"

[Patton State Hospital, San Bernardino]

I pulled my blue Camry up to the guard's booth and rolled down the window. The blast of heat was like opening an oven. The dash read 105 degrees.

"Yeah, uh—I'm here for the concert?"

Behind wire-rimmed aviators, the guard's eyebrows went up, then dropped into a scowl. On the booth door, the California state seal—Minerva, a bear, the word *Eureka*—was the same baked dust-brown of the guard's uniform.

"Who on earth is playing a concert here?"

I was.

In 2007, I was the youngest member of the Los Angeles Philharmonic, three months shy of turning twenty, and already asking the kind of inconvenient questions that made my parents nervous. They'd wanted me to be the other Dr. Gupta. Instead, I'd rebelled and won my first audition, landing a spot in one of the best orchestras in the country. Two years later, I'd earned tenure, which meant that I had a six-figure salary, a pension, benefits for life: a dream job, by any standard. Four nights a week, I got to play with some of the biggest names in classical music—Gustavo Dudamel, Yo-Yo Ma, and John Williams—onstage at Walt Disney Concert Hall, the Hollywood Bowl, on tour all over the globe in London, Paris, Tokyo, and Vienna. Night after night, I played some of the greatest music ever written, with musicians who had dedicated their lives to the craft of classical music.

And yet, I couldn't understand why it all felt so hollow. I didn't know what I wanted—but I'd go anywhere to find it.

I started cold-calling clinics and county jails. I played in VA hospitals, cancer wards, and hospices. I played for kids with Down syndrome and once in a Skid Row courtyard for a man who had turned the Second Street tunnel into a concert hall. After a recital at Occidental College, someone in my audience, who turned out to be a forensic social worker, asked if I'd play at a state hospital seventy miles east of LA. I said yes without giving it a second thought, not realizing that I'd just agreed to perform in an asylum.

And now, I was here, about to play a concert, and feeling not just pre-concert adrenaline, but a gnawing unease. At the booth, the guard made a few terse phone calls. The barrier lifted, and I drove past a row of brick, Victorian-looking buildings. Patton was one of the last remaining state hospitals, a former asylum with a brutal history of shock therapy and Thorazine, lobotomies and forced sterilizations. When patients died, they were buried in a mass, unmarked grave somewhere on the grounds. After President Ronald Reagan gutted the asylum system in the 1980s, places like Patton absorbed the fallout, shifting from asylums into holding pens for those deemed unfit to stand trial in the overcrowded LA courts. And today, they—the "criminally insane"—would be my audience.

I parked my Camry and two lanyard-clad social workers greeted me in a dusty parking lot. I pulled my violin case from the back seat, trying to hide the mound of fast-food wrappers, water bottles, and an empty box of cookies. As we walked toward a drab concrete building that would serve as my concert venue that afternoon, the social workers told me that a janitor had recently unlocked an attic in one of the buildings, in which he'd found a room full of suitcase lobotomy kits from the 1950s. Some of the instruments were still rusted from use.

Despite the furnace-heat that engulfed me, I shivered.

As we approached the swinging double doors of the drab, concrete building, one of the social workers said, with some embarrassment, that this crowd might not "behave" like the typical concert-hall audience I was used to. Some were acutely mentally ill and might do something I'd find disruptive, like talk during the performance or wander around the room. I nodded, thinking of the dozing patrons at Disney Hall, or the pot-smoking picnickers at the Bowl. I had come to Patton wanting to play music for people who'd never be able to hear music inside a concert hall. I was convinced that music, or beauty of any kind, could be soothing, even healing, to people I saw as suffering, maybe even broken beyond repair. I was utterly sincere, naïve—and totally unprepared for what was about to happen.

Even as eighty inmates in brown jumpsuits filed into the room, my focus was entirely on the music I'd be playing for them: Bach's "Chaconne," one of the most difficult pieces of music ever written for the violin, which I'd be playing from memory. The audience was made up of men and women of all ages, and most looked drained of definition, blurred by heavy antipsychotics. Some stared blankly, while others locked eyes with me and didn't look away. I looked back in their direction, and even tried to nod a curt, professional greeting, but really, I was still practicing in my head, imagining all the things that could go wrong: *Don't crunch the first chord. Make sure the bassline is clear. Don't play out of tune. Don't rush.*

I opened my case in front of a heavy black curtain and lifted out my violin, tuning the strings one by one—A against D, D against G, E against A—tightening the fifths. The curtain swallowed sound and I barely heard the staff member's introduction. My chest thumped with adrenaline. The focus I'd learned as a child performer returned on cue, more instinct than choice. My vision narrowed to a single point.

Without a smile, or a bow, or even a single word to my audience, I began to play:

Yaa-ta-tum, taa-ta-lam, yaa-de-dum, da—

Johann Sebastian Bach wrote the "Chaconne" in a moment of devastation. While visiting the spa town of Carlsbad, his wife, Maria Barbara—a gifted musician, as well as his teenage sweetheart, and mother to their seven children—suddenly died. By the time Bach returned home, she had already been buried, and mourned. Even though Bach was no stranger to loss—orphaned at ten, he would later become a father who buried several of his own children—Maria Barbara's death marked a turning point in his life, upending the stability he once knew, propelling him toward a quiet, unfulfilled life as a little-known church cantor. After he died, most of his music disappeared from public view and stayed that way for nearly a century.

In Bach's hands, the "Chaconne"—a Baroque dance with origins in the New World—became prayer and dance, hymn and counterpoint, joy and death. In the work, he embedded four Lutheran chorales, *Christ lag in Todesbanden,* "Christ lay in the bonds of death"; *Jesu, meine Freude,* "Jesus my joy"; *Den Tod niemand zwingen kunnt,* "No one could force death"; and *Auf meinen lieben Gott,* "To my beloved God"—all perfectly apportioned to the Golden Ratio like a piece of musical architecture. This music was Bach's Taj Mahal.

For the violinist, the "Chaconne" demands years of disciplined training, drawing the player into a zone of total focus, where nothing exists beyond the next measure. The double stops, the long runs of broken chords, and the exposed lines require a near-dissociative level of hyperfocus. The piece, the longest work written for unaccompanied violin at the time, runs close to fifteen minutes. For the person holding the violin it can feel like a marathon of terror.

But at Patton, I was playing my heart out. Bach's music rose into a hymn of resurrection, a pinnacle of ecstasy, soaring and singing, before turning back to the grave. It was one of the rare times where I—a serial perfectionist—was happy with the way I was playing. Now, I geared up for the return to Bach's opening line, repeated at the closing, as if to remind the audience that even though they had climbed between hell and heaven, they had really been hearing the same music the whole time.

Yaa-ta-tum, taa-ta-lam, yaa-de-dum, da—

I landed on the last note and unleashed my bow in a flourish, waiting for that familiar crack of applause to shatter the air.

It never came.

The open D hung in the air, unanswered. I stared around the room, dumbfounded. I lowered my violin, smiled, and nodded, a universal cue for "clap now, please." Still, nothing.

For the first time in my life, I had bombed.

In an *asylum.*

Then, from the middle of the room, a Black man with a graying beard—an inmate wearing a tan jumpsuit the same shade as the desert dust that clouded the state hospital—lifted his hand and glared straight at me. I nodded, silent.

"Son," he said, "don't you know any songs we know?"

I felt a searing flush of shame. I had perfect pitch, and a nearly perfect memory. I'd been at Juilliard for seven years. By thirteen, I'd been a soloist on stages from Tokyo to Tel Aviv, New York to Bombay, Saint Barth's to Santa Barbara. I had twenty-five thousand hours of practice and a seat in a top orchestra. But in that moment, all of it failed me. I couldn't think of a *single* song this man knew. Well, just one. The first music that came out of the depths of my grasping, panicking mind was the theme from *Titanic,* and then, the realization that there could not possibly be something *worse* to play in a state hospital than "My Heart Will Go On." I stood, cowering, humbled, and more than a little humiliated.

And then, grace came uninvited, as it always does. The man raised his head and began to sing to *me.*

Jesus is on that main line, tell him what you want.

His voice was a clear and bright baritone. He slid between notes with the ease of someone who knew how to use his voice in a big space. I could tell that he'd probably grown up singing in the church.

Call him up and tell him what you want.

I'd never heard the song before, but it was clear that plenty of others had. A man in the front row who'd been asleep during my "Chaconne" was suddenly wide awake, stomping in time. A woman started rocking herself and clapping in time. Some sang back to him.

Tell him what you want.

He pressed on, stronger now.

If you're feeling down and out, tell him what you want.

My violin slack and useless in my hands, I watched this man—an inmate, a patient, a singer, a stranger—do what I *should* have come there to do: not just to perform *at* people, but to make music come alive *in* them.

I couldn't have known I was witnessing one of the greatest music lessons of my life.

It took me years to understand that the inmate wasn't rejecting me, or Bach, or asking for a song he preferred. He was asking me to *see* him, not just as an inmate, or a cause for my charity, but as someone with his own music, his own desires, his own voice. He was teaching me that music wasn't a one-sided race to win, not a victory lap to be played at him from a safe distance, but an exchange. Just as he wasn't only an inmate, reduced to the worst thing he might have done on the worst day of his life. He was trying to show me that for all my training, I had walked into that room thinking I was the only musician there, and all anyone would want from me was to be dazzled by my calcified, dissociative perfection.

Tell him what you want.

What did I want? I had no idea. I'd never even asked myself that question before. All I knew was that I had to keep asking—keep *practicing*—that question. And to do that, I'd need to keep making music in places that weren't concert halls.

~

Art is not a noun. It is not an object to be bought, sold, perfected, or displayed. Art is not something made by a genius, or rendered obsolete by a machine, because it is not a thing at all. It is an intention. Art shares the same intention as belonging, which is the longing to be: to be seen, to be known, to be loved. The Bengali poet Rabindranath Tagore once wrote that music could fill the infinite between two souls, because even as the distance between beings stretches toward infinity, each of us carries a song we came to sing during our brief visit to this plane of existence.

That song can change us, heal us, and lift us beyond ourselves. Music reaches the broken places within us and the broken places between us. It becomes a living current moving from one person to another, stitching together what we thought was lost. In a world seduced by despair and, as T. S. Eliot wrote, distracted from distraction by distraction, hope cannot be an idea. Hope must become a practice—not a practice of perfection or aspiration—but of making and unmaking through an iterative, spiritual hygiene of attention.

Over the years I have brought thousands of concerts to shelters, clinics, jails, and prisons, playing music for people who were living the hardest days of their lives. And though places like Skid Row carry problems of the most immense human pain and suffering, the deepest practice I witnessed—with people recovering from homelessness and addiction, from poverty and incarceration and despair—was the practice of hope. It is undoubtedly true that Skid Row is the end of the road for many. But for others, rock bottom is a place of beginnings, a place from where things can only get better. Skid Row is a spiritual crucible: a place where one might learn how to remake themself.

And Skid Row became my crucible, too. Even as I chased achievements that left me feeling increasingly hollow, it was in shelters that I learned how to let myself break and be remade. In Skid Row, I learned how to belong. When my own family disowned me, I realized I had been building a different kind of family, one that sang in clinics and played in jail dormitories and danced in the streets. And when I lost my own home, and my life savings, and any sense of connection to the world around me, people in Skid Row taught me that a home is not the same as a house, and that people do not become homeless when they run out of money, but when they run out of relationships. I learned that music, like all art, is not mere entertainment, but a lifeline.

After my first concerts in shelters and prisons, I kept going back as someone doing "community outreach"—to be a musical evangelist or even an advocate for social justice—never thinking I was there to work on myself. But I was. I met teachers everywhere, people who challenged me, leveled me, and humbled me into new understandings of myself, even as I unraveled in public, circling addiction, despair, and heartbreak. I poured my waking and often dreaming hours into bringing sweetness to people living through their hardest days.

In one of America's most broken places, I found a kind of wholeness I had never known in any other place. In shelters and clinics, and later in jails and prisons, I wept with wonder and grief, astonished by the grace I received from people I once dismissed as the least among us, who became my truest teachers. I learned the meaning of hallelujah, a word that carries grief and praise in the same breath.

Tagore wrote in *Gitanjali*, "I have spent many days stringing and unstringing my instrument, while the song I came to sing remains unsung." For years, that was me, stringing and unstringing myself, chasing perfection, chasing approval, chasing love. But the song I came to sing was waiting in the places I had been taught to avoid, in people I was told were unworthy, and in the parts of myself I believed were broken.

This is the story of how I came undone, and how I was restrung.

—Vijay Gupta
Altadena, California
November, 2025

RESTRUNG

Part 1

The first music I ever knew was the sound of Dad, praying.

His voice drifted down from upstairs, where he sat, cross-legged, before a makeshift altar bearing murtis arranged on a strip of silk: a one-tusked elephant, a blue man meditating beside a trident, a red cloth pouch decorated with cowrie shells, a granite pillar smeared with sandalwood. Each morning, Dad pulled on an orange bathrobe and lit a row of flickering deepa and laid out nuts and dried fruit on crystal coasters, sanctifying the offering with a sprinkle of holy water from the sacred Ganges. Then, he'd light a stick of incense, and, trailing fragrant wisps of smoke, begin to chant in a torrent of Sanskrit, starting with a piercing "Aaauuummm."

Years later, I'd learn that Dad had learned the chants by ear from the tapes of old Kolkata radio broadcasts. He didn't understand the words, but he loved how holy they made him—and his home—feel. As the sun rose, he'd descend from his pujo and plant scratchy, mustached kisses on our cheeks, pressing the sandalwood-smoked proshad—the same offering he had made to the gods—into our mouths: our first food, our first blessing.

One morning after his pujo, I crept upstairs and sat at the altar, babbling mantras of my own creation. Like many three-year-old boys, I wanted to be like my dad. I fumbled with a box of matches, striking the sticks and dropping them on the blue shag carpet, thrilled by the sulfurous bursts of light. When one caught and spread to a curl of silk, then to the yellowed pages of holy books, I made a run for it. Behind me, flames leapt fast, devouring scriptures and murtis carried across continents, ancestral heirlooms that had survived famine, Partition, and (colonial) rule. I scampered down the stairs, hands clamped over my ears, chanting "Alahm, alahm" in counterpoint with the screeching smoke detector.

That's how I earned my nickname: *Potka. Firecracker.*

Chapter 1

BORO ASHA KORE, OR, GREAT EXPECTATIONS

"Twinkle Twinkle Little Star"

Perhaps it is music that will save the world.

—Shinichi Suzuki

Suzuki Book 1: "Twinkle Twinkle Little Star"

[Newburgh, New York]

Shinichi Suzuki knew there was no such thing as a prodigy. He believed that musical ability developed the same way as language developed, through immersion, repetition, and love. He called his method "Talent Education," and believed music could be taught like a mother tongue. If a child could learn a language as complicated as Japanese by ear, then there was no reason any child couldn't learn music—what he called "the language of the heart without words"—that very same way.

And so, in a bright, sunlit room overlooking the Hudson River, I learned the Suzuki Method from a dour German woman named Mrs. Vogel. I'd already had one year of violin lessons from Mrs. Larkin, but I looked on as Mrs. Vogel now drew four lines on a piece of graph paper, one for each year I'd lived so far. She named the strings: E. A. D. G.

Then, she fixed thin strips of colored tape on my violin, which would serve as temporary frets. There were four of those, too: red for 1, yellow for 2, blue for 3, and black for 4. I tucked my 1/16 size violin under my chin and curled my thumb around the neck of the instrument. Trying very hard not to let the instrument slip away, I squeezed my chin down on the chinrest. Her correction was swift.

"No clenching, now."

I tried not to clench my chin, which only made me clench my whole body instead. I turned to look at both of my parents, watching me. Dad *tsk*ed impatiently, waving me back toward Mrs. Vogel. Next to him, Mom was folded in half, hiding her face in her hands, the way she had the morning I set the pujo room on fire.

Even though I was only four, I'd already had a few violin lessons. Dad had made me my first violin out of a Cracker Jack box and a ruler. He plucked a twig out of one of Mom's ornamental pear trees for me to use as a bow. I rubbed on it all day long, singing songs of my own creation. When an Irish father-son duo came to lay tile in our basement, I eagerly serenaded them in a made-up language of nonsense syllables, hopping between the blue and white squares. "Babábaa-dalee-de-deee." One of them looked up, raised his trowel, and sang a verse of "Danny Boy." I stood still and listened to the melody: the slow rise and pause, the soft curls on "the pipes, the pipes are calling," rising and curling again. Then, without a word, I sang it back to them, note for note, in my own babble-language, miming along on my toy violin.

They were awestruck. "Get that kid some lessons!"

My first teacher, Mrs. Larkin, was an apple farmer. She taught Suzuki violin in her cluttered living room. Dad replaced the Cracker Jack box with a 1/16 size spruce-and-maple violin and a bow made of carbon fiber. In group lessons, parents bounced along with the kids as we scrubbed out rhythms—"Run-Jimmy-Run-Jimmy," "Mississippi-Hot-Dog"—their eyes screwed up at the horrifying screeches emerging from our violins. After class, Mrs. Larkin laid out treats: fresh McIntosh apples or leftover Halloween candy. I always picked the candy, off-limits at home because of Dad's diabetes—even though sometimes he snuck a piece too. It was our little secret, which made it taste even better. "Don't tell Mommy."

Dad and I were inseparable. I clung to his shoulders and pulled at his thinning flop of black hair. My favorite song was his favorite song, from Paul Simon's *Graceland*:

If you'll be my bodyguard, I can be your long lost pal…

After a few months, Mrs. Larkin told us to find another teacher. I was racing ahead, picking out songs by ear. Neither my parents nor I knew then that I had perfect pitch. Mrs. Vogel, who did not serve up apples *or* candy, was supposed to be the best in the Mid-Hudson Valley.

In her living room, lit by a river glistening through bay windows, Mrs. Vogel knelt on a pale tatami mat and traced the outline of my small, socked feet on construction paper, guiding me to stand *so*—"heels touching!"—toes turned out to make a small "V." The violin was to be held at another perfect angle—"beautiful posture!"—with my nose in line with the strings. Each lesson began and ended with a respectful Japanese bow from the waist—"feet together, back straight!"—my violin and bow tucked under one elbow.

Mrs. Vogel was exacting, often spending the entire lesson on the placement of a single finger: A "1" on the A string—my first finger curled onto the red fret—was a "B". A 2 on the E string was "G" sharp. One day, I'd manage to curl my fourth finger onto the G string, to play a "D", but that note was still years away.

Dad scribbled everything she said into a notebook, and later, he made me go through the whole lesson again in the living room, or in the kitchen while Mom cooked, encouraging me to play songs and notes Mrs. Vogel hadn't yet taught me.

The Suzuki Method came in a pricey bundle: ten slim books, cassette tapes, and a spiral-bound practice journal. Mrs. Vogel, ever cautious, told Dad to buy one book at a time—most kids, she said, never made it past Book 3. If I stuck with it, I might reach Book 6 or 7 by the time I turned ten. The later volumes—concertos, real music—were meant for teenagers. Dad, impatient for me to move faster and convinced he'd found a bargain, bought the whole set anyway: from "Twinkle Twinkle" to concertos by a composer neither of my parents could pronounce. Still in kindergarten, I traced the letters: M-O-Z-A-R-T. Mom, meanwhile, read Suzuki's autobiography *Nurtured by Love*, in which he insisted that parents were musical co-learners alongside their children: "First we teach the mother to play one piece so that she will be a good teacher at home..."

In the back of our beige Ford Aerostar, strewn with unrottable McDonald's fries and crusted ketchup packets, I flipped through the practice journal, which had drawings of a cartoon duck in a sailor suit. Mr. Ducky grinned and wagged his finger, quacking out koans disguised as practice tips.

"March 11: Practice only on the days you eat!"

In my notebook, Mrs. Vogel wrote two words. My first song. "Twinkle Twinkle." I couldn't read music yet, but the first seven notes were easy: open A, open E, fingers "high in the sky." Then came "little"—a first finger curled on the E string. A small, perfect arch. "Star" brought me right back to the open E.

It looked like this:

E: ———0—0—1—1—0—
A: 0—0—

And for "how I wonder what you are"—a climb down the A string, starting with the third finger:

A: 3—3—2—2—1—1—0—

Within a few weeks, I worked out the finger patterns for the rest of the book: "Lightly Row," "Song of the Wind"—and, at the end of the book, three minuets by Johann Sebastian Bach. At one of my lessons, I played Book 1 straight through with the cassette tape, still unable to read a single note of music.

Mrs. Vogel barely hid her surprise. "Vell," she said in her Bavarian staccato, "perhaps it's gut you bought all ze books! But you'll have to vait before you play Book 2. Zere is a method for a reason."

At home, Mom made "the method" the structure of our household. I stood on Mrs. Vogel's green construction-paper foot-tracing and delivered thirty minutes of practice every day. We had group lessons every Thursday after school, and, as a treat, McDonald's on the way home, accompanied by simple Suzuki songs. My little brother, as musical as me—but not yet able to pronounce "violin"—sang the words to "Perpetual Motion" from his car seat.

"All Suzuki children play la play la play la valalin..."

Even though Mr. Ducky cautioned, "*No hurry, no pause,*" I was ravenous for music. If I could hear it, I could play it—and I wanted to play everything. On car rides I begged for the tapes from Book 3 or 4. At home, if I couldn't find the notes, I'd stop playing and sing the rest. Once, in a group class, I watched a few older kids wrestle with a passage from Book 4. Without thinking, I picked up my violin and played it for them by ear. I barely noticed their red faces, or Mrs. Vogel's fury. It's no wonder I didn't make many friends.

My parents had a hard time making friends, too. Once, after class, Mrs. Vogel pulled them aside. We were breaking the rules. She had a system, a schedule. To her, an abundance of talent wasn't an excuse for a lack of discipline. Sure, I could teach myself the older kids' songs, but my feet strayed from her construction-paper footprints, and my fingers crept up the bow. I had to wait my turn. At recitals I was sent to sit "Indian style" on the floor with restless kids who picked the plastic cylinders off their shoelaces while older kids botched the songs I had taught myself how to play. At the next recital, Mom flaunted Mrs. Vogel's dress code, dressing me in bright red suspenders and a matching Mickey Mouse necktie.

Dad didn't understand why his kid, who already knew the songs by ear, couldn't play too. After all, Dad had learned how to chant in Sanskrit by ear, and his son was just following in his footsteps. Dad insisted Mrs. Vogel let me skip a few books and join the older kids.

Instead, she was furious with the upstart Guptas.

"If it is vunderkind lessons you vant, go to the City!"

Suzuki Book 2: Carl Maria von Weber, "Hunter's Chorus"

[Jackson Heights, New York]

Both of my grandfathers worked for Air India. When their children came of marrying age, Dad twenty-three and Mom seventeen, their union was arranged in the Queens Courthouse in Jamaica, New York. In the 1970s, Bengal had been torn apart by communist rebellion, and my parents began their climb up the sheer cliffside of the American Dream, on which my brother and I were born.

To earn their green cards, they took blue-collar jobs at John F. Kennedy International Airport. Dad worked baggage claim, heaving suitcases alongside West Indians and West Africans chasing their own American Dream. Years of street cricket had made him quick and strong. He smoked Camels and picked up slang in every language he heard. My mother, round-armed and quiet, stood at a duty-free register selling perfume and Swiss watches. Her long black hair fell in ringlets down her back. Her stocky frame and dark eyes would become my own.

My parents had come from the bright City of Joy—Kolkata, but in America, they could only afford to eat colorless staples of survival: rice and potatoes, onions and eggs, butter and salt. Every extra dollar they earned was wired to India. As long as they lived in rupees, my parents could earn their worth.

During their off hours, Mom cowered in their Jackson Heights walk-up while Dad worked every side hustle he could find. He became a chakor—an errand boy—running packages across Manhattan, peeling potatoes in the basement of an orange-sauce Indian joint in Midtown, working for a Pakistani clerk named Zaidi, who taught him how to dress smart and talk fast. Dad eventually landed a gig at a top travel agency in Manhattan. When he could, he treated himself to lunch at Gray's Papaya—two hot dogs with grilled onions and mustard—for only fifty rupees.

After a few months of being the office chakor, he'd had enough. He started a travel agency for his own people. By the mid-1980s, the United States was hungry for foreign doctors and engineers, and a new wave of Kolkata Bengalis—overeducated, underpaid, grateful for a visa—had arrived. Dad made himself essential.

As more Bengalis moved upstate to work at the IBM plant in Fishkill, Dad's business boomed. After a few years my parents accomplished their American Dream, purchasing four wooded acres in the Mid-Hudson Valley that would become our home, as well as the headquarters of Travel World International. The instant the phone rang, he'd answer with a curt, "Travel," but the moment he heard his mother tongue on the other line, his voice warmed as he switched into Bangla, "Haan, Bishojit-da..." He'd traipse down a long hallway to his office, chattering away like his bird namesake, the bulbul.

But sometimes his smile faltered and his voice dropped an octave lower. Even as children, my brother and I knew what that meant. Mom, who had grown up in a high-caste Brahmin household, explained it to us: Dad was sending people home, so that they could sing sacred words to the people they loved, the ones who had gone to god. Hindu funeral rites, led by the family's eldest son, required cremation within twenty-four hours. On the banks of the sacred Ganges, the son would chant mantras and light the funeral pyre.

Now, Dad wasn't a mere travel agent arranging vacations. He became a kind of Bengali Charon, guiding the living toward the dead, mending the heart-rend of immigration.

He'd tell the family to pack their bags, and he would take care of the rest. In an era predating dial-up internet, he'd call London, Frankfurt, or New Delhi. He'd slip into a British accent or throw in just enough slang to grease the wheels—"Arey yaar" (Come on, bud), "ey sala!" (you sonofabitch!)—charming and cursing in five languages, ever searching for a lower price or a quicker layover. To sound official, he taught himself the NATO phonetic alphabet—A as in Alpha, B as in Bravo, C as in Charlie—and always: *I, as in India.*

Even though JFK was two hours away, he'd make it in time to greet the family curbside, tickets in hand. From the banks of the Hudson to the shores of the Ganga, Dad was the Bengali boatman: the surest way home.

Suzuki Book 3: Antonín Dvořák, "Humoresque"

[Montgomery, New York]

When Dad's business grew enough for my parents to start living in dollars, he invested in upgrades. Caste didn't matter in America, but appearances did. He traded his Camels for Marlboro Lights, bought a Mercury Cougar, and started wearing a leather jacket and aviators. Mom joined in, albeit reluctantly. With her wages from the duty-free shop, she bought Dad a slender Cartier Tank that almost never left his wrist. He'd bought her a quarter-carat diamond, and soon, she became a QVC-clad tigress. Each morning, Mom and Dad walked a rescue mutt named Raja around the park. As long as my parents looked the part, they could convince themselves that they belonged to America.

But when Dad's parents came from India, staying weeks at a time, nothing he had was enough: not the house, not the dog named for a king, not the travel agency. And definitely not Mom—who still hadn't produced grandsons. Clearly, this was Mom's fault. As collateral for the long-promised arrival of a firstborn son—me—Dad slipped the ring off Mom's finger and pressed it into his stepmother's palm, creating a festering, lifelong grudge between my parents. I'd never see my mother wear a diamond.

Mom, like many daughters of the subcontinent, grew up two steps behind her husband. She was brilliant, of Borendro-Brahmin stock, but after her father ran off with a flight attendant, she was sent to a convent in Kolkata. The nuns taught her to chant in Sanskrit and memorize Tagore. She became a champion swimmer and placed at the top of her class in early medical school entrance exams. But instead of joining the nuns—or going to college—she was married off to a lower-caste family that didn't know what to do with a girl like her. Dad hadn't even finished high school, and a bright girl was a threat. Mom's degrees, her books, even her medals, were replaced by menial tasks, like cooking and cleaning. She would only be allowed jobs as a cashier, a receptionist, a bank teller. Her new in-laws worried: If she got too smart, she might leave. That kind of shame ran in the blood.

Mom was working the reception desk at a pharmaceutical company when her twenty-four-year-old belly began to show the curve of new life—mine. The company fired her on the spot. When she tried to sue, the lawyer she hired turned out to be even crueler than the company, draining my parents of thousands of dollars they didn't have before dropping the case.

The summer I arrived was brutally hot. Mom developed preeclampsia that worsened into toxemia, then endured a long labor before I was pulled out by emergency C-section. Before she was wheeled into surgery, a masked doctor handed Dad a waiver: He'd either have a son, or a wife. When we both made it, Dad took it as a sign that even America was on his side.

Mom's sole place of sovereignty was her kitchen: She learned how to toast and crush spices, how to fry fish, how to bargain and boil. She found a way to silence her in-laws and her husband: They were less likely to demean her through mouthfuls of food. Even while she coaxed fragrant gold out of dried lentils and turned a bag of shrimp into a briny, earthy kiss, her brilliance fermented into vinegary achaar. After a while, even onions couldn't make her cry. By the time my brother was born, she ran her household like a covert kitchen dictator: Her grandfathers had been freedom fighters, marching alongside Gandhiji. Now, her sons would be wrecking balls launched between old culture and new bigotry.

Lining the fence of her new home, Mom planted a row of Norway spruces and scrawny fruit trees hardy enough to survive the winters. After Raja died, my parents replaced him with a German shepherd named Samrat—"Emperor." But the eerie quiet still left Mom spooked, so Dad found a breeder and brought home a golden Alsatian named Silke, who walked without a leash and seemed to know what he was thinking. Then came Prinz—a floppy-eared pup who grew into a hundred-pound bear, kept in line with a clanking choke collar. After a litter of puppies, our house was never quiet again.

But I became the household's chief noisemaker. After destroying the pujo room, I was strictly supervised. On Saturday mornings, while Dad watched TV, I'd crank the dials on my parents' bedroom TV until I found the only thing I cared about: the orchestra. Not *Tom and Jerry*. Not *Barney*. The New York Philharmonic. Face six inches from the screen, my fingers smearing the glass, I watched bows swoosh in perfect sync. Flutes shimmered, and giant white drums boomed across the dark wooden stage. A balding man in the front played a gleaming red violin. And at the podium stood a swashbuckling superhero—Zubin Mehta, the maestro—conducting Dvořák's

New World Symphony. The music moved through him like current. He dipped toward the cellos and they sang back. He flashed his eyes at a clarinet and it took flight. He took on trombones, glared at timpani, and smiled like fire.

That *sound*. I'll never forget that sound. I wanted to *become* it, to *be* it. I mimed along with the orchestra, babble-singing. Dvořák had written the *New World Symphony* while he was homesick in New York, aching for his native Bohemia. He'd filled it with the sounds he heard around him—Negro spirituals, Native melodies, the distant whistle of trains heading west. It was music born from exile and wonder, and even as a kid, I think I heard that homesickness too. I didn't have the words for it yet, but I wanted to make that sound my own, to hold the whole world in it. I copied the conductor, my left fist glued to my hip, chest flared, singing along.

"Duuu du du duuu du daaaa . . ."

As Dad dipped flavorless, tan biscuits into his morning cha, he watched me enter a world he'd never known.

He was my first audience.

Suzuki Book 4: Johannes Brahms, "Lullaby"

[East Fishkill Fire Station, New York]

In Kolkata, the nine nights of Navaratri—a festival worshipping the Goddess Durga, who Bengalis called "Maa"—bring millions to a devoted frenzy. But in the long-shadowed autumnal equinox of the red-maple Mid-Hudson Valley, our Navaratri took place at a local fire station, the only hosts crazy enough to allow two dozen Bengali kakus and mashis from across the tristate area to light a massive ritual fire indoors. The festivities were overseen by Satya Kaku—a rotund, balding IBM engineer who was also our priest.

Pujo was also the occasion for the grown-ups' favorite pastime of adda: fresh gossip. While the mashis chattered—clad in rustling Banarasi silk saris—the kakus bragged about their new Volvos and snuck beedees. Dad, ever game for a smoke break even if he could only afford Japanese cars, handed out business cards to anyone he didn't recognize, eager to collect new clients. Through it all, my brother and I ran wild in our kurtas with the other kids, acting out our favorite gory karate finishers from *Mortal Kombat*. "No, *I* wanna be Scorpion this time! *Get over here!*"

At some point during the roughhousing, I'd sneak back to watch the priest. With his back to everyone else, Satya Kaku sat cross-legged facing a life-size murti of Maa Durga, chanting hushed mantras for hours, offering flowers and bits of sandalwood paste, waving a stick of incense like a baton that left a fragrant trail, as if he were the conductor of his own private music.

Before the end of each night, Satya Kaku would stand to signal the arati—the final round of prayer—when everyone chanted together before showering the altar with marigolds and chrysanthemums. The flames of the five-wick panchapradip flickered, passed from hand to hand, drawn toward our faces like a blessing, ghee smoke in our hair, camphor in our nostrils. Over the singing, a conch blew, bells rang, gongs crashed, and mashis ululated. Then came my favorite part. The food: luchi, aloo posto, and payesh—fried, starchy, jaggery-sweetened memories from a homeland I'd never known.

My half-hearted solo debut came on the eighth night of Durga Pujo in 1992. Mrs. Vogel had forbidden me to learn songs from other Suzuki books, but while her rules governed the churches where our Suzuki recitals were held, those rules didn't apply before Maa. But all evening, while I played with my friends, or watched the pujo, my hands buzzed with nerves. When it was finally time, I pulled a 1/8 size violin out of a case and stepped forward, bowing twice: to the altar, Indian style, and to the crowd, Suzuki style. I played a sleepy "Lullaby" by someone named Brahms, and my violin squeaked more than once. A few kakus kept talking until Dad shushed them. Some of the mashis called their kids over. My cheeks burned when I missed a note, but I kept going, because in the middle of the room, I saw Dad, nodding his head in time with a pulse only he and I could feel.

But during my next song, the mashis fell silent, the kakus leaned in, and Dad's chest swelled. Now, I was playing music the Bengalis recognized. As the tune poured through my violin, I felt the whole room watching, listening. Suddenly, I felt as if I had floated above the room, seeing myself play from some height, feeling the music come from within myself, but also from between me and the people listening.

In the weeks before Pujo, my parents had demanded I learn a Bengali song—"Boro Asha Kore." They never explained what the words meant, or even what the song meant to them. And even if they had, I was five, still learning to read music, but there was no Suzuki notation for this one. Instead, they played a cassette from Kolkata over and over, expecting me to learn the song by ear, the way Dad had learned to chant. At first, I didn't know what to do. I wanted to go outside and play with the dogs, or conduct the TV. Instead, Dad swatted my cheek with a sharp thappor, and my eyes stung. Then he peeled off my socks and stood me barefoot on the teak dining table. My toes slipped on the slick surface and a wave of panic rose in my gut. Tears spilled onto the belly of my violin. I was terrified of falling off that dining table, my first stage.

Later, as a child performer, I understood why I feared heights, why my knees shook on the wooden stages of concert halls, why it felt as if my toes were sliding inside my shoes—and that if I didn't play well enough, the floor itself might give way and I would vanish.

But music pulled me back from my terror. The music they were making me play was beautiful. The man singing it on the tape sounded so happy, and so sad at the same time. The melody was Suzuki-simple. After Dad played it for me a few times, I could tell that the first note was a D—the same as my open D string. After a few more hearings, I figured it out. Most of the song could be played on one single string:

D: *0—1—2—2—23212—4321—00—121—0…*

As I played at the Pujo for the now-silent crowd, I wasn't playing for Dad anymore. I wasn't playing from fear. I was playing for Maa. I played, both toward my audience and behind, toward the murti of the Goddess, I felt as if my playing was the same as Satya Kaku's prayers. I had become sound, I had become song. I had become nothing, and everything, something infinite, in between.

When I finished, the firehouse erupted in cheers. My first ovation. "Wah! Wah! Ki shundor, Potka!" Mashis pinched my chubby cheeks, and kakus appreciatively thumped my back. A few older uncles, the jethus, wiped their eyes and asked for more Robindroshongit—the songs of Rabindranath Tagore, the bard whose anthems still echo across a divided Bengal.

Clutching paper bowls of thick payesh, before a ten-armed Durga, the Bengalis of New York called for more of the music that could send them home.

Suzuki Book 5: Antonio Vivaldi, Concerto in A Minor

[Montgomery/Manhattan]

The Bengali my family spoke at home was round and sweet and layered with contradiction. The words for "yesterday" and "tomorrow" were the same. There were no words for "thank you" or "goodbye." The word "Babu," when spoken with slight changes of inflection, could summon a lover, a child, or an elder. Mom called Dad Babu. Dad called Grandpa Babu. My little brother, tender, golden-voiced, was called Babushona, "Golden Sweetheart," "Shonu" for short. Once, when I was on a play-date, my new friends misheard "Babu" as "Bobby." Soon, their parents started calling me that, too.

One spring morning at preschool, a wrinkled nun who smelled of sour milk led Mass and handed out Communion. I ate the bland wafer and crossed myself the wrong way. As she pressed an ashy cross onto my forehead with her bony thumb, she asked for my "good Christian name." When I said "Bobby," she frowned and scrawled something onto a name tag decorated with an Easter Bunny.

"Hello, My Name Is ROBERT."

That afternoon, I stepped off the school bus and walked past Mom's garden—marigolds for pujo, vegetables for curries—and was greeted at the front door by Dad's disgust.

"Eeesh, Potka! Are you rubbing mati on your head?"

I pouted and shook my head, insisting that it *wasn't* dirt. He pulled me inside. On closer inspection of my name tag, Mom went pale. "Is that a cross? Did those phiringees *baptize* you?!" Dad thundered up to the restored pujo room and returned with a vial of murky brown water from the Ganges. He dabbed a corner of a tea towel and rubbed my forehead raw, chanting mantras fierce enough to undo a nun's misguided blessing. That was the day I learned that new, not-so-sweet word—"phiringee"—a term bearing centuries of colonial resentment: "foreigner."

But *we* were the real foreigners. Later that evening, my parents spoke to each other in hushed, panicked voices and made a life-altering decision. That summer, I became Robert, *legally*. Little Shonu became "Patrick." Mom—named for fragrant sandalwood and the moon's face—shortened Chandana into "Dana." Vivek—wisdom-conscience—became "Victor," or just "Vic."

I'm still "Bobby" at Starbucks.

Blending in would require more than a name change. The other Bengali families we knew, few as they were, lived far away, in Westchester neighborhoods. Amid sprawling fields planted with corn—and, thirty years later, signs that read "Make America Great Again"—we had to be sure we didn't make people uncomfortable by speaking Bengali in public. On the playground—slow at kickball, wary of football, and hopeless at basketball—I became neither "Bobby" nor "Robert," but "Poopta."

Kids weren't the only cruel ones. When a teacher poked at the curled "R" and "T" of my Bengali accent—because we spoke both Bengali and English at home—she considered placing me in the English

Second Language class with the Dominican and Puerto Rican kids. After that, the Gupta boys only spoke English at home. If our grammar slipped, Mom would correct us mid-sentence, sometimes with a stinging gatta to the back of the head. "Murkho chele!" she'd mutter. *Idiot boy.* "Gadha!" *Donkey.* In this country, words didn't just convey meaning: Language could mark you, betray you, and shut you out for good.

Mom wanted us to speak perfect English, but she didn't want us to lose Bangla, either. In the back of one closet was a brown hardshell suitcase, a vessel for bringing India back home. On trips to Kolkata, Dad filled it with boxes of sweet shondesh and sticks of neem, copper and brass plates, and gifts from Didima and Dadu. Once, a kaku had sent Dad home with a blocky 1/4 size violin for me. But my favorite of all were the books, especially the comic-book versions of Hindu myths. Hanuman leaping across the sky with a mountain on his shoulders, the flute-playing Krishna dancing on the head of a giant serpent, and one-tusked Ganesha winning a race with his brother to encircle the universe by encircling his parents instead. One year, my grandparents sent a book called *Dial B for Bengali.* At the kitchen table, Mom taught us letter by letter. ক, খ, গ, ঘ, ঙ. Ko, Kho, Go, Gho, Ngo. We traced the shapes like we traced our ABCs, learning to live in two worlds: Bangla in our ears, English on our tongues. Code-switching was our mother tongue.

Shonu and I had to win every American game. Like Hanuman, our parents had vaulted across oceans, and now, we carried a mountain of expectations. When Mrs. Vogel suggested "vunderkind lessons," my parents found a program in Manhattan called the School for Strings. I auditioned by rattling off three Suzuki books from memory. I was six. No more Saturday Suzuki lessons in Newburgh; now we drove each week to a nondescript brick building in Midtown, a journey that took ninety minutes, one way.

Down the New York State Thruway, Shonu and I stared out the back seat of the Nissan Sentra—an upgrade from the Aerostar—watching the trees of Harriman State Park give way to the cliffs of the

Palisades. We sang along to Suzuki tapes until Shonu, just three—sweet-faced, large-eared—got carsick near Paramus. Then came my parents' soundtrack: mournful Robindroshongit, Kishore Kumar's Bollywood ballads, Paul Simon, Julio Iglesias. We all loved the mandolin lick at the end of that one Rod Stewart song, and Dad beamed when I plucked it out on my violin. Sometimes, they'd play the wailing Qawwali dervishes of Nusrat Fateh Ali Khan, and Dad drummed tabla rhythms on the steering wheel and dashboard. Crossing the George Washington Bridge, he pointed to the Twin Towers at the island's far end. His pride spilled into us, and for the rest of our childhoods, every trip to the City felt like triumph. A decade earlier, Dad had walked those avenues as a chakor. Now he had returned, a conquering hero in Bally loafers.

As we drove into Manhattan, Shonu and I craned our necks, staring up at buildings that seemed to touch the sky. When we looked down, we saw men who looked like Dad on his fanciest days—pressed suits, belted trench coats, shiny shoes clicking against the pavement. But there were others, a kind we had never seen before: slow walkers with frayed, sagging clothes, people curled on grates or pushing carts piled high with what looked like trash. Everyone else rushed past them as if they didn't exist. One man shouted at the sky while doing shooshoo against a wall. Shonu giggled.

When I asked Dad why a grown-up was peeing in public, he said, "Takash na." *Don't look.* But we couldn't look away. Mom whispered that they were dushtu lok, chor, pagla. Mata kharap. Bad men, thieves, crazy, brains rotted from drugs. We were never to get close. They'd kidnap us, prick us with needles. In the back seat I squeezed Shonu's hand, suddenly afraid of this new place.

What we didn't know was that the poverty our parents feared was the kind Bengalis had endured for centuries. Our ancestors had survived famines that killed millions. Under British rule, Bengal grew jute, opium, indigo, feeding wars abroad while starving at home. Bengalis had learned to forage wild spinach and bitter neem, to boil fish heads with millet, or to simply go hungry. Others hoarded rice, watching their own countrymen starve to death.

The American Guptas would never let themselves get that close to poverty again. Mom warned that if we ever talked to the paglas, we would never come home again.

Suzuki Book 6: Arcangelo Corelli, "La Folia"

[West Fifty-Fourth Street, New York City]

By the time I met Louise Behrend, I was six and she was seventy-eight, and she had already raised several generations of violinists through the Suzuki Method. In the 1940s, she was a top talent at Juilliard, and she soon became one of the first women on the faculty. A decade later, after studying with Dr. Suzuki in Japan, she founded the School for Strings, an academy for young musicians in New York City.

A sharp-eyed creature of the Depression, nothing escaped her gaze. If she spotted a crooked bow or lazy left hand, she would swoop in, hawk-like, quickly making her correction, whirling her small frame around the room, keeping tempo with graceful arcs. Correction and praise came in the same breath. Her smile was rare but toothy, only earned by diligent practice. She danced and sang like a Hollywood starlet. I had never seen music so alive in anyone, and all I wanted was to dance with her.

She could also be less than gracious. Once, in the elevator, she surveyed me clutching a blocky violin from my kaku in Kolkata, painted bright saffron. Ms. Behrend wrinkled her nose as if the violin reeked. "Chubby boy with a fat fiddle."

When it came to my playing, Ms. Behrend made me begin again. I had as much to unlearn as to learn. I had been guessing some notes by ear—and guessing wrong. In my eagerness, my bow hand crept up the carbon-fiber stick, and my sound skated into a squeal. So she slowed everything down. In his notebook, Dad wrote down everything Ms. Behrend said: "Straight bow." "Slow down." "Bow grip." Later, he would develop a language of hand signals to remind me of Ms. Behrend's commandments. Mom, as usual, buried her face in her hands. But Ms. Behrend was playing the long game. She'd seen generations of talented children and overbearing parents: Not everyone made it.

At School for Strings, advanced students from all over New York played Books 7 and 8, and some were already on Mozart, which Ms. Behrend pronounced with a sharp "tz" sound and straight vowels, "MOH-tzaht!" The concertos, which Dr. Suzuki had placed in the final two books of his method, were often played by teenagers for auditions for elite conservatory pre-college programs. My parents gathered sleek brochures for each of the schools: Mannes, Manhattan School of Music, and one that started with a J—which they didn't know how to say. Ms. Behrend chewed the word like prime sirloin. "Jewel-i-aahhd." On the ride back from the City, we clutched our sides at Dad's imitation of her, laughing until our bellies ached.

But when he asked when I would be ready to audition for that school, Ms. Behrend dismissed him with a regal wave, laughing off any mention of an audition or jumping ahead to the Mozart concertos. Six was far too young for the "J" school.

First, I'd need less pizza, and a much better violin.

Suzuki Book 7: Johann Sebastian Bach, Concerto No. 1 in A Minor

[Montgomery / Upper West Side, New York]

The summer I turned seven, Dad took up a new hobby: training—then breeding—his German shepherds. I'd watch him strap on a wicker sleeve and shout German commands at Prinz—*Fass!* to attack, *Fuss!* to heel. Samrat, a rock-chewing doofus, was happy to chase anything, including rocks. But for Silke, Dad built an obstacle course of PVC tubing in our front yard. She glided above the hurdles as if gravity had no hold on her. Soon, our household had a litter of gamboling, floppy-eared puppies, but Shonu and I sobbed into our OshKosh B'Gosh when Dad sold all but one to a giant truck that read "ARMY."

While Dad trained his Schutzhunds, Mom put me through a different kind of obstacle course. She stood guard at the stove holding a wooden spatula, its handle permanently yellowed with turmeric, keeping time between stirs and scolds. "Abar kor, Potka. Again." The Gupta Method demanded merciless excellence. Like the shepherds, I would do anything to be called a *good boy.*

Even though Mom's ears caught more mistakes than mine, it never crossed my mind to correct her. Mom, stirring daal and doling out hand-rolled ruti and porota, rarely sat to eat her own meal with the men in her family. Instead, she'd flip the flatbreads on a peeling Teflon pan, laminating dough with spoonfuls of melted ghee on the red Formica counter. Practice ended only when she set a plate in front of me. "Ai, shona, kha"—the only time during the day that she was affectionate. I'd eat extra helpings, to delay going back to practicing. In my Suzuki journal, Mr. Ducky wagged his finger: "Only eat on the days you practice"—so if I practiced extra, could I *eat* extra? I learned early on that food meant love, that food signaled the end of a hard day's work.

My parents had a reason for all the extra practice. Against Ms. Behrend's wishes, they had signed me up for an entrance audition to Juilliard Pre-College. They believed I could beat the classical music system the same way they trained their dogs, the same way they'd muscled their way into the middle class, the same way they'd earned their place in America: like Bengal tigers.

On audition day, my parents dressed me in Gap board shorts and a bright orange T-shirt. I was in desperate need of glasses, and the committee looked like a row of blurry, judgy blobs. I could still pick out Ms. Behrend, her disapproval radiating across the table like the heat from Mom's stove. I played the first movement of a Bach concerto without an accompanist, and within two minutes the fuzzy lumps dismissed me.

After the audition, my parents took us on a Hudson River cruise to see the Statue of Liberty. I spent the whole ride staring out the wrong side of the boat, munching a hot dog and humming Bach to myself. While I gazed at New Jersey, I didn't notice that everyone else—including my family—was busy snapping photos of a giant green statue.

A week later, Ms. Behrend was the angriest, tiniest person I'd ever seen.

"... And not dressing him *properly*, for goodness sake!" The committee had never seen the like. "This is *Juilliard*! You can't audition your boy in *shorts and a T-shirt*!"

Even though Ms. Behrend barely reached Dad's shoulder, I watched him lean back to avoid her glare. She wrung concession after concession from him: no more rote tape drills, no shortcuts, absolutely no performances. A new violin. A better bow. And if I wanted a real shot next time, I'd have to spend two full years on a single piece—Mozart's Fourth Concerto—and take weekly private lessons at her apartment a few blocks south of Lincoln Center. When Dad balked—"Two years on *one* concerto?"—Ms. Behrend glared again. He couldn't yet imagine that Mozart 4, a twenty-three-minute piece of music, would be a lifelong companion.

Dad took me to the outlets at Woodbury Commons, where he made dressing me a full-time job. Button-downs and polo shirts and oversized jeans with rolled-up cuffs. "You look like a forty-year-old midget," he said. He wasn't wrong.

Next came the optometrist, who dilated my pupils and declared I was so nearsighted I was "legally blind." Suddenly it made sense to my parents: the storybooks held inches from my nose at dinner, the playground where faces dissolved into color, the car rides where a deer would be pointed out and I'd be singing out the window, seeing nothing but blur. I'd always known the world in sound first: able to hear the bird, but rarely able to see it. Now, I had giant red-and-gold glasses that swallowed my face—strapped behind my ears with an electric-blue lanyard—and the whole thing only made matters worse. *Cowabunga, dude.*

At our next lesson, Ms. Behrend was not impressed. "Well, maybe now you'll see the notes," she muttered, already halfway down the hallway. Her studio was a living archive: walls lined with black-and-white portraits of her old teachers and prize students staring down in judgment. She didn't offer a tour, or tea, or even a bathroom. She sat in a wicker chair that creaked under her, legs crossed in brown tweed, as a cat appeared from nowhere and leapt into her lap. In the corner behind me, Dad clicked his pen, ready to transcribe. I raised my violin. The audition was over, but the real test was about to begin: the first movement of Mozart 4.

The first note was a grace note: a quick step above the melody, halfway up my quarter-sized violin. I slid toward it, hoping perfect pitch would save me. "Aaapapapapapah! No cheating," Ms. Behrend snapped. I froze, swallowed, tried again—and missed badly. The cat bolted. She shook her head, lifted her violin, set a bony finger on the E string—in exactly the right spot—and played through the first page for me.

Her sound was full, clear, and alive. She had seemed so small, almost frail, but when she played, her sound made her seem immense. When she stopped, the notes lingered in the air, more real than the dots on the page. She was playing the notes on the page, the same notes I was trying to play, but I heard so much more: Chirping birds and bright leaves, a twirling dance. I didn't want her to stop playing, but now, it was my turn.

"Play," she said. "Try the first two notes, like this: *pi-yam*." She played the first two notes, slowly. Trying hard not to cheat, I repeated the two notes, but my sound was hollow and tinny, a pathetic squawk.

"No. *Pi-Yyyam!* Crisp, crisp!! It's a fanfare!"

I played again, thinking of Doritos.

"Good! Now do it again."

We did it ten times in a row. Each time, I felt the wire E string cut into my finger. It hurt, but I knew not to say anything.

"Good boy! Now, play the rest of the bar. *Pi-yam pum-pa-pum-pum-pum.*"

That day, I learned one—*one*—measure of music. But I hadn't even realized an hour had gone by before she cleared her throat and leaned back in her chair.

"All right. That's enough for today."

I looked at the pad of my pudgy first finger, now marked by a thin black line. Ms. Behrend told Dad to buy rubbing alcohol to clean my fingerboard. Dad, his eyes twinkling, asked her if vodka would work instead. I didn't know what he meant, but Ms. Behrend gave him a long, measuring look and broke into a throaty laugh. "*Yes!* Vodka will do. Keep it off the varnish," she said, knocking the belly of her violin with a bony knuckle.

When Dad asked her how many times I should repeat the "*pi-yams*" at home, she said, "About fifty a day should do it. Not just practice now—*perfect* practice." After a week of fifty repetitions each day, my E string had pressed a permanent indentation into my first finger: my first callus. And after each practice, Dad wiped down my fingerboard with a dab of vodka on a cloth, careful not to let the alcohol touch the varnish on my violin. One time, he took a little swig, and winked at me. *Don't tell Mommy.*

Over the next year, Ms. Behrend taught me Mozart's Fourth Concerto, measure by measure. When we got to the lyrical theme, she said, "This is opera—like *Figaro.* Imagine Maria Callas singing an aria!" I didn't know who Maria Callas was, but after I played a few bars, she explained. "All Mozart is opera. It's a story. You have to see the characters on stage, singing, pleading. What is she asking for, this soprano?" Then she played—one long, sweet slur—and the violin sounded like a voice. When I tried, she reached out and adjusted my forearm, moving it until I found the sound in the right spot on the string, and in my body. But Mozart danced too. "Not too softly now, Robert! Give us some sound!" I tried again. "He was a country boy, you know, young Mozart. Traveled everywhere with his father, like you!" We built sound like a painting, over and over again, until the story became etched in the invisible air.

Dad rented Miloš Forman's *Amadeus* from Blockbuster and we all piled into our parents' big bed to watch. Shonu and I had to cover our eyes during the "grown-up" parts, but the grinning black mask haunted Shonu's dreams for years. If I ever bragged about a performance or got too full of myself, Mom would say, "Don't be like Mozart."

As our lessons progressed, Ms. Behrend filled my head with little pictures: a ping-pong ball rolling down a hallway, the pinprick of the devil's tail, a leaf drifting to the ground. Each image turned into sound, and each sound into technique. A bouncing ping-pong ball was a natural *accelerando*. The devil's tail was the bite of my bow to make the string speak. The leaf was the bow moving so lightly that the violin seemed to sing on its own.

I was too young to understand that her answers were always about connection: image to feeling, feeling to sound, sound to listener.

"Remember," she'd say. "People listen with their eyes!"

Suzuki Book 8: Johann Sebastian Bach, "Preludio" from Sonata in E Minor

[Newburgh, New York]

After one of my lessons, Ms. Behrend handed my parents a stack of cassette tapes: narrated fairy tales about composers. In one story, a moody Mr. Beethoven writes to the boy downstairs. In another, a panicked Tchaikovsky flees Carnegie Hall rehearsals on a train, dashing off *The Nutcracker* along the way. Mr. Bach steps off a spaceship to help a bored child practice a minuet. My favorite was *Vivaldi's Ring of Mystery*, in which a young gondolier helps an orphan girl search for a missing

Stradivarius. A nightingale sang in a graveyard. An oar cut through a haunted Venetian canal. Vivaldi himself appeared, reuniting a family through music.

The tales were fantasies, but based in truth. Tchaikovsky really did suffer stage fright so severe he feared his head might fall off while conducting. Beethoven tormented his neighbors, sometimes standing naked at the window, stomping and shouting. Bach wrote music for his children, half of whom he would also bury. And Vivaldi spent most of his life teaching at an orphanage, writing music for abandoned girls who became some of the most celebrated musicians in Europe.

Vivaldi's *Four Seasons* is one of the most overplayed works in classical music—the soundtrack of any good public radio pledge drive—but we often forget for whom it was written. Between 1720 and 1723, Vivaldi composed the *Seasons* while serving as violin master at the Ospedale della Pietà, one of Venice's four orphanages. Carnival made Venice a party town, but it also bankrolled its *ospedali*, its hospitals. Masked dukes and princes paid for their sins—and for their bastard children—through donations disguised as spiritual indulgences. A predictable number of months after Carnival, sex workers delivered unwanted babies through the *scafetta*, a small back-alley window of the orphanage.

At the age of five, those children came under the instruction of Maestro Vivaldi, a priest nicknamed "Il Prete Rosso" for his shock of red hair. According to legend, he'd been born on the day of an earthquake, and in gratitude that they had both survived, his mother dedicated him to the priesthood. He became a virtuoso violinist, though asthmatic and often ill, as well as a shrewd fundraiser, writing florid budget requests to royalty so he could hire the best soloists for his operas and concertos. Patrons flocked to see this cleric who never said Mass but could make bird sounds on his violin, conjure storms and lightning and the winter wind itself.

Instead of the 1980s pop my parents usually played in the car, I begged for the composer stories. As we passed Woodbury Commons on the Thruway, I barely noticed the blur of gold-green trees, immersed in the music's imaginings: spring birdsong and twirling nymphs, sweltering summer nights and monsoon rain. In autumn, as the maples in the Palisades blazed, I imagined Vivaldi's deer running through the forest, chased by horns and gunshots. The thrill of the chase was as real as the deer's death. In the music, like in stories, everything was more real than real. And some part of me knew then: If I could learn music, I could learn life.

I became obsessed with Vivaldi. I wanted my violin to cry, to scream, to shiver. At elementary school, I mimed the concertos constantly, even when my instrument was at home. My left hand wouldn't stop tapping, tracing fingerings across desks crusted with Dubble Bubble. The music played in my head all the time, and sometimes I couldn't help playing along.

One night, outside the Sears in Newburgh, I stood in the freezing cold with my jacket unzipped, trying to imagine how a violin could sound like sleet, as slippery as black ice. I mimed the furious blasts of "Winter," arms whipping in the wind. But we were only there to buy jeans, and I had no violin or bow. I stood outside the doors with a crazed look in my eyes, limbs twitching to thirty-second notes only I could hear. Dad stood inside the sliding glass doors, watching my unheard performance. When a couple walked past and whispered, "Poor kid," he bolted outside, grabbed my hands, and rushed me to the car with a gatta to the back of my head.

"Don't act pagla. What will people say?"

Suzuki Book 9: Wolfgang Amadeus Mozart, Concerto No. 5 in A Major

[Carnegie Hall / Rusk Institute for Rehabilitative Medicine, New York University]

How do you get to Carnegie Hall? We all know the answer: practice, practice, practice.

Ms. Behrend's students got there by the age of eight.

To celebrate the twenty-fifth anniversary of the School for Strings, our group lessons led to a performance on the world's most famous stage, gathering Ms. Behrend's students across generations. A composer named Bruce Adolphe had been commissioned to write a new work for the occasion called "Gut Feeling." It was the first time I'd ever played music by someone who was standing in the room, right next to us. Some of the other performers were my parents' age, now principal players in big orchestras or soloists with major careers. Ms. Behrend had been teaching for fifty years, and as she darted across the Carnegie Hall stage, her blue irises were electric. She ran our rehearsal in front of rows of empty red velvet seats, reminding us that a performance wasn't a show, but an exchange. Our job was to make the room feel what we felt in our guts.

When the lights came up, though, I was blinded by brightness, unable to see any of the people I was supposed to be playing for, even with my glasses. Because I couldn't see a single face, I had to pretend that the people out there were listening. I focused on the few things I could see: my fingers, my mistakes, Ms. Behrend's waving arms. The rest of Carnegie Hall slipped away, too distant to register, and I may as well have been at home, standing in Mom's kitchen.

Dad, on the other hand, celebrated my Carnegie Hall debut at the Carnegie Deli. He took me and Shonu in for pastrami sandwiches which, when they arrived on huge white plates, were bigger than our heads. The walls were covered with signed headshots of celebrities like Jerry Seinfeld, Tom Hanks, Robin Williams. Dad beamed. "One day you boys'll be up there. I know it." He slathered his sandwich with mustard and handed it to me. "Here, Potku. Take a big boy bite." I took the bite, and my nose stung as my eyes watered. Dad cracked up. I glanced at the glossy faces on the wall and wondered if any of them had teared up from mustard, too. Shonu drowned his foot-long hot dog in ketchup, in case Dad tried the same trick on him.

That night, I realized the performance itself had already slipped away, overshadowed by mustard and laughter and the glow of Dad's pride. But the concert that stayed with me wasn't Carnegie Hall. It was the one that came two weeks later.

Ms. Behrend was already planning our next concert, this time at New York University's Rusk Institute of Rehabilitative Medicine. We would play the program from Carnegie Hall again, but now for children with terminal cancer. In a hospital waiting area, we unpacked our violin cases and lined up in Suzuki formation. Mimicking Ms. Behrend, we bowed to that audience exactly as we had at Carnegie Hall. There, I had played for people I couldn't see: donors and proud parents and other Suzuki teachers. But now, I could see my audience: children, all of them around my age, whose eyes glinted from their hospital beds. And now, I could be sure that they were really listening.

We played our Suzuki favorites: Corelli, Bach, and Vivaldi. Ms. Behrend stood between us and the audience. She held her violin, a Guarneri del Gesù from the same century as Vivaldi, under her chin. Behind her, a girl sat bolt upright in a hospital bed, swallowed by an oversized gown, conducting us with wild, jerking arms. Her eyes blazed overbright, and I couldn't look away. The girl, like maestro Mehta, had become the music, and for a while, I followed her wild conducting. The room itself seemed to vanish—the antiseptic air, the steady monitors, the parents' faces lined with exhaustion—and for a moment it was only the girl, eyes blazing, conducting and listening, and us, answering her with sound.

A few minutes later the girl sank back onto her pillow, spent. Her chest barely moved. She was probably ten, yet she seemed older than Ms. Behrend.

On the dark drive home, Dad wasn't his usual clattering, chattering self. He took long drags on his beedee and tapped the ash out the window. When Shonu asked why some of the kids in the clinic were bald, Dad didn't answer right away. He kept his eyes on the road.

"Ek din tora bujbi."

He was right. One day, we would understand.

Suzuki Book 10: Wolfgang Amadeus Mozart, Concerto No. 4 in D Major

[The Juilliard School, New York]

In August 1995, a week before I turned eight, I auditioned for Juilliard Pre-College a second time. This time I wore a black suit, and I could see my judges. Dad had coached me for weeks, quoting Ms. Behrend: "Move, Potka. They listen with their eyes." Before I walked in alone, he pressed a scratchy kiss on my cheek, reeking of Marlboro Lights and Eau Sauvage.

In a chartreuse-carpeted room with heavy velvet drapes, I played a movement of my hard-earned Mozart concerto—nailing Ms. Behrend's *pi-yam*—then the opening of a Handel sonata. The notes felt like a golden thread, running on and on, brighter each time. I forgot it was an audition. Now, all I had to do was make the people in the room feel what I was feeling.

Over the next few years, I learned how emotions sounded before I knew how they felt. Music gave me a way to try on feelings I didn't yet have words for. I heard nostalgia in Tchaikovsky before I had anything to miss. I learned what longing sounded like through *Carmen*, years before anyone explained love to me. The soft, anxious melody of the Mendelssohn concerto—music that would become the soundtrack of my teenage years—felt like praying for something that might never happen. Sometimes it was easier to play the feeling than to feel it. And later, it would be safer not to feel anything at all.

The committee stopped me right before the second movement of the Handel sonata, which started like a trumpet call. I could tell from Ms. Behrend's smile that she was pleased. I had forgotten it was an audition.

"Flying colors" was all she said to Dad, who had been waiting outside the room, wringing his hands and chewing his fingernails. When he leaned down to straighten my bow tie again, I caught a whiff of medicinal sharpness. Later, as I put away my instrument, I found the tiny bottle of vodka in my case, for wiping down the strings, empty.

We celebrated with Dad's favorite meal: masala dosa at Maharani, an Indian restaurant in a Fort Lee strip mall. I ate with my hands and smeared sambar on a cream-colored tablecloth, still dressed in my black suit.

Chapter 2

THE WALL OF ACCOMPLISHMENTS

Mendelssohn, Violin Concerto in E Minor

> The violinist is that peculiarly human phenomenon distilled to a rare potency—half tiger, half poet.
>
> —**Yehudi Menuhin**

Felix Mendelssohn, Violin Concerto in E Minor, Op. 64—i. Allegro molto appassionato

[The Sherry Netherlands, Fifth Avenue, New York City]

Dad was desperate for legitimacy. He had climbed the rungs of an American Dream, but he wanted more. Too many doors were still closed to him, and by extension, his sons. But he was convinced that if he could get the attention of famous people, if we could get closer to the world of fame, then he—and we—would finally be enough.

So, Dad wrote letters to 1990s talk-show hosts, pretending to be me: "Dear Oprah, someday I would like to play for you, if you want me to." The shows responded by sending signed glossies: Oprah in a red pantsuit, Sally Jessy Raphael with her trademark specs, David

Letterman in a letterman jacket. He'd carefully frame each picture and nail it to my bedroom wall, alongside elementary school achievements—"Math Whiz!" and "Spelling Champ!"—and karate trophies. And in the center of Dad's Wall of Accomplishments, in a slim walnut frame and white matting, hung the stoic, unsmiling Clintons. A few years later, I realized their Sharpie signatures looked suspiciously like Dad's.

Dad wrote to Zubin Mehta—the music director of the New York Philharmonic, the same maestro I'd watched on PBS as a toddler. The Philharmonic's publicist sent a signed eight-by-ten monochrome headshot. I'd stare at Mehta's matinee-idol face while I practiced—his coiffed hair, aquiline nose, and piercing eyes, wondering what he looked like in real life.

Dad even wrote to the famous violinist Yehudi Menuhin, who, surprisingly, wrote back, inviting our family to meet him the next time he was in New York.

So one April evening in 1997, Dad and I stood outside a pale blue door at The Sherry Netherlands. My heart pounded. Dad tugged at my bright red bow tie, straightening it. Before Dad knocked, he reminded me, "Remember to touch his feet, Potku. He's a mahatma."

Lord Yehudi Menuhin really *was* a great soul. In 1929, at thirteen, he had debuted with the Berlin Philharmonic, playing concertos by Brahms, Beethoven, and Bach—then, as an encore, the last two movements of the Mendelssohn. Albert Einstein, who was in the audience, said, "Now I know there is a God in heaven."

Though Menuhin became one of the most famous musicians in the world, he spent much of his career wrestling with fate. Playing for troops during World War II left him with a chronic injury that never healed. And when he returned to Germany in 1947, the American Jewish Congress condemned him—even though his very name meant "the Jew." He replied, "There is a Germany other than Hitler's.

I believe in the humanity of the German people, and we must start somewhere."

Later he turned to yoga under B. K. S. Iyengar, famously standing in shirshasana before performances. He championed Indian music, too, recording ragas with Ravi Shankar. We listened to those CDs in the car: Menuhin playing not only Mozart and Mendelssohn, but Piloo and Puriya Kalyan. Dad said he played with dorod—compassion, tenderness, concern. Even at eight, I could hear it: the faint tremble in his bow arm, the same kind of shake I had when I was afraid.

When the door opened, I saw a simple man, dressed in a silk paisley shirt and charcoal trousers. I bent forward to touch his black slippers, and he lightly placed a hand on my back. His eyes were a limpid, clear blue. When I rose, he kept his hand on my shoulder. I looked into his deep-blue eyes and didn't feel so nervous anymore.

"Was your journey difficult?"

Dad answered him with a tight little wave. "Oh no, no, fine, fine."

I looked up at Dad. We had spent three hours driving through a rainstorm, the car nearly spinning out on the George Washington Bridge. Because parking in the City was impossible, Mom and Shonu were circling Central Park in the Sentra. Dad shook his head, indicating I shouldn't say a word.

Menuhin turned, leading us into his room. On the coffee table was a bird's dinner: cracked walnut shells, a half-peeled banana, an apple with one clean slice taken out. I wondered to myself: *How could someone eat so little and look so happy?*

For the next hour I played for Menuhin: first Mozart, then Mendelssohn. His recordings of those pieces were legendary—some of them made even before Dad was born—and yet Menuhin listened to me as if he were hearing the music for the first time. As I played, he closed his eyes. When I finished, he praised my teachers and thanked my parents. He made a few simple suggestions about a fingering or a bowing. He focused instead on how I held the violin. Like all Suzuki kids, I used a shoulder rest—a plastic bar that locked the violin into place—but Menuhin could see that I had a rather short neck, and using the shoulder rest was causing me to clamp my jaw and twist my neck, which was then causing me to corkscrew my entire body. Asking for my violin, Menuhin gently took off the shoulder rest and placed the instrument directly against my body. I tried to hold the violin, but it slipped away. Gently, he placed two long fingers on my collarbone. Then he took my hand and laid it against his collarbone.

"Here."

I played, and Menuhin steadied me, adjusting my shoulder or elbow when I tensed, and I felt, for the first time, the vibration of my violin move throughout my body.

During the lesson, Dad kept snapping flash photos, oblivious to the miracle happening between two violinists, seventy years apart. Maybe he wanted proof he could understand. After I finished playing, Dad asked Menuhin to write me a letter of recommendation. Menuhin looked at me, not saying a word, and nodded.

He turned and took a seat at a large wooden desk. From the drawer, he pulled a sheet of letterhead and slowly uncapped a fountain pen. I heard the nib cut into the paper, and then stop, and then start again. He wrote: "I have heard Robert Vijay Gupta, and believe this young man is possessed of great musical and human talent. He is bound to go far."

Before we left, Dad told me to salute Menuhin again. But this time, Menuhin stopped me, folded his hands, and bent at the waist.

Three years later, Yehudi Menuhin died on a gray March day. I was eleven. I looked out the window of my bedroom while playing his recording of the Mendelssohn violin concerto, gazing out at a sky full of clouds and bare tree branches. I wondered if I could absorb some part of his soul, now released into the world, into mine, but maybe reincarnation didn't work like that.

Menuhin had returned to that Silence from which all music comes.

Franz Schubert, Symphony No. 6 in C Major, D. 589—iv. Allegro moderato

[Room 309, Bruno Walter Orchestral Studio, The Juilliard School, New York]

In a 1996 episode of *Reading Rainbow*—"Zin! Zin! Zin! A Violin"—LeVar Burton watches a rehearsal of the Juilliard Pre-College Chamber Orchestra. Most of the musicians are no older than ten. The towering, baton-wielding terror on the podium is Eugene Becker. When he raps his baton on a stand, the noodling orchestra of children comes to an abrupt pause, instruments ready, their eyes wide with fear.

Today, these musicians will play Schubert's 6th symphony. A few violinists will narrate the episode. Yura will talk about playing as part of a group. Maya will say she always watches the conductor out of the corner of her eye. And a rotund boy with glasses too big for his face and a mild Bengali accent will caution viewers who think playing in orchestra is fun: "If you're careless, and you make a mistake, you're gonna bring *everyone* down."

The entire drive into Manhattan, my parents—who had volunteered me to be interviewed—grilled me in the back seat of the Nissan Sentra. "Ki bolbi, Potka? What will you say when they ask you about orchestra, about music? What? Speak up!"

Their interrogation would be far more terrifying than anything the camera crew would ask me. If I'd falter or stutter—or when my lower lip started to tremble—Dad sent his blade-like palm back toward my knees for a sharp gatta. I swallowed my tears in big heaving gulps.

"Potka, stop crying! Tor boro hote hobe!"

"Boro," like in the Tagore song "Boro Asha Kore," could mean immense or huge, but when it was directed at me, it meant "Grow up!" When I was finally in front of the camera crew, I channeled all the terror I felt toward my parents—and Mr. Becker—into gripping my quarter-sized violin and bow, wide-eyed and completely serious about my worst fear.

I'd only been eight for two weeks.

Everyone—you're gonna bring everyone down.

Eugene Becker, a former New York Philharmonic violist and one of Leonard Bernstein's early hires, conducted with a pout and a tick-tock slash of his baton. He held Juilliard's youngest group to an impossibly high standard. The school had three youth orchestras—high schoolers, middle schoolers, and us—and Becker needed us to be the best.

Under his glare, the pianissimo *clip-clop* of a Schubert second-violin part felt like walking a tightrope. Sometimes, we were more afraid of him than we were of our parents who were closely watching the rehearsal. One slip and he'd pounce: "You do not know the bowings!" Sometimes he'd make a child stand alone and play before the entire orchestra. The one time he called on me—to play an excerpt from the last movement of Dvořák's Eighth Symphony—fear made my bow skitter over the strings and land on the wrong side of the bridge. When my violin let out a horrible squeak, some of the front stands laughed. Becker made me play alone again, and then again. I felt Dad's eyes boring a hole in the back of my head. I knew Mom was already doubled over in shame.

That night, after classes at Pre-College, I cried all the way up the Palisades. "We didn't raise you for this, Potka." Then Dad put on a CD: Kurt Masur with the New York Philharmonic at Avery Fisher Hall. I let it run on repeat all week, practicing my part in the kitchen the way I had with my Suzuki tapes. By midweek, I was singing the symphony nonstop. One morning, I conducted the entire symphony in the shower from memory and used up all the hot water.

By the time we performed it at the Juilliard Theater, I could sing the trumpet fanfare, the trombone chorale, the aching cello lines, the flute solo, and the horn calls. Once my part was so familiar I could forget it, it felt like I was playing the whole orchestra at once.

And once I had become that music, I wasn't afraid of Mr. Becker anymore. In fact, there was nothing—*nothing*—that could bring me down.

Pablo de Sarasate, *Carmen Fantasy*

[North Michigan Avenue, Chicago]

After I graduated from playing Suzuki tunes, Dad started to fall in love with classical music.

If he had a favorite recording, it was the 1987 *Carmen Fantasy*—Itzhak Perlman with the New York Philharmonic, conducted by Zubin Mehta. He'd blast it while cooking eggs and Polska kielbasa, singing along with Perlman. The composer Pablo de Sarasate had taken Georges Bizet's opera, the story of a woman who refused to be owned, and turned it into a tour de force for a violinist and orchestra. After watching a VHS of Perlman performing the *Carmen Fantasy,* Dad dreamed of the day I could perform it on the same stage.

One day, he came home with a napkin signed by Perlman, whose motorized wheelchair he had chased across Fifty-Fourth Street. He framed the napkin, too, and then nailed that to my bedroom wall.

When I finally learned the *Carmen Fantasy* a few years later, I could feel Dad keeping time across the room, comparing every note I played to Perlman's recording. He knew that if I could sound like Perlman—if I could make him feel the way Perlman made him feel—then one day, I could be on the same stages. And I would do anything to make Dad happy, even if I thought the *Carmen Fantasy* was a really stupid piece of music.

Dad kept writing letters to famous people, as me. One day, we received a response from Harpo Productions, Oprah's production company, inviting me to be on her show. I'd never seen a single episode of *The Oprah Winfrey Show* in my life.

A few weeks later, a film crew arrived at our home to film B-roll for a series called "Letters to Oprah." Dad coached me on every syllable of his—my—typewritten letter, which I read aloud to the crew with pretend fire. Behind the producer, I looked for Dad's thumbs-up. The crew camped out in a tent on our lawn, and Mom improvised a Bengali bolognese for them—lamb keema on spaghetti. Shonu eyed the tall cameramen, asking when we could play outside with the puppies. He was told to go to his room, and when he did, he slammed the door. I wished I could play with the puppies, too, but I knew better than to act like a kid.

A few weeks later, I got off the school bus to find two small suitcases and my violin case waiting by the door, packed. I was going to be on *The Oprah Winfrey Show*: my first flight, first hotel, first time out of New York. Naturally, Dad had me perform the *Carmen Fantasy* on the airplane, for the TWA crew. A flight attendant pinned plastic wings to my windbreaker. Our hotel, the Chicago Omni, felt like another planet: The lobby smelled like vanilla ice cream. At check-in, the concierge offered to book us a tour of the city. Dad waved her off: "We're not tourists. My son's going to be on *Oprah* tomorrow!"

Our suite had two perfectly made beds, the biggest TV I'd ever seen, and a view of the Sears Tower, which Dad said was taller than the World Trade Center—but New York was still better because it had two of them. I nodded hard, proud to be a New Yorker. I stood barefoot on the patterned carpet while Dad coached me from a leather armchair: "Smile, Potka! Move your head! Body movement! Abar baja, bhalo kore baja!" He wanted me to play again, and better.

On the day of the taping, Dad fidgeted in our dressing room at Harpo Studios in the West Loop. Other child performers and their parents wandered through a crowded greenroom. A mom with a soft southern lilt asked Dad if he would watch the taping, and when he said yes, I panicked. I didn't want to be alone before I walked into the bright lights. But Dad went to watch. An assistant producer kept me company until it was time to walk onto the set, and when I did, I played, bobbling my head in time, a smile plastered to my face. Oprah greeted me with her famous warmth, exclaiming, "You got that *head thing* going on!" More like *Dad's* head thing, I thought. *Where was Dad?* The audience laughed and cheered. I don't remember if Oprah asked me any other questions and before I knew it, the lights were out, Oprah was gone, and the same producer gently steered me off stage. *That was it?* I felt a jolt of fear. *Did I do okay?*

That night, on Oprah's dime, Dad and I ordered overpriced room-service cheeseburgers bigger than my head, and he let me order cheesecake *and* a fudge-brownie sundae. We sat with our pants unbuttoned, hands on our swollen bellies, watching *Seinfeld*.

Back in New York, Dad turned my appearance on *Oprah* into his own ordeal, telling his Bengali friends that the day I went on the show was the day he went bald. The studio lights, he said, had sunburned his scalp.

Wolfgang Amadeus Mozart, Sonata in E Minor, K. 304—i. Allegro

[Montgomery, New York]

At home, Shonu and I were becoming a musical team. He started on violin too, but when I started playing concerts, our parents quickly switched him to piano. I would need an accompanist. We became a performing duo dressed in matching gaudy vests, ready with a repertoire of Suzuki tunes, and later, Mozart sonatas and a few salon pieces by Fritz Kreisler. At home, Dad coached us on how to walk out with broad smiles and straight backs, and then bow to our audiences in perfect sync. Dad made flyers for our recitals—"The Gupta Brothers Play Suzuki Book 2"—which we performed for retired Presbyterians in Goshen and Wallkill. By the time Shonu turned nine, he had earned a spot at Juilliard. He moved out of our shared bedroom into a room of his own, with a giant upright piano as his new roommate. He too was on his way to the Wall.

We were both rising—Shonu on piano, me on violin—but we were also at the center of hours-long screaming matches. We learned to disappear during those fights, the farther from the house, the better. The arguments were mostly about how much we were, or weren't, practicing. Dad wanted us to be kids. "They need some fresh air," he'd say. But Mom knew that every wasted minute was a step backward. Her sons wouldn't get second chances in this world. Childhoods were a luxury we couldn't afford.

Like every other Bengali kid we knew, we were expected to bring home straight A's. But when a teacher sneered, "Sure, your boys are good at music, but they're probably going to fail at math"—Mom canceled our lessons from *Dial B for Bengali* and taught us algebra herself—four years before we'd encounter it in middle school. I had loved the Bengali lessons, which felt like a game, a secret code. She blamed Dad for going soft. "You're not a real man," she shouted. "I don't want them to end up like you!" Sometimes, Dad would yell back, and the two of them would get into a screaming match that could last for hours.

Shonu and I learned to read our parents' moods. We listened for the tempo of their footsteps, the dynamics of their breathing. Raised voices were bad. Silence was worse. If Mom called one of us by our Anglicized first name, we were in deep trouble. I shrank and tried to smile my way out of it, as if I could change the air in the room by acting better than good.

One morning I practiced in the living room while they screamed on either side of me. I kept playing, hoping the music might stop them. Mid-shout, Mom swung at Dad and caught my bow instead, snapping it in a spray of horsehair. I froze, in case the next swing was meant for me.

In a sunny atelier across the street from Carnegie Hall, a Chinese luthier repaired the shattered bow and polished the salt-trails of tears off my half-size violin. He didn't look up from his work.

"All the best ones cry."

When I was nine, I scribbled my name in Sharpie on an expensive Bärenreiter edition of the Mendelssohn concerto, practicing my own autograph. When Mom found it—"ROBAAAAART?!"—she stood in my doorway holding the defaced score in one hand and in the other, a precious rock collection, carefully mounted on a sheet of cardboard, labeled with torn scraps of masking tape. Tiny treasures: quartz, feldspar, fool's gold, a smooth green pebble I thought was jade, and my favorite: a small spiral ammonite from the Museum of Natural History.

Before I could speak, she bashed the collection against the dresser, once, *twice*. The cardboard crumpled, and the pebbles skittered loose all over the room. I'd never find the ammonite.

But when Dad got angry, he was truly terrifying. When his kind, smiling face twisted into fury, I bolted to my room and cowered in the corner. As he raised an open palm above his head, a warm, soaking shame spread down the front of my Ninja Turtle sweatpants. After the first few strikes, he saw it and stopped, leaving my room without a word.

That night, he took me to Pizza Hut. "Don't tell Mommy."

At night, my parents would watch *Seinfeld* together in their bedroom, their door ajar. Attracted by Dad's laugh, Shonu and I would crawl on our bellies and watch from the floor, hoping the dogs wouldn't give us away. When we giggled at Kramer's antics, Dad would call out "Arey! Dushtu boys! Come here!" We'd emerge sheepishly, expecting the worst. But then, he'd yank the comforter and we'd clamber into the bed. He'd stretch out a bony, expectant leg to each of us and we would knead his tight arches until we found the spot.

"Now do your mom's."

George Frideric Handel, *Messiah*, HWV 56—"Comfort Ye"

[Room 303, The Juilliard School, New York]

Every Saturday morning, as the Hudson Valley autumn slid into a grudging chill, the back seat of our Nissan Sentra became a chapel. Around 6 a.m., after a quick pujo, Dad started the car and scraped ice from the windshield, hollering for the Gupta Brothers: *"Move your asses!"* From our bedrooms, we watched twin plumes of vapor rise, one from the car's exhaust pipe and the other from his fist as he blew into it like it was a conch shell, muttering a string of curses in Bengali.

Meanwhile, Mom packed our lunches—last night's lamb keema on Wonder Bread—and buckled us into the back seat with our backpacks and my violin case, then popped the CD into the CD player: Robert Shaw and the Atlanta Symphony Chorus singing Handel's *Messiah*. The overture began with majesty, like a gate swinging open to something holy and terrible. Dad peeled onto Rock Cut Road, heading for the Thruway as the strings needled a fugue, one voice threading into another, and then another. At the Newburgh on-ramp, where the red maples and oaks and beeches blurred together in a wash of orange and crimson, the car was warm enough for us to start drawing stick-figure dogs and hearts and naughty words on the inside of the windows as the music changed again. The strings pulsed a gentle *accompagnato*. A tenor sang alone:

Comfort ye. Comfort ye, my people.

Shonu and I pulled out the scores from our backpacks. We were ready to sing.

Chorus was my favorite class at Juilliard. Ms. Scott didn't bark like Mr. Becker. She didn't demand perfection so much as show us where it already lived: in our breath, our bodies, our voices. Her classes were met in a bright, sunlit ballet studio and always began with stretches, then warm-ups—"la-la-LA-la-laaa"—three notes up, two down, as if we were greeting the full range of our voices. If we cracked or squeaked, she would smile and tell us to come back to our breath. Singing wasn't about playing in tune. It was about *being* in tune.

In the car, before Shonu and I launched into the first chorus—"And the glory, the glory of the Lord"—we'd press our hands against our ribs and breathe deeply. Our chests rose, our lungs stretched, and the music was already there. All we had to do was let it out.

I also loved chorus for the ways it let me sing—and pray—in other languages. In the seven years I was a boy soprano in her Pre-College

Choir, I sang psalms in Hebrew and Masses in Latin, songs in German, Spanish, French, and Ladino. I reveled in the taste of sacred words echoed across traditions—Domine, Adonai, Deus, Dio, Dei—the way they lit a warm light inside me, like Dad's morning chants: "Devi prapannartihare prasida..."

I had a bright, trumpet-clear voice and chased every solo I could, eager to show off. My brother sang softer, plainer, usually holding his favorite Beanie Baby—a sheep or a piglet—as if he were singing into himself. A private prayer. The first time I was ever moved to tears by music was hearing him sing "Once in Royal David's City" at a church somewhere in the Hudson Valley. He wore a paper crown and a swatch of silk, and his golden voice hung in the air like a suspended drop of light.

But in the car, I tortured him. I corrected his theory homework, invented melodic and rhythmic dictations I knew were too hard, and, worst of all, used my perfect pitch to convince him he was always a half-step flat. He would retaliate by pelting me in the face with a Beanie Baby. Dad's arm would swing back blindly, while he gripped the steering wheel in his other hand, a cigarette burning between his fingers. If the car swerved, Mom hissed, "Babu, shabdaan!," urging him to be careful.

Still, we sang. Red-faced, eyes wet, we picked the melody back up as if nothing had happened.

His yoke is easy, and his burthen is light.

Later, when my voice settled into a clarion boy soprano, Ms. Scott assigned me a solo: the Twenty-Third Psalm, set by Leonard Bernstein. I learned Hebrew words I'd never forget.

Adonai ro'i lo echsar. Bin'ot deshe yarbitseini.
Ahl mei m'nuchot yenahaleini.

When I sang the soaring, bluesy melody of the Chichester Psalms, I disappeared, becoming more than I could ever be.

In a world before most Americans knew the word "Diwali," Ms. Scott had done her homework. She knew my family came from a tradition of devotional song, and while curating a program of international folk music for the Pre-College Choir, she asked me to arrange something by our poet Tagore. Mom and Dad were cautious, but proud. I'd learned a new Robindroshongit for Navaratri, and while I copied out the melody, Mom transliterated the Bengali into Roman script. It was the first time I had heard a choir sing in my mother tongue—maybe the first time Bengali was ever sung at Juilliard.

Akash bhora shurjo tara
Bishwa bhora pran
Tahari majkhane ami peyechhi mor sthan
Bishowye tai jage, jage amar gaan

Sky, filled by sun and star
Cosmos, filled by life
Amid them, I found my place
Awe awakes, awakes my song.

The year I turned nine, Ms. Scott assigned me the solo in Gabriel Fauré's *Requiem*: "Pie Jesu Domine." In the back seat of the Sentra, I practiced, my breath fogging the glass. When Mom asked what the Latin I was singing meant, I explained that *Requiem* meant eternal rest; it was a Mass for the dead. And *Pie Jesu*, the first words of the solo, meant it was a prayer to Jesus. Mom nodded. "He's God too, Potka." I drew a cross on the window and imagined Jesus: not the glittering infant in a manger, but a dying man-god who became the sacrifice instead of demanding one, both pujo and proshad. My eyes filled with tears. At the performance a few weeks later, as I stood between the crucifix and the audience gathered into pews, I didn't have to prove anything. All I had to do was sing for Jesus.

Later that year, I came in as the runner-up for a Juilliard concerto competition, which everything in my world told me was just "best loser." By now, I had learned how to hate myself. As I placed my violin back in its case, Mr. Becker walked past without a word, and Mom and Dad didn't have to tell me how much I had let them down. I had practiced so hard, imagining every note in my hands for months. But it wasn't enough. No one came to tell me that making a mistake was human, or that I could make a mistake without becoming one. On the ride home, I sobbed, pulling my knees to my chest and rocking back and forth against the seat belt. Dad said nothing. As we passed Harriman State Park and took the exit for the Thruway, the sky glittered with stars and he put the CD into the player, and clicked forward to the second track, my favorite.

Comfort ye. Comfort ye, my people.

Harry Belafonte, "Jamaica Farewell"

[New York Coliseum]

After *Reading Rainbow,* a call arrived from a wholly different musical universe. *Billboard* wanted five Juilliard kids to perform at the 1995 music awards. The gig: playing "Gangsta's Paradise"—the year's top-selling song—with a gospel choir and the rapper Coolio. Stevie Wonder would make a surprise cameo. Dad bought the cassette at the Lincoln Center Tower Records and blasted it in the car on the way home from Pre-College. In the back seat, I studied the J-card: Coolio stood in front of blurred skyscraper lights I'd later realize were Los Angeles, wearing a purple shirt, white necktie, and suspenders. Two sharp braids stuck out of his head like antennae. And in the corner, a label I'd never seen on a classical album: "Parental Advisory: Explicit Lyrics."

Coolio's team faxed Dad a single, fragile sheet of handwritten music with a looping rhythm: *daa-dada, da-dada, daa-dada—da-da-da.* I would play alongside four other violinists from Pre-College, among whom I was the youngest, roundest, shortest. A producer picked my outfit: a black T-shirt, screen-printed with a single word, PEACE.

For the next few weeks, I'd come home from third grade and play along to "Gangsta's Paradise" for hours with the cassette. Dad, seeing the Billboard Awards as a once-in-a-lifetime shot for his little superstar, coached me most afternoons: "*No,* Potka, *move! Body movement!* People want to see you have fun. This isn't *Mozart*!"

(If only Dad had known that Mozart had once written a six-part canon for his buddies called "Leck mich im Arsch." You figure it out.)

Meanwhile, Juilliard didn't consider hip-hop "real music," even though "Gangsta's Paradise" blared from every pop radio station in the country. Dad suggested I bring the chart into my lesson. That was a mistake. Ms. Behrend took one look at the curled, pink-streaked fax and wrinkled her nose as if it smelled. "What is this?" Out the fifth-floor window overlooking Lincoln Center Plaza, I fixed on Henry Moore's bronze sculpture *Reclining Figure.*

"Aren't we hearing Mozart today? The second movement?" Her eyes narrowed. I swallowed while Dad—dressed for the occasion in his best tan suit and Gucci tie—stepped in to explain. Even as he spoke, saying something about a "good opportunity," I could sense her disappointment. She had, after all, forbidden any public performances. She sighed. Then she picked a measure from the chart and turned it into an impromptu étude on dotted rhythms, all the while berating the song's unmoving harmony. But before the hour was up, she made her point: Show business and "real music" did not mix.

Back home, though, Dad taught me another kind of lesson. He pulled out a VHS tape of Mom's favorite performer, Julio Iglesias. We sat in front of the same TV I'd watched as a toddler, glued to the New York Phil, while Dad pointed at the screen as Iglesias worked a sold-out crowd in a turquoise satin shirt unbuttoned to his belly. "Look how he moves, Potka. Look how many people love him." A few nights later, when a special of Harry Belafonte aired on PBS, Dad called me out of bed to watch. I sat on his feet, feeling like a grown-up being up so late. When Belafonte sang "Jamaica Farewell," Dad sang along. When I turned around to look at him, tears were rolling down his face.

In early December, at the New York Coliseum, I stood before the largest audience I'd ever seen. The evening was hosted by a young Jon Stewart, who introduced TLC, Goo Goo Dolls, Real McCoy, and Joni Mitchell. Before our number, Luther Vandross and Kenny G stood together at a podium. Kenny let out a *doo-do-do-dooo* on his soprano sax, and "Gangsta's Paradise" was announced as the year's No. 1 song. A Black, bow-tie-wearing conductor snapped his arms into position, and the lights came up over the stage as the strings came to life. For a second, I missed Mr. Becker. I felt out of place, already thinking of what Dad—waiting backstage with a camera dangling from his wrist—would say. Coolio walked out between the gospel-choir risers wearing a plaid flannel buttoned tight to the collar, and the crowd erupted. Soon, L.V. emerged with the now-famous refrain under Coolio's verse. And then, as if it couldn't get any bigger, Stevie Wonder—haloed in gold, escorted by four choirboys—glided onstage. When Stevie unfurled an improvised melisma, the conductor cued the strings to stop playing, and it felt as if time had stopped.

Tell me, why are we so blind to see
That the ones we hurt are you and me?

Everyone in the audience was singing along on their feet, and I could barely even hear my own playing. And then it was over. Backstage, under blinding spotlights and rows of steel scaffolding, people swarmed: crew members shouting into headsets, stagehands rushing to reset for the next act. Coolio's entourage, all in sunglasses indoors at night, stood guard outside the smoke-thick greenrooms.

In the middle of it all, Dad waited, hellbent on his mission: a photo of me with Stevie. He pleaded with an assistant, insisting I was "his biggest fan." I had never heard Stevie Wonder sing a note before that night. But when I repeated the line, Stevie smiled, bent down to my height, and whispered, "That's very nice, young man."

Twenty years later, when I found the video on YouTube, the other kids stood cool and composed. And then there was me, front and center as if the spotlight owed me something. I stomped, swayed, threw in head bobs that didn't quite land on the beat. I knew I was being a showoff, but Dad had me convinced I was a gangsta in paradise, and I ignored everything but the performance in my head.

The *Billboard* gig was the first time I ever received a check for playing the violin in public. Mom, who worked as an on-again, off-again teller at the Hudson Valley Federal Credit Union, opened a joint checking account.

"We'll keep this money safe for you, babu."

They never told me how much I'd made.

Felix Mendelssohn, Violin Concerto in E Minor, Op. 64—iii. Allegro molto vivace

[Huberman and Toscanini Streets, Tel Aviv, Israel]

Dad and I had a secret sign language. During performances, I'd find him in the back of the hall and follow his cues. "Straight bow" was a sharp half-nomoshkar, one palm pressed flat to his lips like a blade. If my fingers crept up the stick of my bow, he'd wag his fingers at me, his eyes blazing. To push me—faster, slower, softer, louder—he'd flash tight, staccato gestures, like a traffic cop with his elbows pinned. His guidance, not actually rooted in any kind of musical training, was a kind of well-intentioned showmanship: He believed he knew how to make me play in a way that audiences would love. When he popped open the heart-button of his shirt and tapped his chest—right where a gold-capped rudraksha bead hung—he was telling me to play from the heart, to make everyone in the room feel what I felt. "Make them cry, Potka." In those moments, my father had eyes only for his son. And there was no one in the world who could matter to me more than my dad.

But Dad's biggest star—his ultimate get—remained elusive: Zubin Mehta, the Bombay-born conductor I'd seen on PBS while still in Pampers. Before serving as music director of the New York Philharmonic, Mehta had been the youngest music director in history of the Los Angeles Philharmonic, stepping onto the podium at twenty-six with a program of Mozart, Hindemith, and Dvořák. As he wrapped his tenure in New York in the late 1990s, Mehta was one of the biggest names in classical music, holding concurrent directorships in Munich, Florence, and Tel Aviv.

Between preparing Mahler's *Resurrection* for a performance at Buchenwald and rehearsing Wagner's *Ring* in Munich, Mehta was spending a few weeks in New York at the Hôtel Plaza Athénée on Central Park South. Dad, armed with Yehudi Menuhin's letter, tried again. In Bally loafers and Mom's Cartier, Dad lingered in the lobby for weeks. Eventually, Mehta gave in. He offered me a twenty-minute audition—in Tel Aviv. No problem for a travel agent.

I was nine, and suddenly everything hinged on twenty minutes. If I played well enough—if I proved myself—maybe, I'd get to solo with the Israel Philharmonic. I practiced four hours a day: scales, arpeggios, Mazas and Kreutzer études, and my audition set: concertos by Mozart and the Soviet-Armenian composer, Aram Khachaturian. I knew I couldn't let Dad down, so I worked like my life depended on it, chasing the dream almost every kid studying classical music secretly harbors: to be chosen as a soloist.

In Israel, at the Fredric R. Mann Auditorium, Dad took a seat one row behind Mehta, to the right of the maestro's imperiously draped arm. I couldn't see Dad at all. Onstage, I played my concertos with a distractible but warm pianist who seemed more interested in giving motherly advice and explaining blackout curtains than playing the right notes.

During the Mozart, Mehta hummed along and tossed out a few air-conducting cues. I glimpsed Dad grinning behind him. During the Khachaturian, though, Mehta was silent. I unraveled. *Was I rushing? Was the pianist behind?* I couldn't tell.

Outside, in the hard Israeli sun, Mehta rattled off his thoughts as if late for his next rehearsal, which he probably was. "Stick with the Mozart," he said. "And what's this 'Robert' business?" When we told him who my teacher was, he furrowed the same brow I'd studied in his headshot. "Why aren't you playing Tchaikovsky? Or Mendelssohn? You should play Bach, too."

Dad, meanwhile, was trying to get a word in, but failing. No one talked over Maestro Mehta. I could feel Dad's panic building as he worked up the courage to interrupt one of the most powerful men in classical music. He was about to ask Mehta for a recommendation letter, the same way he'd asked Menuhin. At first, Mehta, still riffing about Bach, didn't hear. I cringed as Dad tried again. This time, Mehta heard.

He stopped and wheeled on Dad, yelling like a kaku at a wedding: "What?! You're asking me now? I have nothing to write with!"

Without missing a beat, Dad reached into his travel bag and pulled out a pen and a sheet of thick "Israel Philharmonic Orchestra" letterhead, lifted from a backstage office. Mehta froze, his eyes widening dangerously. Then, he let out a full belly laugh, shaking his head in disbelief. "And did you bring a desk for me to write it on?"

Not waiting for an answer, Mehta grabbed Dad's shoulder and spun him around, bending him over to use his back as a desk. I stared up, trying to make out the loops and slashes of the Hebrew letters as Mehta scrawled across the page. The vowelless script felt alien to me, nothing like Bengali. Above me, the street signs read "HUBERMAN" and "TOSCANINI."

Later, I'd learn those names. One was a Jewish violinist who had fled Nazi Europe and founded the Israel Philharmonic. The other was a legendary Italian conductor who had refused to perform under fascism. Within a decade, I'd step into a world they had built, shaped by ideals about how music could be resistance and refuge. And standing under those names, Mehta and my dad—these two men who were the signposts of my own life—felt like their inheritors, carrying on a tradition born from defiance and survival.

Mehta scrawled. Bent to my eye level, Dad winced but gave me a shaky thumbs-up. He didn't dare tell Mehta, but his back had gone out the morning we left New York. He'd complained of a slipped disc for as long as I could remember, but this one was a particularly brutal episode—especially because instead of crawling into bed to rest for a week, he had boarded a ten-and-a-half-hour flight from JFK to Ben Gurion Airport, just so that his son could play for Zubin Mehta. And now, Dad was bent at the waist, pale with pain, holding still while Mehta wrote on his back, gripping his knees so hard his knuckles turned white.

That night, after he carefully placed Mehta's letter back in his travel bag and slowly crawled into the hotel bed, Dad sent me out alone to fetch dinner from the corner stand. I'd learned barely enough Hebrew to order:

"Shnei falafel b'pita, bevakasha."

The pain was worth it. Dad had crossed the globe for one thing, and he'd succeeded. Back home, he framed a copy of Mehta's letter on the Wall, next to his headshot. The Z's matched.

> I've had the greatest of pleasure listening to R. Vijay Gupta—he has a great future—but *must* be guided with love and care by all who are close to him—Zubin Mehta

One year later, at eleven, I made my international debut: a movement of the Mendelssohn Violin Concerto with the Israel Philharmonic, Zubin Mehta on the podium. Four concerts in Tel Aviv and one in Haifa. We were driven around in a diesel Mercedes by an ex-Mossad agent who let me hold his Glock and later brought me a white stone from Jerusalem.

The concerts went by in a blur. I played too fast for fear to catch me, too fast to feel the orchestra behind me. I don't remember the murmur of the strings, the timpani's pulse, or the clarinet's gentle theme. I know my intonation slipped, and that I rushed through transitions, missing the chance to settle into the phrases, or to enjoy myself at all. Still, I played with the flash of a young virtuoso, and the crowd gave a warm ovation. Dad had told me to keep my eyes on Mehta, who stood like a superhero—left hand clenched at his hip, chin jutted out, eyes sharp—holding the band together while I barreled through. I kept waiting for someone to slow me down, to tell me I was okay. But Dad wasn't in my eyeline, guiding me from behind the conductor. Instead, he was in a high balcony, crouched with a camera, trying to capture the perfect shot of his son with his hero for the Wall of Accomplishments.

When Dad stepped out of the auditorium, he gripped the back of my neck, gave me a small shake, and then lit a cigarette. My shoulders dropped. He was happy, and nothing else mattered. I knew I could have played better, but success wasn't measured by how I felt. It was measured by the look on his face. But it wasn't until my second bowl of strawberry ice cream at a nearby kibbutz that I let myself believe I'd done well—that I'd been "boro" enough for him. As I scraped the glass bowl clean, I made a quiet promise: I'd do whatever it took to keep him smiling like that, even if it meant swallowing everything I felt.

Antonio Vivaldi, "Winter" from *The Four Seasons*

[JBS Haldane Avenue, Kolkata, India]

My stomach churned. Dad had warned me about drinking tap water in Kolkata. I'd been sick all day, and now I was breaking out in a cold sweat, my fingers trembling.

I was still eleven, and somewhere in the roiling mass of people I couldn't see were my Dadu and Didima, kakus and mashis and dozens of cousins. I'd spent the past several days being a kid in Dad's old neighborhood, Dum Dum, learning how to play cricket and carrom, gorging on flaky pattys from Flurys and eight kinds of sweet shondesh from Ganguram. I didn't want to go out alone. But Dad leaned down and gripped my shoulders, fixing his dark brown eyes on me, his finger pointing. I swallowed, tasting bile.

"You better hold it, Potka. Tor boro hote hobe." Dad had spent the past two years organizing this concert—his homecoming, my India debut. He'd even found one of the few Western-classical chamber orchestras in the country, and the venue, the Science City Auditorium on JBS Haldane Avenue. Thanks to Mehta's letter and Dad's marketing efforts, the night was sold out. Alongside Dad's family in the crowd, ten thousand Bengalis had crammed in, eager to hear one of their own—me—play music not of their own—Vivaldi.

This was no time to act like a kid. So I held it. I clenched, squared my shoulders, and walked out. *Back straight. Heels first.*

Onstage I blinked against the lights, ears ringing. The cheering sounded like a low-flying jet. I shook the conductor's hand—the way Dad taught me—and wiped the fever-sweat from my palms, then raised my violin. *Smile. Always smile.* Behind me, the small orchestra waited for my cue. My stomach flipped, but it wasn't nerves. *Tor boro hate habe.* I gave the conductor a nod. The music began.

I played "Winter" from *The Four Seasons.* When I finished, the crowd screamed for more, as Dad said they would. He had already planned my encore: "Boro Asha Kore"—the same Tagore song I'd played at the Hudson Valley Durga Pujo six years earlier. But in Kolkata, three notes in, I heard the crowd gasp in unison, drawing me toward them like a riptide. Then the entire stadium sang with me. I still didn't know what any of the words meant.

Boro asha kore eshecchi go kache deke laow . . .

The next morning, over cha and a beedee, Dad let out a shout. He held the front page of the paper, grinning. His name—our name—was printed in big block letters: "GANGULY AND GUPTA—THE LIONS OF BENGAL." I didn't know who Ganguly was, so Dad turned on the TV and flipped to men in white sweater-vests hurling a ball at a helmeted man with a flat paddle. Sourav Ganguly, the Bengali cricket captain, was a national hero. The pride of being mentioned beside him in print was like headlining with LeBron James. When I sat down to watch the match, Dad let me take sip of cha, and a puff of his beedee. I had been formally invited into the world of men.

When we went to visit Dadu and Didima, Dad brought three copies of the paper and slapped them onto the coffee table. "Dekecho?" Of course, they'd already seen the headline. Because of me, Dad might finally be enough. Didima made Dad's favorite—bhetki maach—but she served the fish to me first. I scanned her hands for Mom's diamond ring, but didn't see it.

The next day, Dad took me to the marble tomb of Mother Teresa, where I was supposed to serenade the nuns in their blue-trimmed saris. As we walked through the tiled courtyard, hundreds of children reached out their hands. Dad led me through a bright blue doorway, and inside, I saw the tomb, a raised rectangle. I opened my violin case and started to play the slow movement of a Mozart concerto. Outside, the children pressed up against the windows, their faces framed by iron bars. When I finished, they cheered and shook cups of coins, like applause. Dad said I was playing for the nuns and Mother Teresa, but I knew who my real audience was.

On my way out through the courtyard, someone tugged at my pant leg. I looked down and saw a boy crawling on the tiled floor. Both of his legs ended at his knees, and he called out to me in a clear voice.

"Saar, saar?"

I hadn't expected anyone to call me "sir." One of the boy's eyes was milk-blind. At first, I thought he was begging. But he was holding out his palm, and on it was a diamond-shaped poisha. He motioned for me to take the coin. He wanted to pay me for my performance. I took it, feeling the thick callus of his palm. The boy folded his palms, and I bowed back. I felt proud for a moment, then sick. I was about to get into an air-conditioned cab on my way to a five-star hotel, but where would he be sleeping? Where was his family?

Later, in the back seat of the Ambassador, Dad saw me inspecting the three-headed lion on the coin. He recoiled and slapped it out of my hand into the footwell.

"Het! You'll catch leprosy!"

But when we passed the banks of the Ganges and Dad pointed toward the temple at Dakshineswar, I bent down and pocketed the coin. It would join a small collection of precious things I gathered on my travels with Dad across the globe, from Mumbai and Tokyo to Santa Barbara and St. Barths, Riechersberg and Soesterberg.

A porcelain clown. A white rock from a holy city. An origami crane. A single poisha.

Chapter 3

PRAYING WITH A VIOLIN IN YOUR HANDS

Bach, "Chaconne"

Arise, awake, and stop not till the goal is reached.

—Swami Vivekananda

Niccolò Paganini, Caprice No. 24

[Montgomery, New York]

"Potka! Ki hocchey? Ami shunthe parchina!"

Of course they couldn't hear me practicing. I was lost in a book. For months, I had been escaping into Tolkien, the only way to survive the six-hour gauntlet of daily practice. The first two were for scales, with corresponding arpeggios, thirds, sixths, octaves, and tenths, and after that, *another* two hours of études: Kreutzer, Mazas, Rode, and Paganini. Then, the last two were for repertoire, usually some empty, flashy showpiece—like Paganini's 24th Caprice—that demanded machine-like precision and endless repetition. I'd escape the crushing boredom by becoming engrossed in a book. Sometimes I'd forget that even a moment of silence was forbidden when I was supposed to be practicing. Eventually, I devised a way for me to keep playing, but keep reading, too.

For the last few months, I had been studying with a new team of teachers. Dad had decided that I needed an upgrade from Ms. Behrend in order to become a serious soloist, so he had unceremoniously yanked me out of her studio. I had loved learning with her—learning through her singing and dancing, her images—but now, I was handed over to teachers who sat behind desks, and barely played their violins, and if they did, only grotesquely exaggerated my mistakes. When I asked one of them when I'd be ready to play the Brahms violin concerto, he laughed, saying that I'd have to learn "twenty other concertos" before I'd ever be ready for that one.

But now, all I was learning at Juilliard was how to unlearn joy. Another teacher, sallow-faced and terrifying, once barged into my fourth-floor practice room and said, "You may as well quit now, because every single note you're playing is approximate." He slammed the door, leaving me gutted. Another time, he made me play the same passage ten, twelve, fifteen times in a row, sneering after each attempt, cataloging every slip, every scratch, until the only thing I learned was his contempt. The only time I saw him smile was when Dad handed him a bottle of Johnnie Walker Black.

Another teacher—a fading legend—kept us waiting in the fifth-floor hallway for hours. The accompanist had to be paid overtime, but that didn't matter; hunger gnawed at me until I was dizzy. When she finally called me in, she unwrapped a fried chicken dinner from Citarella and ate with her fingers while I played. When she asked for my violin to demonstrate something, she'd leave a smear of grease across the fingerboard. When my fingers slipped on the fat, she laughed, marking my part with a Blackwing pencil: a dreaded, encircled X. "You'll need to practice that at home, sugarplum, nice and slow."

Back home, whenever I tried to give in to the rush of music, to feel a flicker of excitement, or to let the orchestra rise from my imagination, a yell from the kitchen stopped me cold.

"Eeeeeshh Potku, what are you playing?! Asthey, asthey! Slow *DOWN!*"

I hated slow practice, which felt like choking the music in my hands. Behind my bedroom door, I twisted my face and mouthed an unthinkable, unsayable word back at them. And then, condemned to a six-hour sentence of musical monotony, I turned to my refuge: a book.

I practiced for my parents, but I read for myself. In Middle-earth and Narnia, in Camelot and Hogwarts, I could slip into the childhood I never really had. On my music stand I wedged a novel between Flesch's *Scale System* and the Kreutzer études, with the sheet music of my memorized concerto nearby in case I needed to cover my tracks. Lost in a story, I plodded mindlessly through the notes, slow enough to pass as "good practice."

But every few minutes I had to turn a page, which meant fifteen seconds of silence. My stomach clenched as I braced for the door to swing open, for the shout that meant I was caught. When it didn't come, I played and read again, until I had to turn another page.

Sometimes a yell came from the hallway and I'd call back a half-hearted "I am!" But other times I'd hear the floorboard creak outside my door, and I knew it was already too late.

BAM!

The door would swing open, and before I knew it, Mom could have me by a fistful of my thick black hair, rendering me immobile. To protect myself, I'd hold out my violin like a shield. But then, she'd say:

"Put down the violin."

What I feared most was the quickness—the sudden flash of a hand, the *thud-thud-thud* steps of an attack, the leash hanging on the doorknob, the single raised choti, the sting of a gatta that could come without warning. The fear of her punishments—which could come at any time, anywhere—was enough to keep me constantly terrified.

Mom knew how to make it really hurt. Once, while Dad was away in India, I remember her catching me with a library copy of *Harry Potter and the Prisoner of Azkaban*. I loved that book—the way it opened into another life, a world inside a world. A lonely child, a hunted fugitive, both trying to find their way home: I saw myself in them. What I remember next is the sound—the sharp crack of glue, the flutter of paper, the cold air beyond the window. Later that night, after dinner, I stole a roll of Scotch tape from Dad's office and crept out into the cold with a flashlight, hunting for whatever happened to Sirius Black. The next day at school, I lied to the librarian and said I'd lost the book. She only shook her head.

"No one cares about books anymore."

As children, my brother and I had to find a way to make this kind of pain make sense. Our parents had sacrificed everything so I could succeed. Dad worked nonstop. Mom never missed a lesson. We watched them skip meals so that we could eat. In our house, every dollar had already been spent on gas to the City, parking at Lincoln Center, repairs and rehairs, piano tuning, concert shoes, and a new suit each year. So it was only natural that if we misbehaved, we had earned our punishments. We were bad boys, and needed "discipline."

When one mashi gave us a gleaming set of Corningware, Mom returned it at Woodbury Commons and came home with cash for new violin strings and two pairs of GapKids jeans. Month after month I played those strings until the winding at the bridge unraveled to wire, the core showed through, the pitch soured—and one afternoon the A string snapped with a dry ping, whipping my knuckles. I knew I hadn't broken a string. I'd broken the bank.

I also knew it hurt less if I could pass it on. In the room next to mine, Shonu practiced as long as I did, but his escape was music itself. At times, he improvised, singing a sweet line over a Chopin nocturne, slipping extra notes into Beethoven, making something new. But I knew that anything new—anything fun—was not allowed. From my room

I'd tattle: "Moooom, Shonu's making it uuuup!" Then it was his turn for a thrashing.

When we were finally allowed outside, Shonu wandered off alone, kicking at the grass, still humming the melody he'd been working on. I stayed on the other side of the yard, playing with sticks or chasing the dogs. In another story, we might have been best friends—us against the world—but that wasn't ours. Our parents gave their lives to us, and we paid them with our childhoods. As Shonu and I learned to shape sound, we were also being driven toward careers our parents could barely imagine, not just at the expense of being children, but of being brothers.

But my brother and I were not just pitted against each other and the world. We were also up against something far more unpredictable. It was around this time that I remember things changing about Mom. She started having trouble throwing things away. Dad used to joke that she was a hoarder, but now, the basement was piled with old pieces of mail she insisted were important, or plastic containers from the supermarket she said she might need "someday." She'd spend several hours each day screaming—sometimes at us, sometimes at no one—and then she'd collapse into bed for the rest of the afternoon, saying she didn't know why everyone was leaving her. When Dad traveled to India for business, she would accuse him of having another family in Kolkata. She'd make me practice in her room while she rested, so I couldn't sneak my books. Every so often she'd murmur, "Wrong note." Even when I knew my pitch was dead-on, I said nothing. It was easier to let her be right.

Over the next year, Mom stayed in bed longer and longer. One day, after she bathed, I found dime-sized clots of jellylike blood in the drain. During my lessons in New York City, she sat on a pad of folded towels. She was exhausted all the time, which meant that she was more dangerous, and more terrifying, than ever.

Arvo Pärt, *Fratres*

[Seventy-First Street and Central Park West, New York City]

Of the many books I hid on my music stand, one was a comic-book version of an orange-turbaned monk who taught the surest way to find God:

Shiva gyaney jiva seva—worship people as Shiva.

In 1893, Swami Vivekananda—the turbaned monk after whom Dad was named—delivered a searing address at the Parliament of the World's Religions. The next year, he established the first Vedanta Society in a brownstone on the Upper West Side. But this new Hinduism, soon appropriated by New England intellectuals, would have no clanging bells or fierce-eyed, demon-slaying Devis—not even a single real flame.

After exhausting Juilliard Saturdays, Mom dragged us into the City for Sunday services at the Society. The building felt frozen in early 1960s pallor—musty beige, dim fluorescent lights, a thick brown carpet that murdered any chance of staying awake. A thin septuagenarian man droned hymns from an electric keyboard. From a podium carved with a swan, a tall, bushy-browed, ocher-clad monk we called Shamiji rattled off a staccato catechism of Advaita Vedanta in a thick Bengali accent, sending me and Shonu into giggling fits:

Bedantooo... means that one Divine... is the sole substance
and reality in this world of multiplishity.... Bedanto
says to find out unity in the midst of divershity.

After a while, my eyes drooped. Shonu was busy with the Beanie Baby in his jacket, and even Mom's eyes glazed over with some faraway devotion. Dad, meanwhile—who preferred the kind of pujos I loved, with bells, smoke, and chanting—pretended he couldn't find a parking spot and slipped in near the end, reeking of Marlboro Lights. He said the building smelled like cockroaches.

On the car ride home, Mom would play Arvo Pärt's *Fratres* on a scratched CD. I later learned that Pärt, an Estonian composer, had written it using his *tintinnabuli* technique—music built from circles and bells, a meditation on the space between sound and silence. To him it was cosmic, eternal. To me, sitting in the back seat, the music felt relentless. The same phrases kept returning, like Shamiji's unending, circling sermons. I'd stare out at the dark Hudson, my head against the glass, waiting for some kind of melody I could hum, but all I heard was a failure to arrive.

Shamiji was our family's surrogate patriarch, a stand-in for the maternal grandfather who had died before we were born. Mom said he prayed for us, and that God spoke to him. At Sunday services she made us perform, and we'd walk past rows of stiff-backed wooden chairs and a tan wall inscribed with gold-lettered wisdom from the Rig Veda: "*Truth is one—sages call it variously.*"

At the far end of the room, against a curtain, were three large portraits: the handsome, turban-clad Vivekananda, sunk deep in meditation; a bearded Sri Ramakrishna, the priest of Maa, known as Pagla Thakur, the "Crazy God"; and Sarada Devi, plain sari over long black hair, two thick gold bangles at her wrists, who guided Vivekananda and insisted on the education of girls.

Before we played, Mom had us lie flat on the floor before Shamiji in an act of what should have been reverence, although all I did was gawk at his thick yellow toenails. I wondered if he could read my thoughts.

After the lecture, families would sit with Shamiji in his kutir upstairs. The room looked as if an absent-minded professor lived amid teetering piles of books and papers on the desk, the shelves, even his bed and the plastic folding tables. Yet it was also unmistakably a monk's cell: a deerskin draped over a wingback chair, murtis and framed pictures of saints, and the accoutrements of his daily pujo—incense sticks spilling from cardboard packets, a copper bowl of water, an ever-fresh plate of carnations. In the dead fireplace he had built a shrine to the Goddess.

His tongue snapped like a whip, usually aimed at my midsection. His F's came out as P's: "PAT! PAT! PAT! Cheee! Go run ten laps each morning! Patness is weakness!" If he did pray for us, I didn't understand why he was so damn mean.

Still, I was mystified by Vedanta. The myths of my childhood had turned into a love of Hindu philosophy. Soon, I had traded my music-stand comic books of Hanuman and Krishna for the Bhagavad Gita and the Upanishads, and my Tolkien for Vivekananda's *Lectures from Colombo to Almora*. By then, I'd become inflamed by the idea of renouncing everything and becoming a monk, living in a cave in the mountains, unbothered by cold or hunger or expectations or obligations, focused only on finding my dharma—my purpose. When I mentioned this to Shamiji, though, he dismissed me, calling me "pat" and "undishiplined."

On the day of my initiation—the day he would give me a mantra to guide me through my life—I brought in my treasured copy of the Bhagavad Gita, which I loved for the Sanskrit transliteration I could sound out. I wanted to chant for him. Instead, with a yell, he confiscated my book, ridiculing me for bringing a rival swami's translation. He plucked another from a pile above his headboard, one with no illustrations.

He flipped the book to the first blank page and scrawled: "What you give, you get. What you never give, you never get."

For the past few years, when Dad traveled and Mom was too tired, I'd taken on the daily morning rituals, spending hours in the pujo room chanting in Sanskrit. Later I taught myself to copy the characters into a notebook, enthralled by the sound of my mother tongue's mother tongue. In that dim room that I had once tried to burn down, I began to realize I was learning a Hinduism my parents had never taught.

I would become lost in the two-millennia-old shlokas of the Bhagavad Gita, the "Divine Song" sung by Krishna, God disguised as a lowly charioteer. I felt the world around me restringing itself, like the bow of the great warrior Arjuna. According to this song, there were infinite paths toward God—each of them worthy in their own way—and every being was a manifestation of the Divine, no matter how irredeemable they seemed. Even the paglas were God.

And as I sang Krishna's teaching to Arjuna—that there was no escaping one's dharma, even if it meant going to war with family or teachers—the truth struck like an arrow: I didn't yet know my own dharma, but I knew I wanted my life to become a kind of song, something I could offer to the Divine: not to a murti on an altar, but to the Shiva living in the heart of every being.

Johann Sebastian Bach, "Chaconne" from Partita II in D Minor, BWV 1003

[Newburgh, New York]

When I was eleven, on tour with Dad performing across the globe, I missed a social studies midterm. The teacher refused to let me make it up. According to him, I'd been "on vacation." The Lion of Bengal would fail sixth grade.

Mom and Dad pulled me out of school and hired tutors. The district sent child protective services to our house for "educational neglect." They didn't believe Mom was already teaching us precalculus at home, amid recital tours to Asia and Europe. For months my parents fought the Valley Central School District. After a battery of IQ tests and a year of homeschooling, I earned my GED at twelve, along with a 1200 on the SAT. That was enough to start college at Mount Saint Mary, a small liberal arts school on the Hudson.

Mom chose my major: biology, premed. She said I needed a backup, in case being a full-time soloist didn't pan out. I stayed quiet. But I already knew that if I became a doctor, it would mean I had failed as a musician. Either I'd be the next Yo-Yo Ma, or the other Dr. Gupta.

I barely had any friends as it was, and once my parents pulled me out of school, I never saw or spoke to them again. I couldn't name the wrenching feeling in my gut. My parents told me my teachers were being cruel, even racist, and that I'd be better off earning college credits than sticking around small-minded people. I didn't know how or what or when to feel, but that didn't matter: I had to succeed. I had to survive.

I took my first college classes with Dr. Bill Lahar, who looked amused to see a twelve-year-old in his lecture hall. He gave me a generous B-minus in Chemistry 101. I made sure to earn an A in 102. The science wasn't too hard—learning microbe tables felt similar to learning the Latin Mass—but my real love was literature. I raised my hand to talk about Oedipus, Lysistrata, the hypocrisy of Polonius, the final lines of John Keats. At first, the mountainous jocks laughed at my cracking soprano, but after a few weeks some of them asked me to edit their essays.

Outside class, I felt like a target. No one wanted to be friends with the pudgy child freak-genius. So I learned how to talk sports—Yankees and Red Sox—and crack crude jokes to get people to laugh. I started listening to Ludacris and Blink-182 on K104.7. After a while, I even embraced my new nickname: "fucking Gupta."

I'd duck into the computer lab between classes with a bag of junk food and disappear into whatever I wasn't allowed at home: Yahoo games, porn, AIM chat rooms where I could pretend to be older, normal, someone else.

> **RandomGirl938:** Hey what's your ASL?
> **TheGupster459:** 17-M-NYC, u?

By the time I finished my dopamine binge, the keys had turned Cheeto-orange.

But starting college at thirteen meant that my Pre-College days were over. After seven years of Saturdays, my time at Juilliard ended abruptly. But I knew, at least then, that I was going to be a soloist. And a soloist never stops training. After Dad petitioned maestro Mehta, I had a new violin teacher: Glenn Dicterow, the New York Philharmonic's concertmaster. I'd watched him on PBS since toddlerhood, sawing at my Cracker Jack violin while he played Brahms and Mahler. That year, he became my teacher, and my parents enrolled me in a second undergraduate degree: On top of being premed at Mount Saint Mary's, I'd start an undergraduate in violin performance at the Manhattan School of Music.

In our first lesson, Dicterow handed me his Guarneri del Gesù, a violin older than America. Mehta had bought it for the Philharmonic. The sound Dicterow drew from it was massive, luminous, almost too big for the room, and when I played on it, I could feel his sound in the instrument. I had never heard myself make a sound like that. Dicterow nodded. "You may as well get used to it. You'll be playing on a violin like this one day."

He put it simply: A violin was not an object to be owned, but rather, like the music, a voice to be cultivated. All a violinist could hope for was to be a good steward of a violin, whose life would last much longer than our own. The violin, like the music we played through it, would always be above our understanding. With luck, a lifetime of devoted practice would only bring us deeper into the mysteries of music.

The concertmaster had to be the most dependable musician onstage—part soloist, part leader—and Dicterow was one of the greats. It was the concertmaster's job to transmit the messages of a conductor across the stage, and if a maestro was ever unreliable, the orchestra often looked to the concertmaster to lead. But he was a great teacher, too. He insisted that lessons at his home in New Rochelle were to be a strictly parent-free zone. He'd escort Mom or Dad to the living room, offer them coffee, and then shut the studio door behind him. This was a major adjustment for my parents, who, until that point, had unhelpfully sat in every single violin lesson, usually taking notes they'd enforce later at home. Dad usually went for a drive, headset on, pitching to clients. Mom waited in the McDonald's parking lot down the road—close enough for the bathroom, far enough to be out of sight. Lessons were meant to be an hour, but he often kept me much longer. In our first session—the Tchaikovsky Violin Concerto—Dicterow told me to make the sound *sexier.* "Think Britney Spears. Or Christina Aguilera. Which do you prefer?" I froze. No teacher had ever talked to me like that—as if I were already a grown-up. (Obviously, Christina.)

For Dicterow, devotion meant discipline and wonder in equal measure. His silver tone came from precise control—bow speed, pressure, elbow angle—and enough ease in the body. Every note had a story to tell, and there was always a technical solution to a musical problem. If a melody needed to sing more, he would show me how to flatten my bow hair against the string, drawing a thick sound like ganache. If the sound needed sparkle, he would assign a few lines of a caprice or étude like a musical prescription. His solutions seemed simple, almost inevitable. One time, when I was forcing the sound on the lowest string, he walked over and raised the scroll of my violin. Suddenly, I felt every vertebra of my spine click into place, and the violin—and my body—rang with sound.

If I came in unprepared, though, I'd see it on his face. "What's this about, Robert? Come on. You can do better. Let's start from the top." When I stumbled, he'd pick up the phrase—always from memory. The point of our lessons was not to execute the notes on the page, but to understand them, to learn how to think about music. Just as every note had a story, every phrase, every section, every movement would continue that story. And for the first time, as a musician, I had the right to create my own story: a right to feel something, and trust that feeling.

Before I started studying with Dicterow, I was playing showpieces—usually pieces Dad thought would "wow" people. But Dicterow had other ideas. He wanted me to learn real music. "I think it's time for you to play some Bach."

I'd played Bach before in the Suzuki books. But the music Dicterow wanted me to learn was unlike anything I had ever played before: two, three, sometimes four notes at a time, nearly a symphony for a single instrument.

Our first lesson on the "Chaconne," a movement from the second Partita, lasted three hours. Dicterow spent nearly an hour on the first line alone, adjusting how I stood, how I held the violin, trying to untangle the tension in my body that mirrored the knot in the music. "Relax, Robert. Listen to the bassline." I tried to play the first chord, but my fingers couldn't reach. My pinky kept collapsing. "Make an arch," he said. "It's the strongest shape, see?" He gave me an exercise to strengthen my finger. Over and over, we played together, hammering on the ebony boards of our violins—2-4-3-4, 2-4-3-4—his pinky struck with perfect accuracy each time. Mine was like a noodle. After a minute, I'd wince, feeling my palm burn with lactic acid. I was already beating myself up in my head. Dicterow would cut me off.

"And the moment it hurts, you stop. Immediately. Okay?" I nodded. "You've got to build the strength slowly." No one had ever told me to *stop* practicing before.

The next week, we spent another two hours on the opening page. The "Chaconne" sits on a "ground bass," one simple line repeating under dozens of variations. No matter how the notes were stacked above it, the bass had to be heard. But every time I tried to play a three- or four-note chord, I pressed too hard and made a crunching sound. "Too fast, Robert. Take your time." So Dicterow worked on my bow arm, raising and lowering my elbow, showing me the exact way to play so that the lowest string could sing. When we ended our lessons, we were both exhausted.

Dicterow was initiating me into the kind of practice that could sustain a musician for a lifetime: one of devotion, of perfection. There were some ideals—like Bach—that would always be worth the effort.

~

A few weeks after 9/11, I was practicing the "Chaconne" at home, and Mom and Dad called me into the living room. My first instinct was that I was in trouble. I wasn't hiding books on the music stand anymore. I was so absorbed in Dicterow's lessons, trying to understand Bach's coiled variations. I hadn't done anything wrong. Still, violin in hand, I felt like I should apologize.

Dad's voice was soft. "Potka, ki bajacchish, re? What is this music?"

I explained what I had been practicing.

Mom pointed to a spot. I stood where she pointed and started playing again. It was the only time I saw my parents sit together on the loveseat, listening to me practice.

When I finished, Dad said, "Potka, when I die, I want you to play this for me."

After weeks of finger-and-arm calisthenics, advancing a page or two at a time, Dicterow finally asked me to play the "Chaconne" straight through. When I stopped, he sat back in his chair, eyebrows lifted. He seemed proud, but also stunned, maybe even slightly uneasy. It was as if he'd witnessed someone too young glimpse the sacred and understand it.

I lowered my violin and he nodded. "This is as close as we get to God. Sometimes making music is just praying with a violin in your hands."

Pyotr Ilyich Tchaikovsky: Violin Concerto in D Major, Op. 35—ii. Canzonetta: Andante

[Mount Saint Mary College / Manhattan School of Music]

I did love college—both of them. Somehow, through the combination of courses in pre-medical biology and conservatory classical music, the world was starting to make sense in a way it never had before. I was devouring Thomas Aquinas alongside medieval counterpoint, parasitology, Mozart operas, cantatas, and calculus. These weren't separate worlds at all but interconnected, informing each other. I finally felt like I was being welcomed into the world of learning, of knowledge, and I didn't have to apologize for being curious. Learning made the world make sense, even if my own life made no sense.

But trying to hold all that at once was too much for a fifteen-year-old boy. And my professors were starting to notice. One of the toughest biology professors pulled me aside after an exam. I braced myself for the worst. Maybe I'd misidentified the milk-white plate of bacterial colonies he'd handed me in lab the week before. We all had been given a month to figure out the puzzle, but I did it in four days, checking diagnostics and flowcharts until I knew them by heart. It *had* to be *Morganella morganii*. I waited a few more days, triple-checking my work before I finally turned it in. *Had I gotten it wrong?*

But instead he said, "You're burning the candle at both ends. I'm worried you're not sleeping."

Even though I was acing his class, I kept falling asleep in his lectures. I'd been waking up at 5 a.m. each day to do thirty credits' worth of homework so I could come home and practice. I knew what Dad would say: A teacher's concern could be used against me. Maybe they were looking for reasons to kick me out. I put on a toothy cheerfulness and lied before I could think. "Oh no, no, I'm fine!"

But I knew the truth. If I showed any signs of exhaustion, I'd be "normal"—maybe human—and I would rather pass out in class than do that. Mom and Dad were still driving us to Manhattan several times a week—seventy miles each way—putting tens of thousands of miles on a new Toyota minivan. Burnout was for the weak.

To fuel the overwork, I overate. At Mount Saint Mary College, I binged on all the substances forbidden at home: caffeine, sugar, salt, and grease. Venti Frappuccinos got me through three-hour chem labs. Twix, Combos, and Dr. Pepper kept me company while I studied. If I aced a test, I'd reward myself with a burger, onion rings, and a double scoop of ice cream in the cafeteria. Exhausted? A Mountain Dew and a bag of Cool Ranch Doritos. Overwhelmed? Oreos. Lonely? Two slices of pizza. The fear I'd never be enough? Two more.

Soon, every piece of clothing I owned was too tight, and I couldn't walk past Dad without hearing him suck his teeth in disgust: "Cheee, Potka! When did you get so fat?" Soon, nothing at Woodbury Commons fit me, and we had to find concert clothes for me at Syms, an off-price retailer in Secaucus, where the only clothes that fit me were size 2XL shirts, baggy trousers, and size 40 blazers in "Portly, Short," which is what Dad started calling me.

I didn't need Dad's help to feel ashamed of myself. I learned not to linger at mirrors or windows, to tug my shirttail down and keep moving. I told myself that the only numbers that mattered were grades, credits, test scores. The mirror, like my exhaustion, was just another thing to ignore.

But some problems couldn't be avoided. After 9/11, one of Dad's clients, a Sikh kaku who owned a nearby gas station, was beaten. Someone in our neighborhood started dumping raccoon carcasses to rot outside our picket fence. One morning we found our mailbox splintered and half-buried in gray sleet. To make matters worse, some of Dad's loyal Bengali clients started buying tickets to Kolkata on a new website: Priceline.com. Doubly terrified, Dad plastered the family car in American flag stickers and began driving all over the Mid-Hudson Valley to pitch new clients.

Mom was suffering, too. She was driving more than ever—Mondays, Wednesdays, and Fridays into the City for me, Saturdays for Shonu at Pre-College—and she was always exhausted. But it wasn't just "normal" exhaustion. Her periods had become irregular, and sometimes she bled for weeks at a time. While I studied Renaissance polyphony and played chamber music, she sat in the parked Nissan for hours, perched on a stack of folded bath towels. At night, Shonu and I listened to our parents' low hushed whispers from the bedroom door they now kept shut. Mom didn't trust doctors, and after delivering two children by C-section, she didn't want to be cut open again. Dad finally convinced her to get a CAT scan. The news was bad: several grapefruit-sized fibroids. Benign, but impossible to ignore. They'd barely scraped together the money for a scan. How would they afford surgery?

One night Dad woke up in a panic, after seeing a vision of his worst fear. In his nightmare, I was grown, with a scruffy beard, and dragged my feet through a blizzard wearing a thin, worn coat, a violin case strapped to my back. I knocked on Upper West Side brownstones, begging to teach violin to their kids, offering to become a chakor. Door after door slammed. I was digging through trash. I was pagla.

What I couldn't have known then—what Dad never told me—was that he was losing everything he had built. His American Dream was becoming a nightmare. The doors that had once been open to him seemed suddenly shut. He had been the Lion of Bengal, the one who came to America and beat it at its own game. But now he knew, and we knew, and soon Kolkata would know: America was winning. A few months later, he collapsed at an airport. The ER doctor said he'd had a mild cardiac episode.

On a cold February night—the upstate New York cold that cuts like a blade—Dad called me into the living room. I walked past Shonu's room, where he was working through a Chopin nocturne. Mom and Dad sat close on the couch, closer than I'd ever seen them sit before. Something was wrong.

"Potka, listen."

I stood in front of them, eyes on the beige carpet. One of the dogs scratched at the metal prong collar around his neck.

"You have a choice. You're going to be a doctor."

I stood there, dumbstruck. I knew what he meant. I had a choice, like I had always had a choice: to be boro—to grow up—or stay a child, which is to say, I didn't have a choice at all. My parents had crossed continents and oceans and had sacrificed everything. Now, it was my turn to make the same sacrifice. I did have a choice: to save them or abandon them. To finally become boro, a good boy, a Gupta.

Dad narrated the rest of my life. "No more Mount Saint Mary's. You'll go to Marist. Those teachers can prep you for the MCAT. You need a summer research position. Tomorrow we'll start looking at programs."

The MCAT. Research positions. Summer programs. Okay. Fine. I could do it. I'd wake up earlier. Sleep less. I could make it all work—as long as I could keep playing. As long as I could still see Mr. Dicterow. That's what I asked them—how we'd fit in lessons. *I could lose everything else. I couldn't lose music.*

"No. No more music. No Manhattan, no Dicterow. When you're a doctor, music can be your hobby."

A hobby?

My gut jumped into my throat. I couldn't breathe. This couldn't be happening. Blood hammered in my ears. The room was still, but everything tilted and blurred, hot and cold at once. I didn't know what to do with my hands. The ground fell away, and I slid onto a smooth, slanted plane with nothing to grab.

And when I finally found my voice, it came from some void I didn't even know was there, burning through me until I howled, cursing the parents who had given me everything. But now I wanted everything to end, because everything had already ended, and I could finally say the unsayable.

"*Fuck* you! I wish you were dead! I wish *I* was dead!"

I looked at Mom. She didn't flinch. As I screamed, her eyes stayed fixed past me, down a dim tunnel to nowhere. She looked shut down, as if she had braced for this all along, and now that it had come, she couldn't feel a thing.

But Dad rose. Slowly. He lifted his index finger and leveled it at me like a weapon. He exploded, matching my rage. And suddenly I was afraid of what I'd unleashed, as if I'd cracked something dangerous and inevitable, and now it was rushing for me: *How dare I?* A father shouldn't have to explain himself in his own house. A father shouldn't be questioned—especially by the son he'd bent the world to raise.

I'd turned his innocent child into someone who questioned his authority: I had become a threat. His voice dropped, lethal, final.

"Then go!" he said. "See how it really is for a fat brown boy in this world! Get out! OUT! Get out of my sight, out of my house!"

I ran out the front door. My vision blurred. My legs carried me across the frozen lawn and into the twenty-degree darkness. I hadn't grabbed a coat, but it didn't matter. I was burning and the cold couldn't reach me. My chest heaved, each breath a flare of steam, bright for a moment, and then gone.

I ran across the yard to the fence line and collapsed onto a boulder. The night was so cold, the air so thin, the stars didn't even twinkle. Rising in the east was Orion, my favorite constellation. Betelgeuse burned red from his shoulder, and below him was Sirius, the Dog Star. Sometimes, after pujos or concerts, I'd beg my parents to let me stay out late to watch the sky. On amavasya—the night of the new moon—I could spend hours lost in the stars, until they finally called me in, warning I'd catch a cold. But tonight no one even came to yell at me.

So I talked to the night. I didn't know what else to do. I begged for a sign, any sign, that I could still be who I was, that I might be allowed to find my dharma on my own terms. Somewhere in the singing stars, I could hear Tchaikovsky's *Canzonetta*—that slow movement he wrote after nearly ending his life, a melody so spare it feels like a man talking to the dark, asking for permission to go on living.

I blinked, and tears fell hot, cutting the ice of my cheeks. From the vast space between those ancient lights came a silent, incomprehensible song.

Boro asha kore eshecchi go kache deke laow…

A Presence regarded me, almost smiling at my grief. There was a plan, though it wasn't mine to know—not yet. What would be would be, or not. Either way, the sky would keep singing, as it always had. And I, if I was brave enough, might still find a way to be part of that song.

I don't know how long I stayed before my teeth began to chatter and my cheeks went numb. Soon my stomach growled. Hunger brought me back across the yard, through Mom's dead garden, which would soon burst with tulips, zinnias, marigolds, and irises. For now, I would have to steel myself and wait. I turned the cold handle slowly, easing the door so it wouldn't squeak. I didn't want them to know I was back. One of the dogs trotted over and pressed a wet nose into my hand. At the stove, Mom filled a plate—daal over rice, a handful of crispy aloo bhaja. Dad sat at the table, chomping a kacha lonka, scooping rice with one hand while holding the venom-green chili in the other. He never looked up from his plate.

"As long as you live under my roof and eat my food, you'll do what we tell you."

Mom put the steaming plate in front of me.

"Kha, shona."

Part 2

The story of Saint Julian begins with a curse. A boy born to nobles will, one day, cause their deaths. When a ten-year-old Julian hears the words of the prophecy, he runs away, leaving the warmth of his home for the forest, where he learns to hunt, fish, and survive.

Years later, in the woods, Julian sights the shape of a bear and draws his bow. His arrow, though, does not find a beast, but the hearts of both his parents, who had come, clothed in animal skins, to bring their son home.

Julian is cast out as a murderer. He is reviled, forced to sleep on hard ground, and to suffer cruel words from passersby. In time he marries a kind woman. Together they build a small house by a lake. Their door is always open, offering the warmth of their home and hearth to anyone in need. One winter night, as dusk settles, Julian sees a man flailing in the water. He rows out. The man is misshapen, his skin a map of boils and festering wounds. The drowning man is a leper. Julian hesitates. It would be easier to let him drown—maybe even a kindness—but he pulls him into the boat.

Julian feeds the leper every last scrap of food they have. But because the leper is shivering to death, Julian strips off his own cloak and embraces the man, holding him close. Julian closes his eyes and drifts into a fitful sleep. At dawn, the leper is gone. In his place stands an angel, granting Julian clemency.

Platted by developers a century ago, San Julian Street is a real place in Los Angeles. It is the center of the largest community of unhoused people in America, the heart of Skid Row. Each night more than eleven thousand people sleep on its fifty square blocks—on mats, in tents, under streetlights, on bare concrete. And yet, Skid Row is also a place where people are most likely to find the services they need, services that no one else can provide: a hot meal and a bed, someone to talk to, someone to sing with, someone who will listen.

Saint Julian is the patron saint of innkeepers and boatmen; of pilgrims, hunters, and travelers; of those who offer shelter without question.

He is also the patron saint of violinists.

Chapter 4

WHAT MAKES YOU LEAP OUT OF BED

Brahms, Symphony in E Minor, i

A symphony is no joke.

—Johannes Brahms

Ludwig van Beethoven, Violin Concerto in D Major, Op. 61—i. Allegro ma non troppo

[Poughkeepsie, New York]

The week I turned seventeen, I walked away from Mount Saint Mary College, the Manhattan School of Music, Mr. Dicterow, and the violin altogether. When Dad told him I wouldn't be coming back for lessons, my teacher was furious. He'd been preparing me for the Olympics of the violin: the Tchaikovsky Competiton in Moscow and the Queen Elisabeth in Brussels. He'd said I could have a real shot at winning—at a life as a soloist.

Trying to exist without music, without my teacher, felt like an amputation: like I had once had wings and knew the world from a high vantage point—and now would never fly again. Sometimes the concertos rushed back into my body like phantom pain. So I stopped listening to them and switched to the symphonies I loved—Brahms, Bruckner, Mahler—but that only made me want to play even more. When that didn't work, I turned to Led Zeppelin. And when even *that* didn't work, I started drinking.

One afternoon, I opened the case and tried playing the "Chaconne." While attempting the first chord, my knuckle gave out. My unrosined bow slipped sideways. In a few months of not practicing, the drills Dicterow had carved into me had faded and my coordination was gone. I froze, humiliated, and then reached for the little vial of vodka Dad had tucked in my violin case from when I used to play concerts, from when he and I used to laugh together. I held the bottle up to the window. It was full. I took one scorching sip, then another. After I finished the bottle in a gulp, it was easier to pretend I didn't care that music had abandoned me. Then I tried playing the last thing Dicterow and I had been working on: the Beethoven Violin Concerto. The opening arpeggio of octaves was easier while buzzed, but I knew every note I played was out of tune.

At Marist, surrounded by kids I didn't know, I could pretend to be grown up, passing for a five-foot-seven college freshman, even though I had the worst case of senioritis. For the first time in my life I started skipping class, simply to do nothing. Instead of MCAT review sessions, I spent hours on a nursing major's PlayStation, locked in with Scorpion's combos on *Mortal Kombat: Deception*—"FATALITY."

After a battery of scans and more hushed, late-night discussion, Mom agreed to a "D&C," a scraping of her uterine wall. Dad said doctors pulled out three tumors, but the biopsies were benign. They warned that the fibroids would grow back and that she needed a full hysterectomy, but Dad said she'd be fine. Even I knew what went unsaid: The procedure—which wouldn't be covered by their health insurance—would set us back at least thirty grand, probably more. One day, Dad handed me Mom's medical records—scans, blood work, visit summaries—and asked what I thought, as if I had any authority.

"You're a man now. You need to know these things." He still wouldn't let me drive the family Nissan down Route 52, but he wanted my second opinion on Mom's health. What I realize now is that he had no one else to talk to.

But I was still a boy, desperate to prove I could hang with man-children. At a game of beer pong, I went toe-to-toe with a six-foot-four jock, downing seven cans of warm Busch Light in under two hours. My drinking buds left me passed out in the handicapped stall of a Poughkeepsie McDonald's. When I came to, I panicked, terrified my parents would find out. A nursing major cleaned me up, doused me in Polo Ralph Lauren, and handed me a couple of aspirin for the hangover. On the ride home, I couldn't feel my face, but Mom complimented my cologne.

A few months later, I sat for a round of graduate school entrance exams. I aced the writing portion of the GRE, but the MCAT wrecked me. I'd have to wait for a few months to figure out how I did, but I knew the news wouldn't be good. I sent out applications to biochemistry PhD programs—because Mom had said I should get an MD/PhD—but none of the labs wrote back, either because they didn't want to take a chance on a seventeen-year-old, or because my test scores were too low. In secret, I also put in an application to the Yale School of Music, even convincing Dad to drive me to New Haven under the pretense of an "interview," which would really be an audition. When he noticed the violin case in the back seat, his eyes flickered with surprise. For a moment, I wondered if I should be afraid, but then, something like pride crested his face. "Don't tell Mom," I said. He knew the drill.

The next morning I auditioned with the first movement of the Beethoven Violin Concerto and a Paganini caprice. My playing was only a shadow of what it had been, but I still got in. A few months later the admissions letter arrived. Mom was furious at first, and relented when she realized I'd be the first in our family with an Ivy League diploma.

But she wasn't easily satisfied. "Maybe you should take some biology classes while you're there. See if someone will let you join their lab."

That year I attended a talk delivered by a lean, soft-spoken neuroscientist from Harvard. Dressed elegantly in a white Oxford shirt and a striped red-and-blue tie, he looked like the paragon of erudition my parents wanted me to become. Holding up the cap of a Bic pen, he explained the basic mechanism of Alzheimer's Disease: how memory dies as cells become wrapped in the toxic plaque made up of protein shards—like pen caps breaking off of pens. It was as good a performance as I'd seen from any musician. His presence was magnetic, the inflection of his tone lyrical, and the prop was simple, elegant. When he finished, I borrowed some of Dad's bravado and asked the man—Dr. Dennis Selkoe—if I could intern in his lab for the summer. He said yes.

When I told Dad I'd landed a summer research internship at Harvard's Center for Neurologic Diseases, he beamed. "See? I knew you'd come to your senses."

But I hadn't. I was getting better at pretending.

Henryk Wieniawski, Etude-Caprice in A Minor

[Avenue Louis Pasteur, Boston]

The summer I turned seventeen, I wandered the blocks around Harvard Medical School, spinning my iPod between Carlos Kleiber's recording of Brahms's Fourth with the Vienna Philharmonic and Robin Williams's 2002 stand-up special, *Live on Broadway*. Most afternoons I walked down Camden Street to the theater, where I saw *Revenge of the Sith* at least once a week, waiting for the moment when Anakin finally became Darth Vader: *daa-daa-daa daa-da-daa daa-da-daa*.

Between showings, I read Tracy Kidder's *Mountains Beyond Mountains*, the story of Paul Farmer, the Harvard doctor who had dedicated his life to providing healthcare for HIV/AIDS and TB patients in the world's poorest places, once hiking seven hours through the Haitian countryside to see only two patients. Farmer called his work "fighting the long defeat." The same year I wandered through Boston, filled with teenage ennui, Farmer was testifying before the US Senate, saying that real medicine wasn't just fixing people, but *accompanying* them, "sharing their fate." I remembered the little boy in Kolkata who had handed me a poisha. Since I had failed as a soloist, it would be better to be a doctor, working like Paul Farmer, maybe even in India.

My new labmates were dedicated scientists, but many of them seemed more interested in talking to me about music than solving Alzheimer's Disease. I'd expected Selkoe's lab to be filled with unfeeling automatons, but in my first week, one postdoc, who had recently published a paper in *Nature*, spent hours talking about his favorite recording of Beethoven's Ninth, and why the symphony was the soundtrack for *A Clockwork Orange*. Another postdoc, also a violinist, asked if I wanted to play the Wieniawski Duo in A Minor with him for Selkoe's annual garden party. For the first time in a year, I had someone to play music with again.

Selkoe ran his lab quietly, more coach than conductor. He knew the shape of every experiment but didn't hover, letting lines of inquiry play out even when he disagreed. But during weekly seminars reviewing the lab's progress, his questions were calm but brutal, exposing every weakness. One time, a PhD candidate unveiled a bold research plan that would take ten years to accomplish. Selkoe pressed him, naming every obstacle in his way. The student—who had a buzz cut and a point-guard build—stood his ground. "Yeah, but I want to cure Alzheimer's," he said, as he took his seat, eyes brimming with frustration.

The student was staring down an interminable road: Even if the lab discovered something promising, it would take years, maybe decades—trials, regulators, patents—and in the end, only the rich might be able to afford it. Curing Alzheimer's, even with unlimited funding, even at

Harvard, was Sisyphean. I wondered if there was any point in such grueling, thankless work.

But to be honest, my heart simply wasn't in it. In the boredom and quiet discipline of the lab, I became easily distracted and screwed up routine experiments, misloading reagents, overcooking a Western blot until the protein gel smoked and curled like parchment, destroying weeks of work. In this place of minuscule tolerances, I was becoming a major liability.

The quiet coach noticed. One afternoon, Selkoe took me to lunch at the Harvard Med School cafeteria. He was tall and wiry, with cheekbones and watchful eyes that gave away little. He was at ease, and although we exchanged pleasantries, I was nervous, not sure how to impress him. I asked about his lab's most recent paper in *Science*, trying to sound interested in "signal transduction" and "putative kinases," but I was performing, like a wannabe dutiful scientist. Selkoe listened intently, head slightly tilted, reading me. Then, gently, he set his fork down.

"Robert, listen. You need to do what makes you leap out of bed in the morning."

The next morning, Selkoe sent a short email introducing me to a neurologist named Gottfried Schlaug. Schlaug had been raised as a church organist in Vienna but had dedicated his life to studying how music shaped the brain. Years later I'd see his name in Oliver Sacks's *Musicophilia*. But at the time I was simply relieved: Here was someone who might speak both my languages, someone who could convince me that medicine was my path, so that my parents could be right.

One morning, I walked across the medical campus to Schlaug's lab, tucked into an older wing of Brigham and Women's Hospital. The halls were tiled and gray, with flickering lights and half-empty bulletin boards, lacking the polish of Selkoe's cutting-edge, likely better-funded setup. Schlaug had a square, heavy face, with deep-set eyes and a deliberate manner. He spoke in an accent that reminded me of Mrs. Vogel, rattling off the details of his work without embellishment.

There was a kind of worn-down dignity to Schlaug, like someone who had chosen the hard way on purpose. As I watched him, I realized it was the same look I'd seen on the PhD student in Selkoe's lab: not the quick flash of genius, but an unending burn of patience—exactly the kind of patience I lacked. The people in these labs had apprenticed themselves to failure. They didn't chase easy answers: They kept company with hard questions, stumbling forward in controlled experiments. Over a lifetime, those stumbles became discoveries, each one opening another line of inquiry.

Schlaug explained his research. Patients who'd lost the ability to speak—after a stroke or traumatic brain injury—couldn't form words on their own. But if they sang the words, even something as simple as "Happy Birthday," they were able to enunciate clearly. Schlaug gave his subjects eighty hours of singing lessons, tracking their progress with regular fMRI scans. What he saw was astonishing: Through singing, his patients were activating and creating new circuitry in the undamaged hemisphere of their prefrontal cortex. Music didn't just help his patients cope emotionally: Music was rewiring their brain.

A few years later, I'd hear about Schlaug's work again, this time on the news. Congresswoman Gabby Giffords, a former French horn player, had been shot in the head. The bullet tore through her left temporal lobe, destroying her speech centers. But with Schlaug's protocol, and months of strenuous music therapy, she sang her own voice back.

I had come ready to ask Schlaug the "right" questions—about neuroimaging techniques, about whether diffusion tensor imaging could track new neural connections as they formed, about mapping speech recovery across hemispheres. But when we sat down, all that slipped away. I felt like a boy again. What I asked instead was the real question—the raw, quiet one that put me to sleep at night and woke me in the morning.

"Do you miss music? I mean, do you ever miss playing, you know, the organ?"

He didn't pause. "Every day." Then, before I could say anything else: "You know, science can wait. In fact, science will only get better with waiting. But your violin won't wait for you. If you need to play, if you really need to be a musician, do it. Do it now."

I watched him: his square jaw and quiet eyes, the hands that once commanded organ manuals and stops. This man, who rewired the brain through song but didn't sing himself.

He softened. "We could make room if you change your mind."

But he'd already given me all the permission I needed.

Johannes Brahms, Symphony in E Minor, Op. 98

{i. Allegro non troppo}

[Grand Avenue, Los Angeles]

"Tui ki jitbi?"

I didn't dare answer her. Mom and I both knew the odds of me winning my first orchestral audition were slim to none. I looked down at the menu, cowed by the prices. Twenty-five bucks for a three-egg omelet at the Hilton Checkers, enough to cover breakfast for the whole family at a diner back home. But this was Los Angeles. Sun bounced off glass and concrete outside the window. I looked back at Mom, who had the same shade of muddled-hazel eyes as mine, and even though I knew she was disappointed that I was trying out for a job in music, she couldn't hide being slightly impressed, maybe even proud. Three months shy of turning twenty, I'd made the finals for one of the most prestigious orchestral jobs in the world.

"Let's split breakfast," she said.

Over the past two years at the Yale School of Music, I'd fallen for music harder than ever. I played Bach passions on gut strings.

I played new music for classmates and friends. I learned Byrd and Berg, Shostakovich and Charpentier, Beethoven sonatas, Schumann quartets, Mozart and Messiaen. And all the while, in orchestra, I played Strauss and Mahler—but above all of them, I lived for Brahms.

Mom called me every day to remind me that I was wasting my time. "Why don't you get an MBA instead? Then you can run a hospital when you get your MD!" But before signing on as a bureaucrat, I wanted one last chance—a shot at the big leagues of music. At night, in my small dorm room crowded with takeout cartons and scores, I'd conduct along with Carlos Kleiber's recording of Brahms's Fourth Symphony, tears welling at the ferocity of the last movement. This music, that *sound*, became my prayer. I'd even adopted Brahms's motto for myself: *Frei, aber froh*—Free, but happy.

The previous March, while I was a student at Yale, two orchestras had announced violin vacancies: Auditions for Minnesota's famed St. Paul Chamber Orchestra and the Los Angeles Philharmonic would take place in late May. I told a white lie to my parents, saying that my teachers at Yale thought taking an orchestral audition "would be a good experience." Dad spat. "Good for what? So you can sit in the back of an orchestra, like some bum?"

My parents had groomed me to be a soloist, not a section player, but I shrugged them off. An orchestral chair meant a steady paycheck, and if I played my cards right, I'd have a job for life. The auditions were fiercely competitive, with hundreds of people trying out for a single spot. Meanwhile, Dad was frantically trying to revive his business, chasing old leads, cold-calling former clients, now flying cross-country to pitch new ones. Needless to say, he didn't find the idea of me auditioning for an orchestra appealing.

"Chee. A waste of time. And money."

When I mentioned St. Paul, assuming there was no way the LA Phil would hire me, Dad made the choice by weather. "They won't give you either job, but in Minnesota you'll freeze. In LA, at least you can take Mom to the beach when they kick you out."

They hadn't kicked me out—*yet*. I'd managed to survive the first two days of auditions, which took place onstage at Walt Disney Concert Hall, the home of the LA Phil. In 2007 the hall was only four years old, and I'd never seen anything like it. The halls in Lincoln Center were austere marble with slit windows like gun turrets. But Frank Gehry's stainless-steel sails unfurled at the intersection of First and Grand, and inside, the hall was the hull of a ship, pale wood carved in fluid arcs. It felt as if the building itself was in constant motion.

Auditions for a top orchestra are blind, which means that for the first two days of my audition, I played alone for a committee that sat behind a screen. Onstage, my violin sounded crisp and bright under my ear, but I felt like I was playing for myself. The only person I could see was Mark, the tall, mustached personnel manager, who had walked me across the strip of stage carpet, taken a seat behind me, and said, "Whenever you're ready," in a gentle voice, indicating that I could start playing my first excerpt.

A few weeks earlier, I had sent in a résumé, careful to leave off my age, and to feature my former teacher's name—"Glenn Dicterow"—in bold. The audition coordinator sent back the excerpt list. I'd have to learn them all, ready to play any one of them at a moment's notice:

Los Angeles Philharmonic

Repertoire list for both 1st and 2nd VIOLIN—May 14–23, 2007

Solo Repertoire

Mozart: Concerto No. 3, 4, or 5 (1st movement without cadenza)

and

One Listed: Concerto (1st movement including cadenzas)

Bartók #2, Beethoven, Brahms, Dvořák, Glazunov, Mendelssohn in E Minor, Prokofiev #2, Sibelius, or Tchaikovsky

Orchestral Repertoire

First Violin Parts

Brahms: Symphony No. 4 (Complete)

Debussy: La Mer (2nd mvt: #19 to #20, 3rd mvt: #47 to #48)

Mahler: Symphony No. 10 (Adagio: #19 to #23)

Mendelssohn: Midsummer Night's Dream [Scherzo: mm 1–136 or beg. to 21 after E (1st page)]

Mozart: Symphony No. 38 [2nd mvt (Andante): m 1 to m 34, 3rd mvt: m 1 to the double bar]

Mozart: Symphony No. 39 (2nd mvt: mm 1–27; mm 96–132)

Schumann: Symphony No. 2 (Scherzo: m 1 to Trio I)

Shostakovich: Symphony No. 5 (1st mvt: reh #9–12, 2nd mvt: from #52 until #62)

Strauss, R.: Don Juan [mm 1–63 or beg. to 13 meas. after C (1st page)]

Stravinsky: Dumbarton Oaks [mm 1–40 or beg. to 3 meas. after #6 (1st page)]

Weber, C. Maria: Oberon Overture [mm 1–60 or beg. to 9 meas. after C (1st page)]

Second Violin Parts

Beethoven: Symphony No. 9 (Scherzo: mm 1–150)

Brahms: Piano Concerto No. 1 [3rd mvt: "E" (m 238)—m 274]

Sight reading and/or chamber music may be required.

All participants should be prepared to begin each stage of the audition with any of the listed materials.

Sight-reading—the tightrope act of music—required one to read the notes on the page, cold, with no preparation at all. Luckily, Dicterow had drilled this into me. Sometimes, at the end of a lesson, he'd plunk an orchestral masterpiece on the stand in his studio. "Okay, go for it!"

I'd crash and burn, and we'd both belly-laugh. Then, one note at a time, he'd show me how to prepare each shift, how to set my elbow for a run of fast notes, how to make sure every stroke of my right hand clicked in place. Before the audition, I emailed him for help, imagining all those special lessons on Bach, Beethoven, and Brahms in his studio. Even though I hadn't had a lesson with him in two years, he faxed me parts with his personal markings from four decades in the orchestra. I felt like I might have a chance if I could, even for a few moments, sound anything like him.

Leading up to the audition, I'd thought of nothing but excerpts, steeping in the recordings of the great orchestras. I listened on repeat on the plane, staring out the window, watching the landscape get browner and drier: *La Mer* over the Midwest, *Midsummer Night's Dream* over the Rockies, and *Don Juan* over the desert. I scrawled a phrase at the top of each excerpt to define its character, dropping my body into a zone of focus. For Mendelssohn's "Scherzo" from *A Midsummer Night's Dream,* it was *elves dancing on tripwire*. The finger-twisting opener of Mozart's Symphony No. 39—*royal silk*. The fugue from the last movement of Bartók's Concerto for Orchestra—*punch it, motherfucker*. Before I practiced each excerpt, I visualized the light of the stage, how I wanted to feel, how I wanted *them*, the anonymous committee, to feel. I wanted to be undeniable, *unfuckwithable*.

On the day of my final round, after eating half a breakfast and ignoring the look on Mom's face, I walked out of the Hilton and toward the stainless-steel hall on the hill. All I had was my violin case, a flip phone with a dead screen, and a sheaf of music. The sky was hard blue, and a slight breeze carried the scent of something briny. As I climbed the hill, I sang excerpts in my head. Quirky Mahler. Brutal Bartók. Regal Mozart. Elfin Mendelssohn. And my favorite—Brahms: *Frei, aber froh*.

At the artist's entrance, a flight of stairs up from Second and Grand, I checked in with the security desk and waited in a large greenroom with pleather sofas and prints of concept art from Disney's *Fantasia*. It was quiet there. The air-conditioning was almost too cold, too clean, and I could smell my own sweat. *I should have worn more deodorant.* Mark greeted me and walked me past doors stenciled with names I still couldn't believe: "Esa-Pekka Salonen, Music Director" and "Martin Chalifour, Concertmaster." My dressing room was a mini-*Fantasia* set: I had never seen a couch that shade of clementine. Mark, who towered a good foot over me, handed me a sheet of paper with the final-round excerpts. I took the page and stared at my fate in robin's-egg blue.

May 25: Final Round

Solo

Mozart, Concerto: 1st movement, no cadenza.

I smiled to myself. Today I would play the same Mozart I'd learned with Ms. Behrend when I was seven. The same Mozart I'd played for Menuhin.

I read on:

Excerpts

Brahms: Symphony No. 4 IV. m 33–80

Mahler: Symphony No. 10 Adagio: [21]–[23], no solo

Bartók: Concerto for Orchestra 5th mvt: mm 12–96 (upper staff)

Strauss, R.: Don Juan mm 1–63 (first page)

Mendelssohn: A Midsummer Night's Dream Scherzo: Beginning—[E] (m 99)

Beethoven: Symphony no. 9 3rd mvt: Adagio, mm 42–114

"There are twelve candidates for the final round. The committee will hear from you at 1 p.m."

First up after the concerto: Brahms. The same symphony I'd prayed to play in my dorm room.

Today I'd get forty-seven measures—less than two minutes—to summon the majesty of forty minutes of music. In my greenroom, I practiced. Time seemed elastic, like a rubber band, slackening as I counted seconds, and then snapping an hour forward. By the time I walked onto the stage at Disney Hall, I had no eyes for the bird-of-paradise-patterned seats, the bamboo-tan floor, or the Frank Gehry–designed organ that looked like a carton of French fries. All I saw was the stand at the end of the carpet strip.

"Whenever you're ready," said Mark.

First up: Brahms.

I wanted a sound like molten lava. My markings at the top of the page glowed: *Slow bow. Still a dance. Lugubrious.* The excerpt started on the lowest string, the same rhythm repeated as a thick waltz. *De-daaa-ya-da-yaaa-la-deee. . . .* Something slithering, gliding, thick. Stretching but never strained, never forced. I had to make a sound that could blend with thirty-one other violinists. My pitch had to be perfect. My rhythm, bulletproof. Then, the second variation, quicker swells of eighth notes, rising against the falling winds. *Remember: The clarinets have triplets. Don't rush.* It rose, building—now the triplets moved to the cellos. It climbed again—leaping, running, screaming. I wanted to leap, to run, to scream, but to play the excerpt cleanly, I had to be cool, almost detached. *Above and ahead. Frei, aber froh.*

When no voice came from the other side, I played the next excerpts. Mahler. Bartók. Then Strauss—*Don Juan. Zen/swashbuckle.* A notorious excerpt that began with a swoosh of notes that with a full section sounds like a demon cranking a dial. But exposed, alone, I had to play seven perfectly articulated sixteenth notes in the span of a single second, followed by a long note and then a triplet: *ka-taka-taka-taka-taaa-lakata-tum!*

But when my bow skidded across my strings during the long "taaa," I stopped, horrified, looking down to see that my bow was on the *wrong side* of my bridge—exactly like when I was a terrified kid at Pre-College, playing for Mr. Becker, except now, my Suzuki-squeak was magnified a thousandfold in the crystalline acoustics of Disney Hall.

Shit! That's it, it's done. It's over.

I waited for a voice to dismiss me.

When it didn't come, I moved on to the next excerpt on the list. But I'd lost my nerve. *Shit, shit, shit.* Back in my dressing room, I replayed the round in my head. Mendelssohn could have been quieter, Beethoven better phrased. I wiped the rosin off my strings, producing more squeaks. *If that was it—if that was all I got—at least the Brahms was good.* I packed my violin and waited to be told to leave, staring at my broken flip phone. The screen inside was dead, but the outer LCD still told time. I couldn't bear to call Dad. He'd tell me I was wasting my time and his money, and to leave and take Mom to the beach. I'd rather sit here and let my final moments as a musician pass backstage at Walt Disney Concert Hall.

For the next hour, I heard others warm up, leave their rooms, and return. I didn't dare leave my dressing room. Another hour passed. In the hallway, I heard Mark's gentle mumble, dismissing other candidates. My stomach growled. What if I left? What if Mark came back and my room was empty and they dismissed me?

At 5 p.m., nearly four hours after I had packed my fiddle, Mark knocked on my door. He held a flamingo-pink sheet. I caught the first two words:

Superfinal Round

What? Another final round? And I had made it through? Mark glanced around my small room, his professional visage dropping for a moment.

"Have you been waiting in here this whole time?" I nodded my head as he handed me a new sheet of excerpts. "Have you had anything to eat?" I shook my head and swallowed.

Solo

Concerto: Bartók #2, Beethoven, Brahms, Dvořák, Glazunov, Mendelssohn in E minor, Prokofiev #2, Sibelius, or Tchaikovsky

Part of my heart was already made of Mendelssohn: the music I played with Mehta. I read on, feeling an electric flood of new adrenaline.

Excerpts

Shostakovich: Symphony No. 5, 2nd mvt: from #52 until 1st bar of #63

Debussy: La Mer, 2nd mvt: #19 to #20

Mendelssohn: A Midsummer Night's Dream Scherzo: Beginning—[E] (m 99)

Mozart: Symphony No. 39, 2nd mvt: mm 1-27; mm 96-132

Schumann: Symphony No. 2, Scherzo: m 1 to Trio I

Brahms: Piano Concerto No. 1, 3rd mvt: "E" (m 238)-m 274

Before he left, Mark said, "The screens will come down for this one. You're doing great, by the way." I blinked in a low-blood-sugar fog. My hands were cold, my face in the mirror drained. As he left, the hydraulic door clacked and hissed. I opened my violin case. I needed to warm up, but I still couldn't believe there was another round. At least I'd get another shot at the Mendelssohn Scherzo.

A few moments later—too soon—came a soft knock. But it wasn't Mark. Two middle-aged Asian women met my eyes, smiling with concern—the orchestra's librarian, and the audition coordinator to whom I'd mailed my résumé. They held plates of Trader Joe's jicama sticks, hummus, cherry tomatoes, and soft cookies smuggled from the committee's buffet. By then, word had spread backstage: A teenager had made the LA Phil superfinal. And he hadn't packed lunch.

By the time they brought me back onstage, I felt reset. This time, there were no screens. About two dozen people sat scattered in the orchestra section of Disney Hall, notepads in their laps. Some of them applauded. My fingers were warm again. *Okay. This I can do. A concert.* I could see my audience, and I smiled, polite, and tried to pick out the committee. *That's Chalifour, the concertmaster. And the blond guy—Salonen?*

I played through the round, stepping back after each excerpt, resetting, visualizing the next one. At one point the blond man cleared his throat and asked me to play the fugue from Brahms's First Piano Concerto—*sneaky Bach*—"with more control."

Shit, so that was *Salonen.*

More control?

Unthinking, I fired back a question at him, the sound of my voice surprising me:

"Do you mean dynamic, or tempo?"

What was I thinking, talking back to the conductor during an audition? Shut up, dude!

Salonen called out, clear and curt. "Both." I thought I saw a wry smile on his face. I played as softly as I dared, locked in on the pulse. As I left the stage, the committee applauded.

I spent the evening in a greenroom with five other candidates. We sat quietly, staring at the floor, trying not to meet the eyes of the person about to beat us.

After hours of deliberation, plus a second superfinal round, two violinists were selected—one for each section. One was a Chinese guy named Shawn. He was taller than I was, with a swimmer's build, and I felt like he could see right through me.

I glanced at my flip phone. It had been twelve hours since I had walked through the artists' entrance, since the omelet.

Standing on the sidewalk in front of Disney Hall, I called Dad. I didn't realize it was 2 a.m. in New York. My vision swam, and the reflection of taillights on the shimmering steel of the hall were like fireworks.

"Dad? Dad. I got it."

His response was a sleepy mumble.

"What will they pay you?"

{ii. Andante moderato}

[Barrington Avenue, Los Angeles]

Neither of my parents had ever held a job with benefits. Neither of them had saved for retirement, and Mom didn't understand how a pension worked. My new post, "Rotating Section First Violin," paid $125,000 a year. It was more than Dad had made in the past three years combined. It turned out they didn't mind that I was a musician, not as long as I was making a doctor's salary. The job came with union protection through Musicians Local 47. If I made it through a twenty-two-month probation, I'd get tenure: lifetime job security at twenty-one. I was one of the youngest violinists ever hired by a major American orchestra. Some of my colleagues had already done the math for me: "You could retire at fifty-five and be a millionaire."

Even with the job, my parents stayed in charge. Without asking me, they picked out an overpriced, six-hundred-square-foot condo on the West Side of LA, which, even though it was only twelve miles away from Disney Hall, would often take me an hour each way. I couldn't afford the down payment, so they took out a loan against the New York house. The mortgage, though, would be my responsibility: $3,000 a month, nearly half my salary after taxes.

Since my childhood performance with Coolio at the Billboard Awards, every check I'd earned had gone straight into a joint account with my parents at the Hudson Valley Federal Credit Union. Now, my LA Phil paychecks went there too. From that account, Mom paid bills on both coasts, bought groceries, and paid down credit cards maxed out by furnishing our new condo. She also set aside savings "for the family." To my parents, my salary belonged to the family, slow payback for all the sacrifices they'd made. To me, it was my money, won by audition, fair and square. But I had always been absentminded with money, or so they told me. I'd never made a budget, or had to. I didn't even know my own online banking login.

They decided I couldn't be trusted to drive myself to work, either. I'd barely passed my road test in New York and had only ever driven country roads in the Hudson Valley. So Dad moved to LA with me. He called our cramped condo the West Coast office of "Travel World International" and told his Bengali friends I'd gotten a job with the Walt Disney Company. He hadn't thought twice about the commute when he'd bought the place, but he made sure I heard about it every morning, on our way to Disney Hall, in the brand-new blue Toyota Camry: his choice, my payments.

Before we left New York for good, Dad took me to his tailor in midtown, across from Grand Central. He was outfitting me for my new life in Los Angeles: a white dinner jacket, black tuxedo tails, and a navy shawl-collar suit made of a light-as-air silk-wool blend. Most importantly, my new wardrobe artfully hid my belly—a paunchy, fleshy flab that hung over a size forty-four waist. As the tailor looped his tape around my shoulders, chest, and waist, Dad sucked his teeth in disgust and jabbed a finger into my gut. "Eeesh," he said, shaking his head, not bothering to lower his voice. I stared at my reflection, trying to disappear.

Within weeks I was onstage at the Hollywood Bowl, the summer home of the LA Phil, for my first rehearsals. The stage stretched out in a massive gray plane, banks of lights hanging overhead like anvils. My new colleagues nodded hello with a sidelong, polite warmth that made me feel like I was still auditioning. *Who even is this kid?* Tenure wouldn't only be judged on how well I played, but on how comfortable I made everyone else feel. Now, every moment, even lunch with a colleague, was a performance.

Dad told me not to trust anyone, but to be the nicest person in the room.

"People are fake here. Not like New York."

That first summer, the orchestra cycled through three different programs every week, sometimes as much as ten pieces across six days. We might play a full opera one night, a film score or a pops show the next. In my first two weeks, the three-hour rehearsals flew: Mozart's *Magic Flute*, a show with the Decemberists, Mussorgsky's *Pictures at an Exhibition*, and the Tchaikovsky concerto with Gil Shaham, a soloist I'd idolized as a child. I'd only seen him once from the balcony at Avery Fisher Hall, while Mom circled the block. Now I was onstage just six feet away from him, rehearsing the Tchaikovksy Violin Concerto and staring at his Stradivarius and his running shoes.

The folders on the stands at the Hollywood Bowl were crammed with music I knew—Glinka, Mussorgsky, Rossini, Fauré, Ravel—and others I didn't: Ponchielli, Korngold, Ginastera, Revueltas, Martinů. When I scanned the schedule of upcoming concerts—sometimes four of them per week—I caught more names that I'd never heard in any violin lesson: Tony Bennett and Lady Gaga, Gladys Knight with Wayne Brady, and Earth, Wind & Fire.

Between a three-hour morning rehearsal and that night's concert, I spent the rest of the day practicing—scrambling to stay ahead of the next program. During concerts, I barely looked up from the stand. But once, out of the corner of my eye, I noticed a group in the white-tablecloth boxes at the foot of the stage pointing toward me. At intermission, a red-faced man in a sport coat and a shirt unbuttoned to his belly marched to the lip of the stage, swirling a glass of wine. He raised his voice above the crowd:

"You're the new kid! Are you liking LA? How old are you? Come have a glass of wine with us!"

I would've loved something to take the edge off, but I still had a year to go before I could legally order a drink. Later, after I earned tenure in the orchestra, I visited people in their boxes at the Hollywood Bowl during intermission. Most colleagues stayed backstage, zoning out to KTLA or running their parts for the second half, but I liked walking through the crowd. It felt good when people recognized me, called my name, and waved me over with a slice of cake, a glass of wine, even a plate of food. One couple I met that way—board members of the LA Phil—invited me to their home for my first Seder, and later my first Thanksgiving in LA. They were kind to me in a way that felt earnest and easy. A part of me wished they could adopt me.

Meanwhile, Dad, a proud, lifelong New Yorker, was taking savage pleasure in berating LA. One time, in a violin shop on Ventura Boulevard—Benning Violins—where I'd go to buy new sets of strings or get my bows rehaired, Dad spent the whole time complaining about how terrible the food was in LA. He didn't care that the violinmaker was standing three feet away from me, patiently laying out a selection of violin bows on a display case.

"There's nothing to bloody *eat* here!"

Part of me wished I could crawl behind the display case and disappear.

Dad wouldn't touch Korean BBQ and insisted he hated guacamole, even though he'd never tasted an avocado. I wanted to try sushi, but he was afraid of raw fish, and after seeing the price of raspberries at the Santa Monica farmers' market, he insisted that we shop at Ralph's instead. Whole Foods was out of the question.

But he did manage to find one cramped Bangladeshi market near Koreatown that sold eeleesh mach—his favorite bony river fish—and mustard oil that smelled like home. On Sundays, he'd drive there, humming melancholy Bengali songs under his breath, come back with a plastic bag filled with fish, and take over the kitchen. The first few tries were disasters, but he kept at it, calling Mom for her recipe, tasting and adjusting, until he got it right.

When I came home from rehearsal, the whole apartment smelled like Montgomery: onions and cumin, coriander leaf and kacha lonka. Before I could swallow my first bite, he'd ask, "Better than Mommy's?"—insisting I tell him how good it was. I'd roll my eyes and say it was close, and he'd grin, proud and boyish. Then he'd smoke from the veranda, the beedee glowing between his fingers as Wilshire Boulevard hummed below. Whether I admitted it or not, that meal—his trying, his wanting to feed me—was love.

He did upgrade his cigarettes, though, ditching Marlboro Lights for Dunhill Reds. Mom had instructed me to put an end to his smoking, but I wouldn't dare tell him what to do, and besides, I loved the classy silver-and-burgundy packaging of his new cigs. While I played onstage, he'd sit in the Camry, puffing one after another right beneath a giant "NO SMOKING" sign at the Bowl. Some mornings, he brought a box of Krispy Kremes for the parking attendants, calling them by name. But when it came to the musicians I worked with, he never bothered to learn a single name.

To be fair, many of my new colleagues didn't seem interested in learning his name either. Some assumed he was my driver. One afternoon, a violinist with cropped gray hair and a hawkish scowl stopped him in the Bowl lot and asked if he was "allowed" to be there. Dad and I called her "Crazy Lady." Another time, pulling out of our space, Dad nearly clipped a cellist—and the LA Phil's Guarneri cello, worth several million dollars. The cellist unleashed a magnificent string of expletives. From then on, Dad and I called him *Mr. Holy Fuck*.

{iii. Allegro giocoso}
[Walt Disney Concert Hall, Los Angeles]

Joining the LA Phil felt like stepping inside the recordings I'd listened to as a kid—Zubin Mehta's *Planets,* Carlo Maria Giulini's Tchaikovsky, Esa-Pekka Salonen's *Rite of Spring.* Now I was shoulder to shoulder with the musicians I'd once idolized. But now, I saw that the life they lived was completely unlike what I had imagined. Most of these people were—how to put it? *Boring.* One violist warmed up onstage with scales and arpeggios, his breakfast—half a pita—dangling from his mouth as he played. Percussionists pounded out basic rhythmic patterns on thick pads backstage. In the brass room, players held long tones, warming up before concerts—and warming down after. Some stood backstage waving their arms in wide circles or figure-eights. Others braced themselves against walls and stretched like pre-race marathoners, tending to their bodies as carefully as their instruments. And one violist twisted herself into a quick vinyasa of yoga poses to limber up before rehearsals and concerts, which everyone called "services."

I had imagined these people as high-voltage rock stars. What I found instead were seasoned professionals committed to the long game of their craft. Many had taken a dozen, sometimes dozens, of auditions before landing a chair in the LA Phil. Many, who had come up through hard years in countless regional orchestras, knew exactly what it took to keep a musician whole. But at nineteen, all I saw was a lot of old people doing calisthenics, like Chinese didimas at Central Park.

But for all the hard lessons I had learned at Juilliard and Yale, none of my teachers had ever taught me that my real instrument wasn't just my violin but my body itself. But I treated it like a machine that could take whatever I fed it or demanded of it. When I wasn't eating Dad's eeleesh mach, I still ate like a teenager, fueled by burgers and ice cream, assured I would bounce back by the morning.

But I was already having a hard time keeping up. Two weeks into the LA Phil—after seven concerts and ten rehearsals—I started feeling a tight, clawing, burning sensation along the right side of my rib cage. I had never played that much music before. During rehearsals I'd clench my way through the ninety-minute halves, barely daring to breathe, locked in on the conductor or soloist. At concerts the stiff sleeves of my tux dug into my shoulders until my arms ached, feeling like they were being pried from their sockets.

The grind took a toll on everyone. Many of my colleagues seemed indifferent to how much music we played. Instruments often stayed in lockers between rehearsals, even through long breaks and vacations. The symphonies were pieces they had played dozens, even hundreds of times, music they no longer needed to practice. Still, the injuries came: torn labrums, shoulder surgeries, dystonia, nerve pain, tendinitis. Whether we practiced too little or too much, our bodies kept the score.

Others became bitter and bored, and didn't try to hide it. During one of my first Hollywood Bowl rehearsals, I looked over and saw a violinist doing sudoku while the conductor rehearsed the winds. Some muttered when a soloist got carried away, taking too much time at the end of each phrase. Others rolled their eyes when a young conductor waxed poetic about a piece they'd played a hundred times. An old bassist cawed like a crow. A busybody violinist answered with a dead-on Daffy Duck. A few didn't show up at all. One guy in my section was nicknamed "Mr. Saturday Night," because he called in sick every Saturday. Rumor had it that he was moonlighting as a Shakespearean actor. One Tuesday night at the Hollywood Bowl, twenty minutes to the concert's downbeat, I sat beside him, running a few bars of Strauss's *Till Eulenspiegel* under my fingers—a piece I'd be playing for the first time. With this fiddle wedged between his chin and shoulder, he turned to me, sneering:

"Cool it, Showoffski."

After that, I practiced offstage.

{iv. Allegro energico e passionato}
[Hollywood Bowl, Los Angeles]

Heraclitus said no one steps into the same river twice: It's never the same man and never the same river. Music is like that, too. The notes on the page may stay fixed, but music itself is fleeting, existing only in vibration, in our perception and memory. Maybe that's why we return to the pieces we love, not only to remember who we were, but to hear how much we've changed. Music confronts us with both infinity and impermanence. The music ends only when we stop listening.

When I was a student, one of my professors taught us to hear Brahms symphonies in layers. We marked our scores with highlighters: purple for melody, yellow for accompaniment, red for dynamics and expression. With each listening, we heard something new in the music. A purple line in the flutes was mirrored in the basses, but at half speed, like a secret code. A yellow figure in the violas would be handed to the clarinets, stitched into the music's warp and weft. A melody that had begun *piano, dolce*—soft, sweet—returned *fortissimo, marcato,* like sadness transformed into joy. Every note, articulation, dynamic, and tempo marking had its own meaning, worthy of total reverence. After an evening of study, my score glowed like a Kandinsky: full of meaning I would have never heard unless I had listened again, and better.

When I saw that Brahms's Fourth was on the schedule three weeks into my new job, I bought a fresh score and took out my highlighters. I wanted to walk into that first rehearsal knowing every seam of the music from the first bar. I had asked for this music. I had prayed for it.

The first movement is a slow-burning miracle. It begins with a plaintive sigh in the violins, a restless figure that never settles, like a secret muttered in half-sleep. Under it, the winds answer in fragments—oboe, clarinet, horn—nudging the theme down a long corridor of memory.

Onstage that morning—back stand, first violins—I watched for the bassoonist to set his embouchure and matched the flutist's breaths with my own.

The second movement started with horns and low winds speaking over bare octaves, like a prayer said inward. Then the clarinet solo, playing an ache that lingered long after the phrase passed to the violins. When my section took the theme, I felt as if my sound had become more like a wind instrument, buoyed by breath rather than bow.

The third movement is a bucking, skittering romp, a dare. Fluid arpeggios sent our hands shooting across our instruments, sudden stops and slashing chords across our strings, and accented off-beat syncopations. When the conductor stopped, I marked my part with fingerings, but when we played again, I didn't know where to find the pulse. I looked across the stage for the timpanist, the triangle, the blaring horns—the back of the concertmaster's head—anything to catch the pulse before it turned wild. We leapt anyway, and at the last chord, even Mr. Saturday Night let out a low grunt of approval. We'd made it across.

All rehearsal, though, I had been waiting for the last movement, in which Brahms built a passacaglia—a repeating bassline—from Bach's cantata "Nach dir, Herr, verlanget mich"—"For Thee, Lord, is my longing"—into a roiling, inevitable whirlwind. Where Bach's music is a solemn dance, Brahms sets the bassline as a trombone chorale, unfurling into thirty restless variations with flickers of Hungarian folk dance, a tender flute interlude, and a final surge that feels like the world collapsing in one wave. In March 1897, this symphony was the last music Brahms ever heard in public, seated at his box in Vienna's Musikverein. During the final ovations, the composer, jaundiced with liver cancer, wept openly. To me, this was sacred music, made more sacred by the fact that it was my dream come true.

But at the Hollywood Bowl, our guest conductor cut us off halfway through the movement, right after the flute solo. I froze. There were still thirty minutes on the clock. "Gotta beat traffic," he said. The Cardinals were playing the Dodgers that afternoon, and he wanted to catch the game. He waved us off, and my colleagues cheered like students let out early ahead of an exam. "You all know how this goes anyway!"

Wait—was it over? A few of the wind players were disassembling their instruments, threading long silk swabs through the dark wood to wick out the condensation before it warped the wood. A few stands ahead, Daffy announced, "That's all, folks!" The bass player beside me cawed. The conductor closed his score at the podium, chatting with the principal cellist. I turned to my stand partner, spluttering.

Mr. Saturday Night barked, "Hey, Maestro! The New Kid doesn't know it yet!"

As he turned to face us, he hollered, "You'll love it!" across six desks of violins, and a ripple of laughter went through the orchestra. Then it hit me: I would be playing the end of Brahms's Fourth for the first time—essentially sight-reading it—with no rehearsal, live, in front of ten thousand people, magnified by the massive, high-definition screens that hung on either side of the orchestra—which we called the "megatron."

I went home and practiced the last movement with the recording of Carlos Kleiber and the Vienna Philharmonic—the same one I'd listened to in my dorm room a year earlier—but now, without the sound of a real orchestra around me, it didn't help much. I didn't know what tempo the conductor would take, or how the sounds would project across the stage, or how Mr. Saturday Night would—or wouldn't—play the notes. Honestly, it wouldn't have mattered whether Carlos Kleiber, Leonard Bernstein, Zubin Mehta—or even Johannes Brahms himself—was on the podium. For the rest of my orchestral life, the most important person onstage would always be the one sitting immediately to my left or right.

Throughout the afternoon, I let my gut knot of anxiety tighten, which meant that by the time we reached the passacaglia—nearly an hour into the concert—it felt like every flub was being broadcast on the megatron in high definition.

That night I finally exhaled during the flute solo—a single, plaintive line drifting into the summer dark, beautiful and terrifying in its solitude. I watched the flutist shape each note with tender, exacting care, and for a moment I forgot I was onstage, and that I would have to play again. Then the trombones answered and my chest tightened. It was coming—the coda—and even though I'd run it alone a dozen times that afternoon with a recording, the ground fell away from under me. My hands went numb. The conductor's baton blurred.

When we started playing again, Mr. Saturday Night sawed away a full beat ahead of everyone else. I couldn't hear anything else, and I couldn't even see the front stands. The back of the violin section was a pileup, and no one seemed to care. During a few bars of rest, my eyes caught on a box where patrons were eating—salads, steak, three bottles of wine—laughing and talking loudly while we played. They were picnicking and drinking while we played Brahms, and I felt like the joke was on me.

Then, in an instant, it was over. The conductor gave a whooshing, dramatic cutoff and waved us up. I stood, dizzy, stomach in my throat. Applause surged, but I felt ghosted from my own body—absent from the music it had just made. Down in the boxes, patrons who'd dropped a grand for dinner and a show were already slipping out to beat the lot. Waiters cracked jokes as they cleared half-eaten ribeyes and glasses of wine. The conductor returned for another bow, but most of the crowd had already turned away, headed for their cars.

Backstage, in a room crammed with instrument cases, I wiped powder-white rosin from my violin, thinking of the score I had marked with highlighters, the care I'd taken in preparing music for one concert—and now—the humiliation I felt for the wasted effort. Mr. Saturday Night clapped me on the shoulder. "You'll get used to it." I swallowed hard, mouth dry, eyes burning.

Don't let this asshole see you cry.

The bass player crowed. "Get used to it, or get over it!"

Chapter 5

PLAY *SUPERMAN*!

Beethoven, "Cavatina"

John Williams, "Title Sequence" from *Catch Me If You Can!*

[Hollywood Bowl, Los Angeles]

As a child, I'd march outside Dad's office window, singing tunes by John Williams at the top of my lungs. One of my favorites was from *Indiana Jones and the Raiders of the Lost Ark.*

"Daadedadaaa, daadedaa..."

A window would slide open, and Dad, clutching a receiver, would call out.

"Potka, chup kor! I'm on the bloody phone!"

A few minutes later, I'd march past his window again, singing louder, and this time, he'd yell again through gritted teeth—"Pot-*ku*!"—and I knew he meant business.

Now, weeks after my humiliation with the Brahms symphony, one day before my twentieth birthday, I sat under the massive gray shell of the Hollywood Bowl, watching the composer of those tunes—John Williams himself—raise his baton. Behind him, ten thousand lightsabers swished and roared. I raised my violin unthinking, ready to join them with the next cue: Darth Vader's "Imperial March."

Daaa daaa daaa daadedaa daadedaa…

The notes, though, weren't child's play. John Williams's music held in it the history of the symphonic tradition. Through concerts and rehearsals over the past year, I'd heard Williams's themes reflected in beloved pieces of classical music. The horn theme from *Star Wars* was an homage to the poignant slow movement of Mahler's 6th Symphony. "Mars" from Holst's *The Planets* gave birth to Lord Vader's march. The ominous underwater chomping in *Jaws* was, undoubtedly, the opening of Dvořák 9's last movement, and the exploits of Kevin McCallister in *Home Alone* were set to "Trepak" from Tchaikovsky's *Nutcracker.*

Next up was the "Flying Theme" from *E.T.* Mr. Saturday Night rolled his eyes. During rehearsal that morning, he'd grabbed my pencil to change the "L" in "FLYING" to an "R." Still, during the concert, I wanted to join the audience as they cheered for the alien in the bicycle basket.

After a half-dozen ovations, through a haze of pot smoke, a man in the audience screamed:

"FOR THE LOVE OF GOD, PLAY *SUPERMAN*!"

The lightsabers issued a swishing roar of agreement. Williams, ever gracious, laughed and turned to the orchestra. I quickly rifled through the folder of music, careful not to spill loose pages across the stage. For weeks I'd been deluged with new repertoire, barely keeping pace with my 108 colleagues, most of whose names I still didn't know. During the summer season, the orchestra played three programs a week, a total of ten different symphonic numbers in six days.

As a student, I'd spend months on a single movement, fussing over every turn of phrase—a perfect bowing to match the phrasing, the ideal fingering for the perfect expressive slide. Now, I was learning ten times that amount of music in one-tenth the time, and my body began to mutiny. A dull ache bloomed beneath my right collarbone, then down into the elbow—what I'd later learn was the beginning of tendinitis.

And tonight, after nearly three straight hours of performing, I was about to sight-read the *Superman* theme—which was a lot like the overture from Wagner's opera *The Flying Dutchman*—for eighteen thousand people, with the composer himself on the podium. It felt like a ninety-mile-an-hour joyride without a seat belt. Part of me loved it. Another part wished I were in the audience instead, cheering the soundtrack of my childhood with the crowd, with Dad and a bucket of popcorn, like a normal kid.

But Dad and I would never get a chance to be normal.

Even after a year into my job at the Phil, Dad was still living with me, and being treated like a little kid was getting old. Every morning he rose at 5 a.m. to chant loudly in Sanskrit, keeping East Coast business hours for his failing travel agency, uncaring that I was sore, exhausted, and wired from the previous night's concert. Or that I was wide awake and seething. As a kid, I'd wanted to pray with him. Now all I could hear was his off-key, mispronounced drone. I buried my head under the sheets while he mangled the words. He kept chanting.

Still, I wanted to be his buddy. On nights after double rehearsals of Mahler symphonies, or on rare days off, he'd suggest grabbing something to eat—Carl's Jr., maybe, or Cold Stone for dessert. I always wanted to go. It felt like being a kid again, like the world was briefly safe. But halfway through a burger, he'd suck his teeth and say, "Cheee, Potka, you've gotten so fat." I stayed quiet. I wanted to remind him that *he'd* been the one who'd wanted to get burgers in the first place, but a good son didn't talk back. I didn't want to ruin how much I still loved him, how much I still needed him to be my dad.

On the walk home I'd surge ahead, full of quiet fury, pretending not to hear. Then his voice cut across San Vicente: "Eyy, Potka! Slow down!" The words were like a leash, pulling me back in step, my face burning as the night swallowed the echo. I hated how my body obeyed him, like another of his well-trained German shepherds.

But now, we were no longer the globe-trotting father-and-son duo: I wasn't the dutiful son, willing to do anything to please him so that he'd buy me ice cream or take me to the beach. We both knew Dad had no reason to stay in Los Angeles, except to avoid Mom back in New York. So he turned himself into a chakor again—but this time, for me. He ironed my tuxedo before concerts, cleaned the condo, cooked meals, and filled the empty hours however he could. He'd ask what time I'd be home, as if I were going to hang out with friends rather than playing four concerts a week. Between rehearsals I avoided him by staying downtown, crouched in a corner of the Disney Hall lounge playing *Dungeons & Dragons* on my laptop.

I was looking for ways to be the man of the house, and soon, I got my chance. After a *Los Angeles Times* columnist named Steve Lopez wrote a front-page column about me as the youngest violinist ever to join the LA Phil, my career took off like a Roman candle. It was the ultimate letter of recommendation, and it eclipsed Dad's carefully curated Wall of Accomplishments. People recognized me at the airport. I got stopped at Whole Foods. Strangers asked for autographs at the Hollywood Bowl. Everyone wanted to know what the prodigy would do next.

Over the next few months, I fielded interview requests from national outlets, eager to frame me as the boy genius who still lived with his father, who was still teaching him how to drive. When the *NBC Nightly News* crew mounted cameras on the windshield, hoping to catch some heartwarming banter between father and son, they caught Dad slapping my hand at the steering wheel. When they asked if he was proud of me, he waved them off. "You know," he said, "he used to be a soloist."

One afternoon, he tried to move the dining table—my writing desk, where I'd started keeping journals—and I snapped: "I don't want my condo to look like that." He froze mid-step, a can of Pledge in one hand, a rag in the other. His face, once debonair, was worn thin by diabetes, ulcers, and heart disease. His rage had only festered, becoming more dangerous. He raised a finger and locked his eyes on mine, and I felt my shoulders at my ears, my back against the dresser. Suddenly, I was seven again, ready to piss myself with fear.

"Tor bari?! Your condo?! Na re, Potka. Without me, you have no home. Konodin bhulish na."

But I wanted to forget.

When I was a kid, Dad was my best friend. *If you'll be my bodyguard, I can be your long-lost pal.* Onstage around the world, I didn't care who was in the audience. All I cared about was Dad: where he sat, if he'd flash our secret thumbs-up at me, and whether he'd take me out for ice cream after the show. I learned how to read every expression on his face. In previous years, he'd beam whenever he told his clients about when I'd made a Kolkata stadium sing Tagore, or how I'd met the Crown Prince of Japan after my solo in Ikebukuro. But now the clients had stopped calling. Priceline.com had gutted what was left of Travel World International. His last scrap of pride was being my father. Which meant that, for him to be a man, for him to be anything at all, I had to remain a child.

Ludwig van Beethoven, String Quartet in B-Flat Major, Op. 130—v. Cavatina

[San Julian Street, Los Angeles]

After a rehearsal at Disney Hall, Dad handed over the keys to his (my) blue Camry. Finally granted a license by the Department of Motor Vehicles in Culver City, I'd be driving us home on Interstate 10 after the morning's LA Phil rehearsal. As soon as I exited the Disney Hall parking lot, Dad grabbed the dashboard and groaned—"Asthey, asthey!"—as if I were about to drive into a brick wall at one hundred miles per hour. He slapped my hand like it was on fire. Disoriented, I blew past the left turns that would have put us on the freeway. At a last-chance yellow light, I looked up at a street sign—"Arey jaa, Potka, gas de!" Instead of flooring it like he'd asked, I hesitated and the light turned red. He sucked his teeth in disgust. "Cheee." I gripped the steering wheel at ten and two and pulled a long breath through my nose.

Dad fumbled with the lighter, cracked the window, and lit a Dunhill, cursing every jerky brake. I wished he wouldn't smoke in the car. Now stuck on San Pedro Street, I gritted my teeth and said nothing.

At least I could still pick the music. The car's stereo was playing the Emerson String Quartet's recording of Beethoven's "Cavatina," the heart-wrenching aria from one of the last things Beethoven ever composed. If I could listen to one piece for the rest of my life, it would be this. The astronomer Carl Sagan had chosen it as the final track on Voyager's Golden Record: a farewell from Earth, a greeting to the stars. The melody drifts between the two violins, part hymn, part song. Beethoven said it was the only music that had ever "cost him tears."

Then everything changed. Inside, Beethoven's music became *beklemmt*—oppressed—a voice out of sync, searching for a pulse, for a way out. Outside, tents appeared on the sidewalk, and from within their blue tarps and flats of cardboard, people stirred. What looked to me like trash was actually someone's home. Outside one tent, a sun-faded American flag served as a door flap.

The light turned green.

Tents narrowed the sidewalks on both sides. Empty food wrappers, bundles of clothes, shoes—life—spilled onto the street. The colors of this place were both faded and too bright, and blank warehouses stood behind it. People formed a short queue. Then someone shouted, and Dad snapped his head to look. A shirtless Black man walked straight into oncoming traffic, parting the river of cars. Dad flicked the butt of his beedee onto the street and jabbed at the switches, locking doors, rolling up the windows, killing the stereo. In the taut silence, the last phrase of Beethoven's hymn-song wouldn't stop playing in my head.

He clutched the passenger side handle as if the door could be yanked open.

"Takash na. Pagla hoigachey."

I pretended to look away from the man who had lost his mind, but peered over my glasses instead, sneaking a closer look. The man's chest was muscled, and he limped steadily, holding his bandaged arm at a wrong angle. His eyes were bloodshot, and his loud, slurred words sounded like a Baroque recitative, the kind that comes before an aria of reckoning. With his good arm he banged on hoods and windows. I gripped the wheel. He kept coming, screaming, though to no one in particular.

The light changed. I swerved past him, turned onto Sixth, then ducked into a narrow alley. As I turned, I caught the sign: San Julian Street.

At the next red light, a woman walked barefoot through the intersection, one breast slipped free of a faded pink dress. Behind her, a man in a wheelchair pumped one leg as he rolled. Behind him, another queue formed outside a concrete building. I realized they were waiting for a meal. Others sat in camp chairs in the shade, chatting with a calm I couldn't understand. A man in a red baseball cap coasted through on a bicycle, singing an R&B tune with unabashed joy. In counterpoint, a police cruiser let loose its siren from the opposite direction, and in my head Beethoven still sang, *beklemmt*.

The light turned green.

"Ja, Potka, ja. Get us out of here."

I hit the gas. We were quiet the whole drive home.

I'd finally seen it, the neighborhood my colleagues had warned me about. Less than a mile away from Disney Hall, nestled within a city that contained the untold wealth of Beverly Hills and Pasadena and Hollywood, hidden by freeways and overpasses, there it was: the largest population of homeless people in America.

Skid Row.

Franz Schubert, Quartettsatz in C Minor, D. 703

[Pine Street, Santa Monica]

On days off from the Phil, I learned to enjoy myself the way my California colleagues did, with loquats and lemons from Pasadena backyards, farmers' market jams and fine cheeses, and home-brewed beer. On international tours—*senza* Dad—I tasted Japanese single malts, smoked my first Cuban cigar, and had a suit made in Seoul. It felt like relief to be free of him. After sold-out concerts, colleagues led me to Michelin-starred tables: sushi in Roppongi, *dourada* in Lisbon, Peking duck over Kowloon Bay.

Every few months, an LA Phil violinist hosted a lavish chamber music soirée in his Santa Monica home. Sometimes he'd approach celebrated soloists, like Emanuel Ax and Joshua Bell—once even the entire Berlin Philharmonic on their American tour—to read chamber music. His guests, made up of orchestra patrons, neighbors, and amateur musicians, potlucked salads made from homegrown persimmons and avocados, and a celebrity chef baked her famous tarte tatin. Once, I saw Frank Gehry, the architect of Disney Hall, sitting on a couch in the living room, drinking Caymus from a red Solo cup. Another guest showed up with a Stradivarius and a Guarneri, plus a box of fine French bows worth several million dollars for us to try at will. On those nights, I sight-read Schubert with Leonidas Kavakos, Dvořák with Sir Simon Rattle, Brahms with Lynn Harrell. Once, we played the Mendelssohn Octet, with three players on each part: twenty-four world-class pros crammed into a single living room.

Between movements, I grazed from charcuterie boards heaped with Camembert, cave-aged Gouda, and jamón-wrapped melon. When Dad wasn't around, my colleagues taught me how to drink: Rieslings that pulled my cheeks into a grin, golden Chardonnays with a finish like honeyed oak. My sight-reading only improved with Syrah. The day I got tenure—at twenty-one—Mr. Holy Fuck popped a bottle of Opus One and poured a glass the color of garnet, all smoke and leather. "Welcome to the rest of your life," he said.

During these parties, I felt like we'd slipped back to the salons of Vienna, where Mozart dazzled aristocrats and Weber gathered friends late into the night. Schubert's circle called their gatherings

Schubertiades, where he tried out new songs and quartets among friends, poets, and the people who loved him during his thirty-one-year-long life. James, a Philharmonic violinist, saw that we could do the same and said we should set up regular readings. Eager for friends, and for more cheese and wine, I smiled, buzzed on my second glass of jammy Central Coast pinot. It was on.

Once, and only once, I made the mistake of hosting a reading party at our West LA condo. Dad insisted on ordering an orchestra's worth of Indian takeout from a joint on Pico Boulevard, laughing loudly on the phone in Bengali while we rehearsed. My colleagues picked at saag paneer and chicken tikka while Dad told stories of my childhood, like the concert where I went onstage with my fly down, and how he thought I could do better than the LA Phil. He didn't want me to turn into "some old bum" who played in an orchestra the rest of my life.

"When is that concertmaster guy going to retire?"

My colleagues remained silent, but exchanged looks. James, who was gaunt and lanky, with thinning, salt-and-pepper hair, had joined the orchestra the year I was born. Dad either didn't realize he'd insulted my colleagues, or he didn't care. He pressed on as I turned scarlet with embarrassment.

"If he misbehaves in rehearsal, just slap him. I give you the permission, see, like this!"—and he cracked me with a gatta to the back of the head. My colleagues stared, alarmed. I dropped my eyes, which were watering from at least two kinds of pain.

A few months later, I found out Dad had been reading my journals while I was at rehearsal. I exploded. He shouted back, lunged, tried to slap me. This time I caught his wrist, holding his hand inches from my face. And then, for the first time, I tightened my grip, holding him firm, until *he* yelled in surprise and pain. The worst part was how easy it was. He swung at me with his free hand, but I didn't let go. Neither of us had realized how weak he'd become, or how strong I'd always been. When I let go, he came at me again, and this time, I didn't flinch.

"Maybe you should go back home," I said, trying to sound calm while my whole body trembled. I was finally saying the thing I'd been holding back for years: that I wanted him to leave, that I would be fine without him.

I didn't want to be a Bengali son anymore. In our house, love was never unconditional. Affection came knotted with expectation. I'd learned early to read my parents' faces, to shrink to fit their moods, to become a version of myself that wouldn't set them off. I'd folded myself into obedience so thoroughly that I forgot it was a performance. Maybe I was wrong: Maybe I was angry enough and American enough to believe in the kind of fresh start my parents could never have. But I knew I couldn't become myself as long as my dad was still in the room.

At the orchestra rehearsal that followed my party, James looked up from his morning warm-up at the back of the first violin section. On that Paris tour, between programs of Sibelius symphonies, he'd once treated me to a three-tiered plateau of fruits de mer and a bottle of crisp Muscadet at a brasserie off Faubourg Saint-Honoré—a recommendation of Salonen's. The whole meal, I couldn't stop smiling at what tasted like pure freedom: the briny oysters, sweet wine, and the crack as we fished the soft flesh out of a langoustine's tail. It was the first time I felt like I had a friend, who was an adult, who was not Dad. I liked James, and I wanted him to like me back.

He reached for a cake of rosin from his violin case, and I met his eyes.

"Man, your dad is . . . uhh . . . *intense*."

I managed a laugh, apologizing for the shitty food, and not mentioning the gatta. I changed the subject—did he like spicy food? Maybe he'd want to try the new Sichuan place in Arcadia.

James flicked his bow, cutting me off.

"We are about to hold a concertmaster audition—the No. 2 chair—and you'd have a real shot. If you're still rotting back here with me in five years, I'm gonna fucking kill you."

Johannes Brahms, String Quintet in G Major, Op. 111—i. Allegro non troppo, ma con brio

[The Village, Long Beach]

A few months later—about a year and a half after we first moved out to LA—Dad went home for good. I pretended not to miss him. I kept up with my reading parties and my Philharmonic concerts, and when I called home, as I was expected to do several times a day, Dad's voice on the other end of the line sounded distant, as if I had condemned him to return to Mom and her volatility.

But in Dad's absence, I finally had my own quiet for the first time in my life, a private world I could shape by myself and for myself. And yet all that this new freedom revealed was a hollow space that I only knew how to fill with food.

In my newfound Dad-free life, I could eat whatever I wanted: After most LA Phil concerts, I'd stop at drive-through windows still dressed in my tux—polishing off two Double-Doubles in the car and tossing the evidence in the condo's dumpster. On days off, I'd order from the dim sum place across the street. The waiter knew my order by heart: XO shrimp, shu mai, egg rolls, fried rice—enough food for a small family. Soon, I was in pain all the time. I'd often wake up with numb fingers because the fat had cut off the blood supply to my arm. Soon, I couldn't walk around the block without stopping to rest.

Still, something was missing—in my life on bright stages, in this land of relentless sun—and it was then that I began looking for new places to play music. I didn't know what I was looking for. Maybe I wanted an audience I didn't have to impress in tuxedo tails, an audience I could meet face to face. Either way, I was lonely, and didn't want, or know, how to deal with this new feeling. Or maybe I was trying to re-create playing for some old version of Dad, the one who still came to my concerts and fumbled with his heart while I played—the Dad I hadn't kicked out of our/his/my condo.

I started at hospitals. At Providence St. Joseph's in Burbank, I walked down the hallways of chemotherapy wards, playing a Bach sarabande for people whose skin had turned ash-gray, their eyes dull with exhaustion. In a modest stucco community center in North Hollywood, with red clay roof tiles and faded murals of saints, I played for adults with Down syndrome. When I arrived, they handed me a large piece of posterboard that read "Welcome Mr. Gupta," with a drawing of what I supposed was supposed to be me performing, but looked instead like a beachball devouring a twig. I couldn't bear to throw the poster away. A few months later, I'd go to the Patton State Hospital in San Bernardino, where I'd bomb with Bach's "Chaconne." And on a November evening in 2009, when James mentioned he was organizing a benefit concert for a mental health agency in Long Beach, I said yes before he could finish the sentence.

The Village, founded by Dr. Mark Ragins, was a place for people living with schizophrenia, depression, addiction, and the fallout of years in psych wards or on the street. The people living there weren't considered "patients" but "members," because they could choose their own pathway to healing. Many members could work in the bakery adjoining the facility, to earn a small living while seeking care, shelter, and rehabilitation. Part of me kept thinking about Gottfried Schlaug's lab, and the stroke patients whose brains he'd rewired with music. Maybe the music we'd play—a quintet by Brahms—could also regulate neurotransmitters like dopamine and serotonin. Maybe music would be healing for people. I'd have another chance to play Brahms, too.

But when we arrived at the church, I was surprised to see that most of the audience members were the same friendly old blue-haired socialite types that attended our concerts at Disney Hall. A politician's wife, wearing a lilac pantsuit, spoke at length while my eyes drooped, and from the greenroom—which had a thick, sickly teal carpet—I listened to her praise The Village's "workforce model," then introduce our quintet: "And we have the Philharmonic here to serenade us!" We walked out to a half-empty church, and for a moment, I wondered. Why hadn't they filled the church with people from The Village—like the members, or even the staff? At the time, I didn't understand what a "benefit" was, but I had expected that we'd be playing to "benefit" the people who lived, or worked, or sought care at The Village, not more season-ticketholders at the Phil. I took my seat in the second violinist's chair, and before I knew it, James had given the cue, and I was lost in a surging blaze of G major.

Even though Johannes Brahms had declared his second string quintet his farewell from composing—telling his publisher that it was "the work of an old man on the threshold of death"—the music starts in a blaze. The opening cello solo catapulted across the entire range of the human voice in just two phrases, and then James took over, soaring into heights that felt almost too bright.

Even Brahms's farewells refused to sound defeated. He drafted the quintet while walking through Vienna's Prater Gardens, sketchbook in pocket, listening to waltzes drifting from the cafés, the rhythm of carriage wheels, the pulse of ordinary life. He once said that he wanted music to sound "as though it had always existed," and this quintet—what he had expected would be his last piece of music—was equally joyful and rending, bittersweet and inevitable.

At fifty-seven, Brahms felt spent. Decades of discipline and doubt had hollowed him out; his beard had gone white, his hands shook. He had lived his whole life under the shadow of giants. As a child, he'd composed little tunes at the piano even before he could read music, and later, his father—a bassist in the Hamburg Symphony—had sent his young Johannes to play in rough taverns amid sailors and sex workers. Brahms never spoke of that time without pain.

Whatever happened in those early years, Brahms grew into a man who struggled with intimacy. He kept people at arm's length, hidden behind sarcasm, jokes, cigars, and the craft of unassailable effort. When he was twenty, the famous composer Robert Schumann had hailed him as the "young eagle" who would bring German music into a new era. After Schumann's madness and death, Brahms took up the mantle—and the burden—bound forever to his mentor's widow, the brilliant pianist Clara Schumann. Clara became his closest confidante, his sharpest critic, the only person whose praise he trusted. He visited prostitutes, drank too much, and kept his loneliness hidden—but everyone knew Clara was the only woman he ever loved. By the time he composed the G Major Quintet, their correspondence had thinned to short, tender notes. Her hands were failing from arthritis; his spirit from isolation. Brahms thought that the quintet was his last great surge of life—the sound of a fire burning itself out.

After our performance, we went next door for the reception. In the warm-lit kitchen, the shelter's bakers—its residents—moved with slow, steady purpose, hairnets and flour-dusted aprons, the air thick with the scent of brown butter and burnt sugar. On a plastic folding table their work waited: a towering chocolate-frosted cake that was piped, "THANK YOU, MUSICIANS."

One of the bakers pressed a box of cookies into my hands, smiling.

"We wish we could have heard you play, honey."

I could have taken out my violin and played for her, but instead I posed for a selfie with the mayor's wife. On the drive home I ate the whole box, then tossed it into the back seat of the Camry, where it lay for months, tipped on its side.

Chapter 6

MR. AYERS

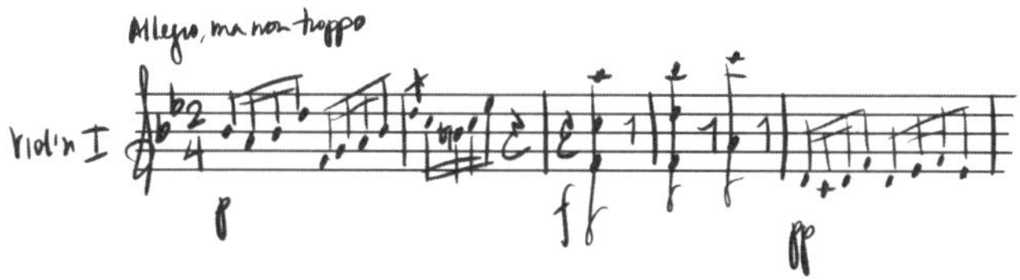

Beethoven, Symphony No. 4, iv

Through suffering and joy I have learned to know what music is.

Ludwig van Beethoven

Ludwig van Beethoven, Symphony No. 4 in B-Flat Major, Op. 60—iv. Allegro ma non troppo

[All Star Lanes, Eagle Rock, Los Angeles]

At the bowling alley, fluorescents buzzed overhead, casting everything in alien green. Nathaniel Ayers sat by the ball return. He greeted me like an old colleague. "Mr. Gupta," he said with a regal nod. I still didn't know how to talk to someone who had spent twenty years living on the streets of LA, but because he insisted on calling us by our last names—Mister this, Ms. that—we all called him Mr. Ayers.

Nathaniel Ayers had been studying at Juilliard when he was diagnosed with paranoid schizophrenia. After being treated at Bellevue Hospital with shock therapy, Thorazine, and handcuffs, he lived on the streets of LA for nearly two decades. Steve Lopez, a columnist for the *LA Times*, told Nathaniel's story in a series of articles and later in his book *The Soloist*. As the book became a movie starring Robert Downey Jr. and Jamie Foxx, many of my LA Phil colleagues grew close to Lopez and Ayers, and that winter I was invited to join them in celebrating Nathaniel's fifty-seventh birthday—on December 16—not his actual birthday, but the birthday of his favorite composer, Ludwig van Beethoven.

I had met Mr. Ayers for the first time just a few days earlier, backstage at Disney Hall, right after the last show of the orchestra's winter season. The orchestra, eager to finish our last concerts of 2008, was in a festive mood. Even Mark, the tall, stoic personnel manager who'd sat beside me during my audition, walked onstage before the entire audience wearing enormous fuzzy red elf slippers. Esa-Pekka Salonen had conducted Beethoven's First and Fourth Symphonies. During the concert, his gaze had swept the first violins, and each time it passed, I made myself meet his eyes, my part nearly memorized, shoulders stiff and burning as I played fistfuls of sixteenth notes from memory, too eager to keep up with Beethoven's bouncing pulse. Afterward, the maestro stood backstage in his usual posture—reserved and self-deprecating—when Mr. Ayers appeared in a doorway with Steve Lopez, the columnist. Without hesitation, Mr. Ayers, who wore army fatigues and a lacy purple D-cup bra draped around his neck like an ascot, twirled his hands and dropped into a deep curtsy before Salonen, who looked faintly alarmed.

At the bowling alley, I tried my best to strike up a conversation with Mr. Ayers, which unraveled into a tangled braid of Beethoven symphonies, Cleveland Indians trivia, and the conducting style of George Szell. His mind looped through music and baseball as if they were the same language: and even though what he said seemed untamed, it made a sort of elegant sense to me. To him, the concertmaster was a shortstop, the third horn an outfielder, the conductor an umpire calling balls and strikes. Naturally, the LA Phil was the Dodgers—and were we ever going to win the World Series? The last movement of Beethoven's Fourth Symphony, he said, was like a batting lineup that couldn't stop striking out. Somewhere between a tray of nachos and a neon flicker over the lanes, he and I were suddenly back in the orchestra together discussing violin technique: the last movement of Beethoven's Fourth, where the first violins race through passagework, twisting like thread on a loom.

"How do you all do that? How do you make your fingers move so fast?" he asked.

Nearby, his shopping cart held a trumpet, a flute, a cello, and a violin case scrawled in white marker: LA DODGERS.

I opened my case and pulled out my violin under the holiday lights. A few LA Phil colleagues looked up from their beers, wondering what the hell I was doing with my violin out in a bowling alley, especially after the last concert of the season. I knew some of them were eager to start a few weeks of instrument-free vacation. Disregarding the glances that screamed "Showoffski," I walked Mr. Ayers through the way I would practice the passage: one finger, then the next. Control the bow. Prepare the elbow before the string crossing. Release the left thumb for the shift. Keep the hand soft. Breathe. For a few minutes Beethoven kept time with Jay-Z and Alicia Keys's "Empire State of Mind" blasting through the speakers.

A few weeks into the new year, I got a call from Steve Lopez: Nathaniel Ayers wanted a real violin lesson. The timing was strange—he and Steve weren't speaking. Mr. Ayers had been swept up in a wave of paranoia and turned on him, lashing out with sudden violence. Steve decided it was best to give him space. When Ayers showed up at Disney Hall with his shopping cart of instruments, he was already muttering about poison gas being pumped into his apartment. The moment I mentioned Steve, his eyes flashed. His words came fast, sharp, veering in every direction. The gracious, bowing gentleman I'd first met was gone. In the padded, soundproof practice room behind

Walt Disney Concert Hall, he loomed over me, unpredictable, eyes burning.

I lifted my violin and played. My hands were steady, even if I wasn't. I couldn't have named it then, but the fear I felt around Nathaniel wasn't new to me. It was the quiet dread that lived at home, that could tip a normal day into chaos without warning. Mr. Ayers's sudden turns, the way his voice could tighten and rise—felt familiar and familial. I knew how to use music to make myself small and safe. Even though I hadn't lived under the same roof as Mom for a few years, I could still hear her shouting when I practiced. Every so often, I'd stop in a sudden fear, hearing her thudding footsteps, even though she was on the other side of the continent. So even though I had no idea what to say to Nathaniel, I did know, somehow, that music was the only language I trusted to hold the world together.

I also knew his favorite composer: Beethoven. The violin concerto was sacred to me—music I'd only half-studied with Dicterow, music I'd once tried to play buzzed on vodka from my violin case—but now I played it for Mr. Ayers. The violin began alone, like a bird breaking into the open sky, then settled into the weave of the orchestra, sometimes vanishing, content to guide from within. I kept my eyes on the page as the scales climbed, their arc and fall supporting the orchestra's melody. In Beethoven's concerto, the soloist was the accompanist. When I finally risked a glance back at Ayers, his eyes were wide. He had softened into his listening, and I could see that he had returned to his own curiosity.

His violin was already in his hands. It was battered, and darkened with grime from years on the street. He had pasted a black "Fu Manchu" sticker on one of the ribs. Once, he'd walked eleven and a half miles—one way—to buy a new set of strings from Benning Violins, the shop in Studio City, but now, his strings were so worn they looked like used dental floss. Nathaniel held his violin tight under his chin, the bow in a cramped, awkward grip. I stepped closer and eased the angle of his elbow. His eyes stayed fixed ahead, but he let me guide the joint the way my teachers had adjusted mine. I moved the violin a little closer to his collarbone.

"Straight bow, Mr. Ayers. Drop your shoulder. Want to play some scales?"

Not yet twenty-two, I had never taught a violin lesson in my life. I stood there unsure of what to say as Ayers's wandering scales unraveled into melody fragments of Beethoven's most beloved works, like the slow movement of the "Emperor" piano concerto, or the hymn from the "Archduke" trio. Then he lowered his violin and called out an opus number: Opus 130. It caught me off guard: It was the same quartet I'd once played in my car while driving through Skid Row, the one Carl Sagan had sent into space—the "Cavatina." I lifted my violin and began to play.

Then he asked for Schubert. Then Dvořák. Brahms. Mozart. I played.

Then Sibelius. My violin sang a long, unbroken line over a frozen plain. As I played, Mr. Ayers placed his fingers, exactly the way I had shown him, on the A string, and began the opening of the Sibelius Violin Concerto—slowly, ever so slowly—with me. His eyes were clear, fixed on his strings. And my eyes were on him, focused on how I could coax even more music out of him. And for that moment, we were two violinists, playing one melody, note by note, together.

After our lesson, he wheeled his shopping cart out of the artist's entrance at Disney Hall. Before he started walking down Bunker Hill toward Skid Row, I reached into the pocket of my violin case and fished out four slightly squashed envelopes labeled E, A, D, and G. One hand still gripping his precious shopping cart, Mr. Ayers pressed the strings to his chest.

"Thank you, Mr. Gupta."

Antonín Dvořák, String Quintet in G Major, Op. 77—iii. Poco andante
[10 Westbound, between the 405 and the 110]

My Camry inched along the 10 Freeway, stuck in rush-hour traffic. I thumbed through the screen of a new smartphone while watching the green exit signs slide past: Fairfax, La Cienega, La Brea. After my most recent lessons with Mr. Ayers, I had started to wonder how many more people like him might be living on the streets of LA. I used my daily commute to cold-call potential venues for my concerts, hoping to find another Nathaniel. Earlier that morning, I'd already left voicemails at the VA in Long Beach, a clinic in Malibu, and a hospice in the Valley. By the time I hit the Crenshaw exit, I'd finally reached someone at a downtown shelter, hoping my recent *LA Times* piece would make my name ring a bell.

"Hi, my name is Robert Gupta? I'm with the LA Philharmonic? I'd like to put on a concert for you. Could you let me know a good time we could come by?"

The line was silent at first, and then: "You're going to bring your Philharmonic here? Do you even know what we do here?"

I had no idea what they did there. I didn't know that the staff of shelters, already stretched thin caring for people with almost nothing—people battling addiction or serious illness—had no time to arrange "entertainment." I didn't know the constant sirens and pops of gunfire, the shouts from tents and corners, or the howling delirium tremens of detox. I didn't know the summer stench of rot and Pine-Sol, or the wet-dog smell of blankets soaked by winter rain. I didn't know that sometimes people died alone on the sidewalk, discovered only by neighbors or a clinic outreach worker. And I never stopped to consider how a word like "underserved" might sound to people already overworked and underpaid, people who had to use what little energy they had to protect their clients from the well-intentioned.

"No one wants that kind of music." The line went dead.

I didn't realize that I was another one of the "well intentioned."

After a fifty-five-minute crawl across twelve miles, I made it to Walt Disney Concert Hall. Upstairs, in the orchestra lounge, I poured coffee and opened my laptop to search for places I could play. Shelters, clinics, anywhere. The Downtown Women's Center. The Midnight Mission. LA Christian Health Centers. Union Rescue Mission. Most sat downtown, less than a mile from my chair. Some were on San Pedro—I knew that street. That was where I'd made the wrong turn with Dad, where a man had pounded car hoods and where sun-faded tents lined the curb. Skid Row.

Before rehearsal, I left a few more messages—skirting receptionists to leave voicemails for executive directors and program directors—making my case for music. I even offered to corral a group of Philharmonic musicians to perform. I hoped that players like James would agree to playing in places like Skid Row. Maybe they wouldn't mind if I took them out for pastrami and beer at Cole's French Dip after our concert.

A few weeks later, someone called back. One of the calls I'd made had landed with the director of LA County's Department of Mental Health. He asked me if I understood what I was asking. "You sure you want to play for folks with psychiatric holds?" I told him I was. So he offered us a performance during the county's annual mental health conference. It wasn't exactly what I'd imagined, but I thought it wouldn't hurt to play for a room full of caseworkers, therapists, and administrators—people who I was sure would love our music and invite us into their clinics.

"Come to the Wilshire Grand Hotel," he said. "Salon B. You can play during the lunch hour."

But when we arrived at Salon B—a hotel ballroom with a long buffet stretched along the far wall—I realized that I had just offered to be the afternoon's entertainment and not a plenary session. Round tables were double-draped in thick white linens, as if for a wedding. Each centerpiece sagged with pale, soft roses. Guests were already midway through the meal. Forks clinked against porcelain, the room hummed, someone laughed too loudly.

My ears burned.

We were used to a handler—a volunteer or stage manager—to walk us to a greenroom, hand us water, and tell us when to go on. Instead, a tall, bearded man in Tevas looked up from his salad and blinked at us like we were the ones who were out of place.

I wedged our quintet between a window and the dessert table, next to a dish of flan and a pyramid of cookies. I tried to introduce us, but my voice sank into the green-and-yellow paisley carpet. No one looked up from their meals.

I avoided my colleagues' eyes, and I could feel the violist's chill. She'd driven all the way across town for this, and now we were boxed in by chafing dishes, ignored, worse than Muzak.

Way to go, Showoffski.

I had to pull us through. I started with the simple, rising shape from Dvořák's string quintet, the third movement. The bass kept time with soft pizzicato, but the notes felt damp, swallowed by carpet and wall panels. In a hall, they would bloom. Here, they sounded like dull thunks.

Dvořák had written the quintet in 1875, while living in poverty. He was working as a church organist, raising six kids in a cramped Prague apartment, composing at night. Years later, he came to America and declared that the future of American music would come from Black and Indigenous traditions. He knew something about clawing beauty from the edges of life.

After I played the first phrase, James joined. He and the cello rose in echoing cascades. The melody rested for a moment, and just as we shifted to a darker key, a fork clattered loudly against a plate, and I flinched. Now the violist and James took up the theme, rising, falling, rising again against the dead, carpeted air. But slowly, the room began to shift. Despite the hum of conversation, people were starting to listen.

The cello tried to sing out, its line threading through the dense air while the other voices cascaded. Soon the music lifted into E major, and I played a melody that soared over all the instruments, as if I were suspended on a thermal of sound. I could have stayed in that soaring place forever.

When we finished, our small audience, still chewing, offered a half-hearted round of applause. The bearded man in Tevas let out a whoop. I took my chance and stood, ignoring the chill from my colleagues. Dad had trained me to meet cold rooms with pretend warmth, to feign confidence with a broad smile and a straight spine, especially when I felt the opposite inside. "We want to come play for the people you care for," I said. A few caseworkers nodded, polite but curious. "I've been playing concerts at hospitals and VA hospitals," I added, "and we'd love to play a few clinics, too."

One of the therapists, a woman my height with a sharp bob and kind eyes, gave me a quick hug and handed me her card. After a quick glance at it, I realized that her offices were on Maple Avenue, just a few blocks away from Disney Hall. The bearded man pumped my hand, thanking me for the way the music hit him. I didn't know much about their work, the lives they lived in service of others, but something about being around them made me feel like the idea I had—of playing music for suffering people—wasn't so crazy. I almost asked James if he'd play a duo with me, but he had already packed up and was halfway through the double doors.

That night, backstage at Disney Hall, just before the second half of the concert, James found me. His usually friendly face was knitted in concern, and I felt a stab of fear. He pulled me aside into a corner, and spoke softly.

"You know there's no point playing for the homeless."

I stayed quiet, unable to find anything worth saying back to him. My eyes burned. I knew I had let him and the rest of the group down.

"If you're going to do this kind of thing, you may as well use high school kids. Those people won't know the difference."

I stood in my tails, violin in hand. I didn't know how to say it then, but some part of me understood that many people in Skid Row, who may never have heard classical music or a violin played live, wouldn't know the difference between seasoned professionals and high school students. That wasn't the point. The point was how playing in Skid Row might change *us*, or how we played the music itself. And if that changed, even a little, then perhaps what we did onstage each night, the rote ritual of classical music, might feel like it meant something again.

James turned toward the wedge of light at the stage doors and walked away. Right then, I decided I was going to prove him wrong. I just didn't know how.

Ludwig van Beethoven, String Quartet in C Minor, Op. 18 No. 4—i. Allegro ma non tanto

[Department of Mental Health, Maple Avenue, Los Angeles]

I arrived at the clinic with three other musicians, wearing concert black. In the basement of the Department of Mental Health clinic in Skid Row, our audience sat in rows of creaking plastic chairs. Most of them were clinic patients, people who had spent their nights on the streets or in nearby shelters. The social workers had taken up a collection to buy sodas, sandwiches, and cookies. In the windowless basement conference room, thirty or forty people filed in, clutching paper plates, settling into cracked chairs for forty minutes of peace before returning to DMV-long lines for IDs, Medi-Cal forms, or food.

After the quartet tuned, a social worker wearing a dark dress and thick-rimmed glasses opened the program with a quote from Plato: "Music gives a soul to the universe, wings to the mind, flight to the imagination." We sat in the same plastic chairs used by our audience, the front row less than a yard from the mother-of-pearl button at the end of my bow. I looked to my left at Shawn, the violinist who had replaced James in my quartet. Shawn and I had met at our audition a few years earlier, and over the past few months we had become close friends, bonding over Beethoven.

With a sharp inhale, I cued a soft "G"—the lowest note on my violin—answered by anxious, quiet pulses from the cello. The others were caught between us, unsure whose side to take. Then, every so often, we all issued subtle *sforzando* stabs in perfect synchrony. We were superathletes of micrometers.

I became the melody, erratic and seeking, one question after another. But I was trapped by the cello's cruel, unmoving "C." I wanted to break free—now the second violin and viola took the cello's side. Against them, my soft line rose higher, my fingers stretched across the tightrope of my steel-wire E string, pulling the music higher, building with an octave leap into a careening crescendo—before a brutal, abrupt arrival at *fortissimo* exclamations:

C *minor!*
G *major!*
C-G-C!

A hand shot into the air, stopping inches from my face. I recoiled so fast I nearly fell off my seat and into Shawn. A woman in the front row thrust her arm straight up into the air, her palm taut like a blade. My bow skittered and I missed a handful of notes, causing our cellist to look up at me in surprise. The woman in the front row was so close that I could see the deep brown indent of her heart line, her short, wrinkled fingers, and, behind them, an oval face topped with a bun of black hair streaked with gray. My chest tightened with fear and surprise. After my performance at the State Hospital in San Bernardino, I knew to expect the unexpected, but I had still hoped this audience wouldn't be disruptive. I had no idea what she would do, and for a moment, I wondered if I had put us in danger. Her cheeks were wet with tears, which dripped past her small, round chin. But she was smiling, and all the while, her hand remained in the air.

We kept playing. The second theme went to Shawn, and I responded to his violin with quick, chirping calls. The music became playful, almost like a game of peekaboo, but then it turned dark and dramatic again. This wasn't music for Haydn's courts, or Mozart's parties. Beethoven didn't care about entertaining: He wanted to grab his audience by their ears.

But now, everyone was staring at this probably homeless—*probably crazy*—lady and her thrust-out hand, which—toward the end of the opening number—still showed zero signs of fatigue. I managed to eke out the swoop of notes, a syncopating skip spanning the lowest and highest sounds of the violin, even though I was roasting with embarrassment.

By the time we culminated with our *fortissimo* slashes of C minor, the woman exploded out of her seat, shouting over a tumult of applause.

"WHAT *IS* THIS MUSIC?!"

No one spoke. The cellist plucked at a string, as if to check it was still in tune. The violist tightened her bow. People weren't supposed to talk between movements of a concert. I swallowed my dry tongue and tried to find my voice. When I did, I muttered some inane, conservatory-trained details about the year Beethoven was born (*Germany, 1770*) and an opus number (*18, 4*), then a bunch of words in Italian (*Allegro ma non tanto*)—but she wanted to know something else entirely:

"Whoever wrote this song was going through hell!"

Isolated and uncured, Beethoven retreated to Heiligenstadt and wrote his brothers a letter—half apology, half goodbye. He would have ended his life if not for music. Humiliated and furious, unable to hear a flute playing right by his ear, he kept writing. That quartet she'd just heard? He wrote it while quietly wondering how not to exist. And maybe that's what the music held—not some triumphant answer, but the sound of someone trying to stay alive.

"It was like you read my mind. I needed that music so bad today—how did you know?" She was a torrent. "How did you know this is *my* story? That music you're playing—it's everything—it's *ME*! You know those hits y'all played—*bam, bam?*—that was my parents screaming, beating each other every day. And that soft bit—that *dididi-deerididiiddeee?*—that was me, hiding my sister from Daddy. When he drank he was a monster. I made up sweet games so baby girl wouldn't cry. Then I started drinking, and those demons came for me, and *I* wanted everything to end. I wanted to end it. But I said, you gotta keep going. *God said you gotta keep going...*"

I looked at the woman, still having said nothing. *Was she really still crying?* I looked toward the back of the room at the social workers for some kind of guidance, the way I looked for Dad at the back of halls. I'd been expecting one of the case workers to rescue me, but instead, I saw that many of the staff were also wiping tears from their eyes. Other patients in the clinic audience began encouraging the woman to keep speaking, keep telling her story. And that's when she turned back to us, took a shuddering breath, and sat back down. Her shoulders dropped. She wiped her face with her sleeve and turned to speak to us.

"Could you please play some more?"

We still had three movements left. During the pauses—usually filled in the hall by coughing and awkward ass-shifting—our clinic audience raised their hands. Some said that the slow movement felt like the love scene from *Sleepless in Seattle*, and the pirouetting third movement, puppets mimicking each other. Others shared scenes from *Tom and Jerry* or *Tombstone*, of forgotten childhoods, and better times.

When we finished, the woman in the front row asked if she could hug me.

A few weeks later, the social worker who had introduced our concert sent me an email. The woman who had interrupted our performance, she explained, had been living in Skid Row for years and had resisted every form of treatment, sometimes even becoming violent during therapy sessions. But our concert was the first time anyone in the clinic had ever heard her tell her own story. The social worker added that a record number of people had asked for therapy after our performance, and that for two weeks the residents had talked about little else. Clearly, the music had opened a door.

"If y'all wanna come back, you're welcome anytime."

Igor Stravinsky, *Petrushka*

[Long Beach, California]

In Stravinsky's *Petrushka*, a puppet comes to life and realizes he's still trapped by his strings. Stravinsky wanted the orchestra to evoke the cacophony of village life—the call of vendors and fistfights in the brass, shrill winds, and even the groan of a leashed bear. I felt like I understood Petrushka, the lame, tragic clown who wants so badly to love, and be loved, and yet, in the end, can never escape performing.

After my lesson with Mr. Ayers, I was invited to speak at a TED Conference to share my experience working with the real-life subject of a Hollywood movie. As I descended the steps of an auditorium in Long Beach, I muttered the opening line of my speech under my breath. The night before, on the forty-minute drive from LA to Long Beach, I ran it eight times. In the hotel, I paced between the desk and the minibar and did ten more rounds before room service arrived. The next morning, as I launched into my canned speech like an audition excerpt, I ignored the filmmaker who'd eaten McDonald's for thirty straight days and the dude who'd started CD Baby. A few sentences into my first TED Talk, I had no idea that in five minutes the room would be on its feet, and that I'd be stepping into a life I could not have imagined for myself.

I'd given talks before. As an undergraduate in biology, one of my courses had required us to co-present dense neuroscience papers to a room of half-dead premeds. I'd printed out the original articles—tiny fonts, double columns from *Nature Neuroscience* or *Neuron*—then spent days annotating them with highlighters and Post-its, turning the paper into a script. Eventually, the others in my science quartet had let me write their scripts, which they'd mumbled into the microphone.

I, however, with my conservatory boy-soprano training, knew exactly how to enunciate, curling my words like whips to electrify the back row. Something about speaking felt musical to me. Each sentence was a phrase, with its own dynamics and tempo—each idea a movement. Even if I was talking about synaptic plasticity in the hippocampus—and not playing the Mendelssohn octet the way I'd once hoped—this was just another performance.

Back in Long Beach, with five minutes left on the clock, I was telling the story of my first violin lesson with Mr. Ayers in perfectly choreographed jolts. I'd spent months preparing for the talk, as if it were an audition. I'd watched three talks a day, taking close notes on how the speakers used the same staccato rhythm of short, digestible sound bites aimed at dramatic, simple takeaways, always veering toward the optimistic. I realized I'd already been obsessed with TED without knowing it—especially Sir Ken Robinson's talk on creativity in schools, which I'd watched over and over long before I even understood what TED was. I'd be on the same stage as powerhouses like Seth Godin, Simon Sinek, and Brené Brown, and now, I had to deliver every word like a soloist. I even rehearsed my hand gestures, casually keeping one hand in a pocket.

But a five-minute TED Talk would never be enough time to tell the whole truth. I left too much out. I didn't say that Nathaniel Ayers talked about poison gas in the vents, about setting his room on fire, or about being trailed by police cruisers. I didn't tell this audience of billionaires that when Mr. Ayers's eyes blazed with that ripping fire, I backed up against the Steinway grand in Studio F and made myself small, bracing for the belt, or the shoe, or the open palm, the memory of childhood violence. He was never violent toward me, but the shadow of the snake in my gut, the gripping fear of feeling hunted by my own parents, welled up in me, and for a few moments, I didn't know what to do with my cold, sweaty hands.

No, I knew what would impress the TED audience. With fiery conviction, I landed my talk's punchline: "Music is medicine, music is sanity." But what I couldn't have known was that what I had done in that practice room with Nathaniel was exactly what I had done in my bedroom as a child: that I had been terrified, and I had played the violin. And the music that moved between Nathaniel and me, the song that resonated along that taut, fraying braid, had become a lifeline: Music was *my* medicine, too, *my* sanity, *my* refuge.

I didn't say I'd known kids at Juilliard who'd had psychotic breaks, or that some of my Philharmonic colleagues drank after rehearsals and took pills before concerts. I didn't mention the one violinist who'd missed a weekend of performances while on a 5150 psychiatric hold. I didn't say how confused I was that someone like Nathaniel Ayers—brilliant, trained, as deserving of music as any of us—could have spent twenty years living on the streets of LA. Why? Because he had schizophrenia? Because he was Black? Because he was poor?

And I certainly didn't tell them that Dad had told me to stay away from Nathaniel Ayers, as if his paglami were contagious.

But when my six minutes were up, the audience was on their feet, giving me a standing ovation. On the way out of the theater, serial entrepreneurs and venture capitalists slapped me on the back. A filmmaker from Argentina handed me his card. The founder of Priceline.com—the same company that had put Dad out of business years earlier—pulled me aside to give me advice on becoming a better speaker. Just a few months later, he'd invite me to speak at *his* conference.

Before I knew it, I was on the lecture circuit, speaking and playing amid some of the world's most important thinkers. Backstage at the Kennedy Center, I watched a tall Black civil rights lawyer pace the floor, quietly rehearsing his talk. When he stepped out, Bryan Stevenson spoke about meeting Rosa Parks, and I sat dumbfounded that I was sharing a stage with a real hero. Later, in Stockholm, between talks delivered by Martha Stewart and Elizabeth Gilbert, I played Bach and met a doctor treating tuberculosis patients in Haiti—like my hero, Paul Farmer. I discussed Skid Row at alpine resorts, gave talks in Santa Barbara and San Diego, and even launched a TEDx for Skid Row.

My newfound fame came with unexpected perks. While speaking at a university, I met a blonde woman who I'd later realize was flirting with me, although I was completely oblivious to it. She asked for my number, and I thought it was because she wanted to speak at my TEDx. I could never have believed that a few months later, she would ask *me* out.

The morning after my TED Talk, at a breakfast reception, I played a movement of unaccompanied Bach and told my story again. I didn't think I was pitching anything in particular, but after my speech, the heiress of a publishing empire offered what felt like a ridiculous amount of money for my "homeless music project." I didn't *have* a homeless project, or any kind of plan to start a project, but not wanting to seem ungrateful by turning down her generosity, I asked for advice from other TED Fellows. One of them sketched a five-year business plan on a napkin. "If you can get that kind of money on a handshake, you can find nine more hands to shake. Then just keep doing that. If you can speak the way you did today, fundraising is easy." I blanched, but nodded, my eyes spinning with the thought of dollars and donors, without any idea *why* I would need that much money to keep playing Beethoven quartets at the Maple Avenue clinic.

I found the nine other hands to shake. And then I found nine more. Fundraising was easier than I thought. All I had to do was memorize a fundraising pitch and practice it like a TED Talk. But I had no idea how I would spend their money.

I thought the first thing we'd need was a logo, so I hired a graphic designer who created a treble clef that looked like a Sanskrit character. I designed a website that used the tagline "music for the undeserved." I'd accidentally left the "r" out of the word "underserved" and didn't even notice until weeks later, when a donor—a recovering addict and pianist—wrote to me pointing it out. I immediately invited him to join the organization's board of directors. A few months later, an official letter from the IRS arrived at the condo, now the headquarters of my fledgling nonprofit: Street Symphony.

Once, and only once, I called Dad to ask for his advice. He was skeptical. He'd never heard of someone giving away money. Was it a loan? Would I have to pay it back? It couldn't be true.

"Don't take it," he said. "There's no such thing as free money."

Hector Berlioz, *Symphonie Fantastique*

> Common life cycle rituals of Hindus in the United States, which typically involve the extended family whenever possible, include prenatal rituals, birth and childhood ceremonies such as naming the child, marriage, and cremation within 24 hours after death.
>
> —**Raymond Brady Williams, *Religions of Immigrants from India and Pakistan: New Threads in the American Tapestry***

[Montgomery, New York]

"Now we have to find you a good bou. My grandchildren will make good Suzuki kids, don't you think?"

Bou? A wife? Was she serious?

Mom ladled a second helping of malai chingri and piled several freshly fried luchis onto my plate. She *was* serious.

At the dining table, Dad chewed on crustacean innards, sucking his teeth. "Dhur! You see how fat he is. What girl will even look at him?"

There was a reason I came home as infrequently as possible. Dad didn't even greet me when I walked through the front door, and when I walked past his office, all I heard was him *tsk*ing at my belly, saying, "Aro mota hoigecchish." He'd called Mom mota my whole childhood, and now it was my turn.

And yet, he'd turn on anyone who had anything negative to say about me. Once, when an uncle joked about my weight, Dad snapped—"He's a Philharmonic musician. What are you?" The room went quiet. He could shame me with one hand and shield me with the other.

And even though we'd never talk about it, I also knew Dad was watching my talks on YouTube, defending me against trolls. His handle was a dead giveaway for "Travel World International."

@CringeKing96: It looks like this guy's neck is eating his violin.

@Twintl1: Please educate yourself.

Even with all the resentment between us, I was still my parents' child—and very much living under their control. I had to call home at least four times a day: morning, lunch, evening, before bed; and if I didn't, I was the cause of a crisis. Once, while I was onstage at Disney Hall, my mother called so many times that a worried stagehand rushed me my buzzing phone the moment I stepped offstage. After eighteen missed calls from "MOM," he'd finally answered, only to hear a woman screaming in rapid-fire Bengali on the other end. "Dude," he whispered, "I think something's happened."

During intermission before *Symphonie Fantastique*, I took her call in a backstage practice room and swallowed her paranoid fury. In Berlioz's piece, the *idée fixe*—an obsessive musical theme representing the artist's beloved—returns over and over, interrupting every movement, no matter how far he tries to escape it. My mother's voice felt exactly like that: a theme I could not outrun, insistent, intrusive, crashing into whatever music or life I tried to make.

Mom was relentless: She demanded I send her a selfie in tuxedo tails to prove I was really at work—or else, she told me, she'd jump off the Mid-Hudson Bridge. I didn't smile for the picture. That night, after the concert, I put away four Maredsous, going drink for drink with the LA Phil's brass and percussion—the band's self-proclaimed "professional drinkers"—until my face went numb. The beers were dark, Belgian relief.

My time wasn't mine, and neither was my money. Despite my age and income, despite living three thousand miles away, Mom and I still shared a bank account. It was the same one I'd opened as a kid at the Hudson Valley Federal Credit Union in Newburgh, where I'd deposited my first performance checks, and now, my LA Phil salary went into that account. And because my paychecks supported the entire family, Mom kept close watch on the account. She had saved $80,000 of my earnings and forbade me to spend any of it. It was her goldmine: No other account in our family had ever held that much money.

Now the next step in my "duty" as a firstborn son was to start a family of my own, which, naturally, would be under their strict supervision. Apparently, Dad had already purchased her a ticket to Kolkata, so she could scope out Brahmin brides. According to Mom, or some outdated tradition, this unfortunate person would live in New York, not in LA—learning the ways of our household—until she could bear grandchildren.

As she spoke, some of the shrimp I was eating struck up a Bollywood number in my gut. I didn't understand. I'd never even been allowed to look at a girl, much less date anyone. When I was thirteen and Mom caught me holding hands with my first crush—a freckled, redheaded pianist at Pre-College—she screamed at me the whole car ride home: "Oshobhyo chele! Don't let me catch you with that girl again!" Her fear of anything outside her control often turned into paranoia, especially about sex and disease. When the girl went to Aspen that summer without her family, Mom chided me over dinner. "See? She'll probably come back with AIDS." When I found out my pianist crush had found a boyfriend that summer, I stole a family-sized box of Ferrero Rocher from CVS and ate it alone in my room.

Later, when I moved into the dorms, Mom's fears worsened. In graduate school, she'd call me every few hours to check on where I was, and then, if I missed our obligatory evening call, she'd keep calling throughout the night. "I know you have a girl in your room!" she'd scream, while I looked around at the piles of books, my laptop screen open to porn and a thesis on late Beethoven string quartets, the floor strewn with empty boxes of Papa John's and Dunkin' Donuts. No, no girl would ever want to be in that room. If Mom called during a party, I'd scope out a quiet corner and disguise my Jack-and-Coke slur as exhaustion.

And now in LA, I was decidedly uncool, content to hang out with guys in their fifties, sixties, and even seventies, pretending to be a connoisseur of Talisker, Partagas, and Rhone varietals while still ducking away to call Mommy every few hours. Even though I spent several nights a week onstage in front of thousands of people, I wasn't brave enough to poke around on dating apps, much less inflict myself on the LA club scene.

I tried to let Mom down as gently as I could.

"Mom, I don't have room for anyone right now."

But I was lying. Secretly, I was texting a girl I'd met at a conference, the one who had asked for my number: Maggie. Blonde hair, blue eyes.

Hellenic and curvy, with a pierced nose and thin lips. Flirty, witchy, and totally confident. After she asked me out, I fell hard and fast. A week later I was in her parents' living room which was decorated like a Sedona ranch, replete with angels peering out from the wall and mantelpiece. While I talked, oblivious at her please-stop-talking-and-fuck-me-now eyes, Maggie, fresh off a breakup, cupped my cheeks and pulled my face into hers. That was my first kiss. I was twenty-five.

That night, I asked her not to call me Robert. I wanted the woman I would love—because, of course, I was already in love—to know me by my birth name, Vijay, which meant "victory." Later that night, when she called me by her ex's name, I didn't correct her. I knew how to meet and exceed anyone's expectations. I could become anyone for love, or something like it.

After a few weeks of dates and headlong, unending text chains filled with emojis I'd never seen before, Maggie introduced me to her friends. I was now her "partner," which they accepted immediately, without question. Under a rainbow flag hung from a Pasadena church and a sign that read "Love is love is love," a Unitarian minister asked when she could officiate our wedding. I clutched Maggie's hand in panic as she tinkled a laugh, stroking the bulging expanse between my shoulders.

"Yep, he's a good one, isn't he?"

I was trapped in a double life. I couldn't say no to Mom, and I'd never say no to Maggie. I didn't know who I was if I stopped being a good Bengali son, but I was also happy that I was no longer a twenty-five-year-old virgin. But the truth was simpler and harder: I had no idea who I was, and I didn't know how to be anything other than what someone else needed me to be. It was a skill that made me a consummate performer and also a really bad boyfriend.

So when Maggie suggested we take a one-monthiversary trip to Sequoia, I was quick to calculate how long I'd be out of Mom-calling range: eighteen hours. *Too long.* I tried on excuses aimed at impressing. Wouldn't it be more romantic to cook for her at home? Now I could pretend to be a chef, orchestrating a perfect evening, starting with a cheese plate, three perfect courses with wine pairings, a pot de crème for dessert. It would just be a different kind of performance.

But, unimpressed by my prosciutto and figs, saffron risotto and a bottle of Grüner Veltliner, Maggie insisted on a picnic getaway. I felt the dread rise like bile. Until now, I had been hiding my obligatory four-calls-a-day from Maggie, because what could be more pathetic than checking in with Mom four times a day? Yet I also knew this moment was the line I'd have to cross. My rubicon. I wanted Maggie's love more than I wanted to keep being the "good boy" my parents expected, so I kept pretending I could manage both. I packed my car—now a sleek Lexus hatchback—with Two Buck Chuck and Trader Joe's charcuterie, tolerating both the soul-numbing four-chord progressions of inane pop songs and the knot in my stomach that tightened with each hairpin turn. By the time I saw my first giant redwood, its trunk wider than the width of my car, I was in a silent panic attack that kept escalating all the way to our cabin until I chugged half the bottle of bad white zinfandel and inhaled an entire triangle of truffle brie. She wanted to fuck. I said I had diarrhea.

Later I found another lie to tell Maggie so I could sneak down to the Wi-Fi-equipped main cabin. There, surrounded by the mounted heads of deer and bears, I sent a different lie to my mother: I was on an impromptu trip to the mountains with the guys in my quartet and we needed quiet to rehearse. I prayed to whatever god would listen for good luck. The next morning, while I trudged through the first fall snow, Maggie hugged each tree trunk, taking in the butterscotch scent of the bark, her laugh muffled by fresh powder as she held icicles to my forehead like horns. "Who's my horny boy?" Not this guy, who didn't own a single pair of athletic shoes, let alone hiking boots, and was still dressed in a tweed sport coat, leather oxfords. We snapped selfies from every angle of streaming sunlight, my smile forced, woolen dress socks thoroughly soaked. When Maggie insisted on posting them to Facebook, using the same Wi-Fi I had just used to lie to Mom, I didn't dare stop her. I was terrified she'd think I was hiding our relationship, which I absolutely was. But the moment she published the post, I knew I was doomed.

On the way home the next day, we stopped at an IHOP in Tulare. We ordered, and while Maggie was in the bathroom and the waitress poured coffee, I turned on my phone and saw it: the endless stream of missed calls from the night before. Every few hours, there were increasingly curt, threatening voicemails. Thanks to a congratulatory call from an old family friend—"I see on Facebook that Robert has a girlfriend! You must be so proud!"—Mom knew everything. She and Dad had already combed through years of Maggie's posts: backpacking trips with former boyfriends, church visits to India, and the coup de grâce of disgrace, Maggie in front of a temple miming our tongue-lolling Maa Kali, the Destroyer of Worlds.

To Maggie and her girlfriends, it was solidarity with a badass Goddess.

To my parents, it was blasphemy.

I listened to their voicemails.

"Potku, pick up the phone."

"Potka, who is this girl I'm seeing on Facebook?"

"She's made our Maa into a Mickey Mouse!"

"Don't tell me you're with this girl. Where are you, Potka? Pick up the phone!"

"Potku, if you don't answer the phone, I'm going to jump off the Mid-Hudson Valley Bridge."

"If you're going to be with some phiringee who mocks our Maa, then go live with her family."

All parents want a better life for their children. But for immigrant parents—especially those shaped by poverty—the American Dream cuts both ways. Parents want their children to avoid the very pain that shaped their lives, and yet, in shielding their children from pain, they can bind them to it.

But what happens when a dream begins to think and choose for itself?

What happens when a parent's dream becomes a child's nightmare?

~

The very next morning, Mom emptied my bank account: $0.00. All of it, gone.

She called it payment for her sacrifices. Thousands of miles of driving. Tutors and lessons. The tuition for two colleges. The home equity line of credit that became the condo down payment. Twenty years of instruments and bows and skipped meals. Of blood and towels.

She said she didn't want all that money to get spent on a white girl's diamond.

I called the bank, then the police, then lawyers.

Each answer was the same: "It's a joint account. There's nothing we can do."

Chapter 7

WHAT'S EATING AT YOU, BABY?

Bartók, String Quartet No. 2, i

The power of art lies in its refusal to despair.

—Albert Camus

Johannes Brahms, Clarinet Quintet in B Minor, Op. 115—i. Allegro

[The Midnight Mission, Skid Row]

Georgia Berkovich turned to introduce our quartet to a roomful of guests on blue plastic chairs in the dayroom.

A smattering of applause followed as I stiffly bowed, dressed in black. I'd first heard Georgia's voice coming through my car's speakers on a Christmas National Public Radio program in 2011. She'd said that music could bring a bit of sweetness to people, a bit of hope. And if people had hope, they were more inclined to ask for help.

Music had once given Georgia hope. She'd started drinking and partying at the age of eleven, but music had kept her and her mother connected, despite her mother's own drinking and isolation. On days when they otherwise might not have said a word to each other, they sang together. Now, nearly two decades into her sobriety, Georgia's weekly art, comedy, and music programs at The Midnight Mission in Skid Row offered connection to people walking through the loneliest days of their lives.

Georgia's events were open to anyone from Skid Row. Some had spent the night sleeping on cots in the Mission's courtyard. Others were residents of the Mission, living the early days of their newly sober lives in community. She insisted on calling the attendees of these events "guests," refusing to let circumstance dictate anyone's dignity.

Like her, many of the Mission's staff members were in recovery. Some had lived on the streets of Skid Row themselves, arriving without shoes, or clothes, or hope of any kind. After I'd played at the Mission a few times, Georgia told me, "There is no us and them. There's only *us*."

It took me years to understand what she meant. During my first few events at the Mission I'd look out at the audience at the Mission and see them—the homeless, the poor, the ones I believed needed saving. I saw people who, in my mind, had to change, had to get clean, had to get off the streets. People who, whether I admitted it or not, I believed needed me and my music in order to heal.

Some of the guests had been sleeping on the streets for a while, and they carried their lives with them in suitcases, backpacks, or bulging black plastic bags. As they entered the dayroom of the Mission, many seemed unaware of the music. Others talked to each other, or sometimes to themselves, for the first fifteen minutes of our events. I got used to playing through the buzz of conversation, something that would never have been allowed in the hall. But halfway through these performances, I'd sense a calm falling across the room, a serenity. Then, I'd hear snores. One man tilted back his enormous, grizzled mane, fast asleep in the front row. Another figure in the corner hugged their belongings and barely stirred, leaning against a wall. If my colleagues noticed, they didn't say so.

Usually, when people nodded off at Disney Hall—which happened more often than anyone liked—it was taken as a slight. The musicians whispered about it backstage, as if the audience had failed a basic test of attentiveness. *"Did you see that douchebag in Orchestra West?!"* Concertgoers were expected to sit up straight, stay alert and polite, and earn their cultural enlightenment.

Once, I pulled Georgia aside and asked if I should be doing something different to keep people from falling asleep during our shows. Maybe we could move the sleeping guy to the back of the room, or ask people to pay more attention. She fixed me with the patient gaze reserved for a confused second-grader.

"Oh nooo, Robert—or, no, sorry, Vijay, right?"

I shrugged it off. I had chosen my name, but hadn't yet grown into it. "Victory" was just a costume.

Georgia went on: "This is good. So many of these folks haven't had a safe night's sleep in weeks—maybe months. They finally feel safe enough to close their eyes around you. They trust you."

A few years into playing concerts in Skid Row, I was beginning to understand that the rules of engagement were different from the Hall. At Disney Hall, people assumed I was a star because of the tails, the violin, and the fact that many already recognized me in the lobby. In Skid Row, I was just another guy. From Patton and later at the Department of Mental Health clinic, I had learned that connection did not happen automatically. But I didn't know how to connect with people in Skid Row. Part of me wanted to ask blunt questions: *What's your story? Why are you here? Don't you have anyone?* But most of the time it became obvious that people needed to be left alone to hear the music.

After a few concerts at the Mission, I started to recognize the regulars. And they started to recognize me. One man, who called himself Brother Jubilee, wore round glasses and a black bowler hat, and slowly pointed his index finger at the ceiling after each movement, his eyes fixed on the concrete floor. Another was a trim, sweet-faced Black woman named Cynthia, who wheeled a small suitcase with an angel-winged cartoon princess affixed to the front. When she came to our concerts, she sat in the front row in her bright pink tracksuit, which had been freshly laundered just for our performance, a neat white golf cap pinned to her graying hair, held tight in a bun. She crossed her legs and smiled brightly at me, calling me "Sugar." She was happy to have us be her special occasion.

When she raised her elegant hand between the movements of a Brahms clarinet quintet, she spoke into the twinge of the music's gracefully bounding arcs, mentioning how the clarinet sounded to her like light rising from the ground. Brahms had written the work in the autumn of his own life. A year earlier, he had said goodbye to composing—but then he heard Richard Mühlfeld play the clarinet. Brahms couldn't help himself: He came out of retirement to work directly with Mühlfeld, creating new works that offered an altar to the clarinet's luminous sound. Later, Brahms gifted Mühlfeld the manuscript and the lifelong performing rights to the work—an unimaginably generous gift from the otherwise sour Brahms.

In response to our playing, Cynthia quoted Louis Armstrong—words that felt as tender as the music we had just played. "I see leaves of green, red roses too..."

At The Midnight Mission, it was never uncommon for someone to burst into song in the midst of our concerts, like some kind of soulful counterpoint. As we started to play more concerts in Skid Row, and later on, in jails, I learned that music lived close to the surface, a gift shared freely—and at times, with more generosity than I was willing to accept. In truth, hearing people sing back to us at Street Symphony felt strangely destabilizing, as if our audience there had refused to buy into the myth of decorum, or the myth that I—purely because of my own assumptions—was supposed to be the "musical expert" in the room. After all, that's exactly what I had been taught: *Keep your head down, practice your excerpts, execute perfectly—and silent, powerful people will give you money, a nice violin—and applause.* But slowly, I was starting to see the reactions of people in Skid Row as a sort of reciprocal music, a mutual gift.

Weeks later, Cynthia would walk up to me and pull me into a warm hug, after a performance of a Mendelssohn string quartet that ends with a hymn. She told me about her family, how she'd sung in church growing up, how much she'd love to sing again someday. As she hugged me, she told me how she'd lost her job. She had been a physician's medical assistant, handling basic clinical and administrative tasks, but when the company was absorbed by a bigger corporation, her job was cut. Then she lost her apartment.

Over the next hour, she told me her story. She was living at the Downtown Women's Center, waiting for a single-room unit at the Skid Row Housing Trust. She told me how some days, she took three buses to the housing bureau to keep her spot on the waitlist. If she missed her appointment, the apartment would go to someone else. If she made it, she'd head to the DMV for an updated ID—because every employer needed an address—then to a social worker in Koreatown to sign off on her General Relief: $221 a month, her only income until someone took a chance on her. Each trip across town would've taken me an hour by car. For her, riding the LA Metro, it would take three times as long. Homelessness was a full-time job.

And still, Cynthia was making time to listen to us play. "I wouldn't miss this for the world," she said, as she covered my hand with hers. I thought she was going to say more about the music, or her day, but instead she tilted her head and looked at me.

"What's eating at you, baby?"

What was I supposed to say to Cynthia? That I was surviving on drive-through binges and nightly bottles of wine? That I was white-knuckling my way through concerts, barely able to breathe backstage?

After a lifetime of performing and knowing exactly how to manage my pre-concert nerves, the stress of losing my life savings, the barrage of terrifying phone calls from my parents, and the events of the next few weeks that would change my life forever had pushed me into a state of vertiginous terror. I was suddenly afraid that if I sat too close to the edge of my perch at Disney Hall, I might fall off the stage.

I may have been learning how to listen to people in Skid Row, but there was no world in which Cynthia could ever know what was actually happening to me.

"Oh, me? Oh, no, I'm fine!"

She held my gaze, still holding my hands. She had just given me her story, and I had refused to give her mine. She could tell I was lying, or that I thought I was too important to share my pain with her.

I wished she would let go.

Antonín Dvořák, Symphony No. 7 in D Minor, Op. 70—i. Allegro maestoso

[Walt Disney Concert Hall]

Over the past few months, my world calved like a glacier. My parents sued me for their stake in the condo, and I hired an expensive lawyer to file a suit for partition: I would walk away from the condo. They could have it.

My bank account emptied, I was now living paycheck to paycheck, barely able to pay my bills, and drowning in overdue credit card bills. Even though I still had a stable salary, and I knew I'd be financially stable again within a few months, I was dodging calls from collection agencies and barely able to pay my bills.

Since childhood, my parents had insisted that I was too irresponsible to handle money. Now, at twenty-five, I was managing my own finances for the first time in my life.

And all the while, Mom kept calling. At any moment, the phone would buzz itself across a table, then start again the moment it stopped, as if she were trying to force her way into my life again. She'd call every half hour, through the night, and even into dawn. After weeks of this, I had to block her number.

Dad said he'd hired a private investigator to "look into" Maggie. He repeated things I already knew about her, but twisted them with a lurid edge, as if her past made her unworthy of me, as if I were betraying him and the family by being with someone like that. When he finally felt my veneer of certainty crack, his tone softened, almost gentle, as if he were offering comfort:

"You know you're a good-looking boy. A catch, right?"

It was the first time he'd ever said anything like that to me. But he had called me mota enough times that, now, I knew better.

Mom rampaged. She called Street Symphony board members and Beverly Hills donors, former teachers and LA Phil colleagues. She even called Steve Lopez at the *LA Times*, screaming overblown accusations about me and Maggie. A violinist in the Phil gave me the number of his therapist.

"Your mom is fucking crazy!" Maggie sobbed one morning as I was trying to get to rehearsal. Her family was horrified: They were Good White Liberals, active in their Unitarianism, earnest in their anti-racism. But everyone had a limit.

"We think your mother is sick, honey. She needs help. But you have to cut your family off. We won't tolerate what feels like abuse, toward us or our daughter. And we won't tolerate any toward you, either."

Abuse.

A word that cracked my world along my heart's fault line. When I finally went to therapy—breaking the long-held family rule about never sharing secrets—I began to hear myself describe what I had always taken for granted: the years of discipline, the sacrifices I claimed as proof of our family's devotion, the endless performing that had replaced anything resembling a childhood. I had never once thought of myself as someone who'd had to survive anything. I found myself trying on the idea of having endured a turbulent, difficult childhood, and some part of me liked the idea of being a victim. It was compelling to see my life through that lens: to cast my parents' behavior in a frame where their control transformed into domination, their volatility into instability, and their sacrifices into abuse. It was so easy, perhaps too easy, to let the story I had lived—but never questioned—calcify into clean lines about boundaries and blame where they were always wrong, and I was always right.

But whenever I was alone—when I was onstage at Disney Hall mindlessly playing symphonies I'd now memorized, or at night after Maggie had fallen asleep—a still, small voice needled me. Had it been abuse? Hadn't I been delivered to my lonely heights by what they had done to me, for me? Didn't I owe them everything? I did everything I could to ignore that voice.

But onstage at the Phil, I started to notice that my body was rebelling. By then, the pain I felt while playing had become constant—a low, searing hum that started in my shoulder and ran down through my elbow into the palm. From the first note, my arm felt as though it were filling with heat. It no longer mattered who was on the podium or what we were playing. I was somewhere else, far outside my body.

During breaks, I would Google some of Mom's behaviors—the ones I had taken as normal, as "just Mom," which Maggie, her family, and a string of therapists now believed were the hallmarks of something called BPD—borderline personality disorder. *Fear of abandonment. Explosive anger. Manic swings followed by depression. Unstable relationships. Unable to keep a job.* I'd feel nauseous and slam the lid of the laptop. During the second half of the concert, I'd zone out while playing and fixate on my upcoming order from Jack in the Box.

That Thanksgiving, Mom and Dad tried to ambush me. At the time, I was with Maggie, two hours away, and I had changed the locks to the condo. From what I could understand, they expected me to leave her, to leave LA, and come home with them for good. They were on a mission to reclaim their son. I finally confronted them with the word I had learned in therapy.

"*Abuse?*" My mother seethed on Barrington Avenue, outside the condo she believed was hers, surrounded by my things she believed were hers, because in her mind, my life was hers, too.

"After all my blood and miles and hunger so you could eat, you lock your own mother out? You've made us homeless. When I die out here remember it was your hands that killed me."

I could find a way to call Mom crazy. But Dad's voice was deadly. "Are you going to make your mother shit in the street like some *pagla*?"

I stammered, unable to find anything to say. Then, Dad spoke again.

"Stop using our last name. Don't call yourself my son ever again."

They called a locksmith and forced their way into the condo, then stripped it of anything they considered a family heirloom: murtis, the volumes of Tagore, and photo albums of me as a child. They scrubbed the condo of any evidence that I had ever been their son. The next day, my parents flew back to New York with everything they could carry. Everything, that is, except the most important thing they had come to collect: me.

But Mom wouldn't leave empty-handed. Two weeks later, she returned to LA to reclaim me. In December 2012, Zubin Mehta was celebrating his Golden Anniversary with the LA Phil, repeating the first program he'd ever conducted with the orchestra in 1962: Mozart's *Don Giovanni* overture, Hindemith's *Mathis der Maler*, and Dvořák's storming Seventh Symphony. In the Disney Hall locker room before the performance, a goateed Russian violinist approached me sheepishly. "I think your mother is looking for you." Clutching my tux pants around my knees, I told him my mother was in New York. "No, she is here."

Somehow, Mom had sweet-talked her way past security, and for twenty minutes my mother had been screaming at the top of her lungs outside the orchestra lounge while my colleagues—chatting or warming up or sipping pre-concert coffee—either scattered or watched in stunned horror. The worst of it: She'd managed to secure a private audience with Zubin Mehta. A security guard later told me that Mom had collapsed at Mehta's feet as if he were a swami, begging him for help with her son—her sweet, lost son who had fallen for the wrong girl. Her son was out of his mind. And, just as Dad believed that Mehta was the only one who could launch me into a career as a soloist, Mom believed that Mehta was the only one who could save our family.

When Mehta called me into his studio, I took Maggie with me, thinking that if he met her, it would be clear Mom was way out of line. But the maestro wouldn't hear any of my spluttering justifications, my accusations of "abuse." I swore that I wasn't out of my mind, laying my hand on the score of his Dvořák symphony like it was the Gita.

He turned to Maggie. "This is a holy family. Please don't destroy them."

Through the whole symphony, I stared at Mehta, willing him to believe that I was still the boy he'd known in Israel, innocent and trustworthy, eyes glued to his baton, playing the entire symphony from memory the way I'd played with Mr. Becker. Mehta never met my gaze.

Mom, though, sat in the third row, tears streaming down her face. It was her first time watching me play with the LA Phil. It would also be her last.

After the New Year, I cut my parents off. After a brief conversation with Shonu—in which he told me that our childhood had never been abusive, but that we were "bad boys, and needed discipline," I stopped talking to him, too.

I had a new family now, Maggie's family. American love was busy work. Dinners at Olive Garden, shopping sprees at Nordstrom, brunches, mimosas, vacations to Laguna. I sang in church. I vacationed in Bali. I convinced myself that every overpriced dress she bought at Anthropologie was stunning. I joined her parents in the nightly bottle of wine without realizing I needed it just to fall asleep each night.

I wanted to spoil her, to be easy, agreeable, generous—the antidote to everything I'd escaped. I thought love meant never saying no. If she wanted to try a new restaurant, I booked the table. If she even mentioned wanting a tropical vacation, I'd surprise her with a first-class flight and hotel. I was trying to win at love, because for my whole life, love had to be won.

But why did winning at love make me feel like such a loser?

Every night, I had the same recurring nightmare: me, in my childhood bedroom, in the dark, bound to a wheelchair, limbless, powerless. Mom would come and force-feed me my favorite dishes: Luchi. Chingri. Daal. I couldn't even lift a hand to stop her—couldn't even hang myself if I wanted to.

During the day, I would show up to rehearsal at Disney Hall numb, usually hungover. When we had breaks, I'd go into the handicapped stall to hyperventilate in private. I ate, I drank, I stopped practicing, and I drank some more. Everything I did felt muffled and numb. Rehearsals. Concerts. Applause.

When she wanted to announce our engagement on Facebook.

Sure, baby, whatever you want.

When she wanted to get married in her mother's backyard.

Yes, I do.

I had expected to be saved by love, and maybe Maggie knew that all we had was a quick infatuation with the idea of being married. But I was still trying to conquer love. I kept finding ways to blame the gaps and inconsistencies on my own shortcomings. I over-forgave, overexplained, and treated her distance like a test of patience. In my mind, she could do no wrong. I made it easy for her to stray further and further, so easy that when she finally walked away for good, I mistook the hollow space she left behind as proof that she had been right to leave.

By the end, I had become unworthy of even my own anger. I wasn't a son anymore, not really, and I wasn't a lover either. I felt like a chakor waiting for instructions that would never come. Weak. Obedient. Alone.

The divorce, when it came, felt like a relief.

It's not you, it's me.

Béla Bartók, String Quartet No. 2, Op. 17—i. Allegro moderato

[The Midnight Mission]

So that no one could tell my life was falling apart—including myself—I turned to growing Street Symphony into a legit nonprofit. I'd start by expanding our musical roster. A jazz guitarist called out of the blue and asked if I'd read *The New Jim Crow* by Michelle Alexander. After I finished it, I started organizing monthly concerts at LA County jails. After a few weeks, I watched in awe as Brandon Bernstein, the guitarist who had called me, performed Howard Alden's "I'll See You in My Dreams" at the Pitchess Detention Center. Under a banner that read "The Serenity Warriors," men in blue jumpsuits closed their eyes, while others nodded their heads in time with the pulse. When the jazz band played at The Midnight Mission a few weeks later, one of the guys in the audience shouted to us, "Hey, didn't you guys play for us at Pitchess? I'm out now—can I join your symphony?"

My now-constant panic didn't let up, even with the nonprofit or organizing monthly concerts, so I took on something even more consuming: learning and performing the six string quartets by the Hungarian composer Béla Bartók—a daunting project that would take several years to complete. Bartók was born in a Hungarian town near the Romanian border and spent his life listening. He traveled the countryside with a wax-cylinder recorder and captured the songs of farmers and shepherds. He believed folk music wasn't primitive but vital and worth preserving. He absorbed the music into his own style, and across his six string quartets, written over the course of his career, those raw rhythms and modal turns resurfaced, transformed. The quartets held the shadows of war, fascism, and exile, and through his works, Bartók remade harmony and form, folding in the strain of folk tunes and dance rhythms, setting modes against chromaticism, music in the rhythms of spoken language, set beside a nocturnal hush. Listening to Bartók's eerie, expressive music, I felt like my wrecked inner world wasn't so strange after all.

A few days before my twenty-sixth birthday, three colleagues from the Phil joined me at The Midnight Mission: Shawn—now a close friend—on violin, Matt on viola, David on cello. David was taller than the rest of us, with big, kind hands that drew a thick, lyrical sound from his instrument. He usually wore a long frown, quick to scowl at blowhard conductors, but in quartet rehearsals he softened, bending his whole body toward the music.

Summer in Skid Row is punishing. Heat ricochets off glass and asphalt until the streets themselves shimmer. As we set up our quartet, I saw Georgia framed in the doorway, her hair lifted by the blast of the Mission's industrial fans. She welcomed each guest as if into her own home, pressing an eight-ounce bottle of water into every hand.

The music we played—Bartók's Second String Quartet—was soft and unsettling, a soft syncopated pulse with no gravity. In the crowd, a woman stood, wearing the kind of gauzy cotton house dress Mom wore at home. The cello sang while Matt and I played a low, steady pulse. Shawn answered, singing until we all sank into a swelling sigh. We hovered at the edge of tension, pleading for a resolution we knew wasn't coming. Shawn's line surged upward, and David's cello caught him midflight, trying to change the subject.

The woman in the dress took a sip of water, then snapped into sudden, erratic motion. She had started dancing, in perfect sync with Bartók's pleading melody. Something clenched in me—the same dread I'd felt whenever Mom lingered outside the practice room, silent, seconds before the door flew open and her hand came down.

Shawn and I tried to hold the center, but my attention was split in two. My fear kept rising, then David's cello cut through the violins in a slow, aching descent.

Then, as if waking from a trance, the woman emptied her water bottle onto David's head. We all stopped playing. A splash hit half a million dollars of eighteenth-century wood. I bolted out of my chair, staring at her, unsure what I could say. David let out a low groan.

"Oh, come *onnn*!"

The woman took one look at me and let out a laugh. Someone in the audience started applauding, and I didn't know if they were clapping for our music or for the woman who had stopped it.

That night, I stayed awake. My throat was dry, heart pounding, mind racing through every worst-case scenario. What would David say? Did he feel attacked? What if the woman had had a knife? What was I thinking, bringing these musicians and their priceless instruments to Skid Row? Could David sue me?

Skid Row could be a violent place, and in those early days I was often afraid, even if I didn't yet understand that the people living there were in far more danger than I had ever known. But that night, safe in my bed next to Maggie, I spiraled into a different fear: What if Street Symphony, the one place where music still felt alive to me, might be taken away because of my own carelessness?

Did we need to hire private security? Did I need insurance? Who could I even talk to about this?

I missed Dad. I missed being his son—the part of me that could hand over the chaos, knowing he'd take charge. What would he have done? Who would he have called first? A lawyer? I could already hear his voice, confident, even if he was pretending. *Arre, Potka—don't worry. I'll handle it.* But now, all I did was worry.

The next morning, on my drive to the Hollywood Bowl, I rehearsed my apology like a TED Talk. I'd lost my family, my last name, my money, and my home. I would not lose Street Symphony. I prayed David wouldn't demand that I shut the thing down.

When I started to blurt out an apology, he waved me away. "Hey, Vijay. Hey, don't worry about that, listen: Do you think I can bring my kids next time? I know they're young, but they need to know what's happening in their city. They need to see Skid Row."

"Wana Baraka"—Traditional Kenyan

[The Midnight Mission]

Joshua fit the battle of Jericho
And the walls come tumbling down

About twenty minutes into the concert, a woman stepped into the dayroom at The Midnight Mission clutching a towel to her chest, her face creased with pain. It was 110 degrees outside, and the air inside wasn't much better. She dropped into a chair at the back, gasping for breath. I looked away. Skid Row offered little privacy, so people suffered openly. The room smelled of bleach and sweat, with urine and something rotting underneath.

Eight singers stood in a semicircle. On another day they might be in a studio recording *Star Wars* soundtracks, or singing at Disney Hall with the LA Master Chorale. But today they were here, singing for Street Symphony at a Skid Row shelter. Months earlier, Amy—a mezzo with a dazzling smile and sequined gown—had cornered me backstage at Disney Hall. "Hi! Have you ever thought about using singers for Street Symphony? I think I sent you a few emails." She had. I'd ignored them.

The idea of bringing a whole choir into Skid Row had felt impossible. But in person, I couldn't turn her down.

That afternoon, the sweltering air filled with benedictions in Latin—"Ubi caritas et amor, Deus ibi est"—and Russian—"Bogoroditse Dyevo, raduysia." The singers nodded their heads to the applause and exchanged quiet nods. Amy raised a small, round pitch pipe to her lips and blew a soft note. With barely a breath, the choir began an antebellum gospel song—its roots in slavery, its story drawn from a battle in the Old Testament—beginning in a whisper, as if whipping up a storm from ancient dust.

Go blow them ram horns, Joshua cried
'Cause the battle is in my hands…

Great performers become music, and these singers were some of the best: Karen shattered the air as the ram's-horn shofar, and Scott and Ed were the deep bass of tumbling walls. Elyse and Amy and Alice kept time, and Tim and Daniel were infallible. The singers' eyes were wide, their rhythm perfect, their words cutting through the air like weapons.

A few months earlier, I had visited the church of St. Martin-in-the-Fields in London—where Handel had once performed—and a chaplain told me that her title traced back to "chapel"—and, by a long route, to *a cappella*. In an act of charity, a mounted soldier had torn off his military cloak and clothed a shivering, emaciated stranger. The tattered cloth became a relic, passed between the hands of poor wanderers who gathered to pray over it with song in small makeshift places: places of the cape. Their unaccompanied prayers became songs, and their songs became a refuge. Cappella, chapel, chaplain: Any place could be made holy with intention.

As the singers began "Shenandoah," the room fell velvet quiet, and a tenor stepped forward for a solo. This often happened at Street Symphony—fifteen or twenty minutes into a program, when a shelter slowly turned into a sanctuary. An unsuspecting audience, mid-meal or mid-thought, would begin to lean in. I'd played with many of these singers before, on stages like the Hollywood Bowl or Disney Hall, in Mahler's *Resurrection* and Beethoven's Ninth. They always seemed possessed by joy, erupting into laughter and hugs the moment a performance ended. Daniel was a buoyant, handsome man whose giggle-shout I recognized from across the Bowl's parking lot or backstage in the wings, and here at the Mission he was the same: radiant, irrepressible, pouring his whole body into song. The last note he sang hovered in the air, something too beautiful to be real, a thing with feathers you didn't dare touch.

The room applauded the singers, and Daniel bowed quickly, blowing a kiss to his audience.

Now they were singing in Swahili—an arrangement of a Kenyan folk song:

Wana baraka wale waombao, Yesu mwenyewe alisema.

I heard an echo in the room, and smiled. The small rooms at Street Symphony often had lively acoustics—all glass and concrete—but after a moment, I realized that I wasn't hearing an echo. There was another voice in the room, rising in harmony with the others—clear, confident—someone else was singing with us.

Wana furaha wale waombao, Yesu mwenyewe alisema.

The woman from earlier, who had staggered past the singers, was now sitting bolt upright in a chair against the back wall, her bundles of belongings—once strapped to her—finally resting at her feet. Her eyes blazed.

Wana uzima wale waombao, Yesu mwenyewe alisema.
Alleluia, alleluia.

She was on her feet, in her own realm of joy. *Alleluia, alleluia,* she intoned, her palms raised in praise. Clutching my violin, I felt drawn to her across the room of the Mission.

"I am so glad I came here today," she said to me as I approached, her face radiating with something more than heat. "I grew up singing in Tanzania," she said, anticipating my question in a throaty, rich contralto, a staccato accent demarcating her *t*'s and the sibilant *s*, the richly rolled *r*. "I came here for school, to study at USC. I was living in my car." I had heard about students at celebrated schools like the University of California, Los Angeles, and the University of Southern California unable to afford housing on campus, living and studying out of their cars instead. But she was the first person in that situation I'd ever met.

"I never thought I'd hear Swahili here," she said. "It was forbidden in Tanzania. My grandparents were forced to speak German, and I hated it. Such an ugly language." She paused to wipe her face, then smiled. "So I learned Swahili. I taught it to my grandparents. I'm proud to know my mother tongue."

She beamed. Minutes earlier, she'd run into the room seeking shelter. Now she stood tall, steady. To my eyes she seemed transformed—no—*unveiled.*

Then I realized: The next song—the concert's last number—would be... in *German.*

My quartet would join the choir for a motet by Bach known as *Lobet den Herrn* (Praise the Lord), a setting of Psalm 117: "O praise the Lord, all ye nations: praise him, all ye people." *Shit,* I thought, sprinting past a row of lanyard-clad men from the Mission, residents taking the first steps of sobriety. How would my new friend feel about German—right after Swahili?

As we played the motet, my mind wandered. It was impossible to know who we'd meet in Skid Row, impossible to read a life from their appearance. I felt ashamed for the times I had driven past homeless people waiting at freeway underpasses and ignored their cardboard signs—"Please, anything helps." Sometimes I fished out slips of green paper from my center console, thinking that's all people wanted or needed—and felt worse about paying off my own guilt with a few dollar bills. What did people *really* need?

During a few bars of rest, I stole a look over at the woman at the back of the room. She sat in thoughtful attention. She didn't seem to mind—or even notice—that the singers were singing in the tongue of her family's oppressors—she seemed to be intoning the final word of Bach's motet, set to a capering gigue—a word that could hold worlds.

Alleluia.

Chapter 8

IN A PLACE LIKE THIS

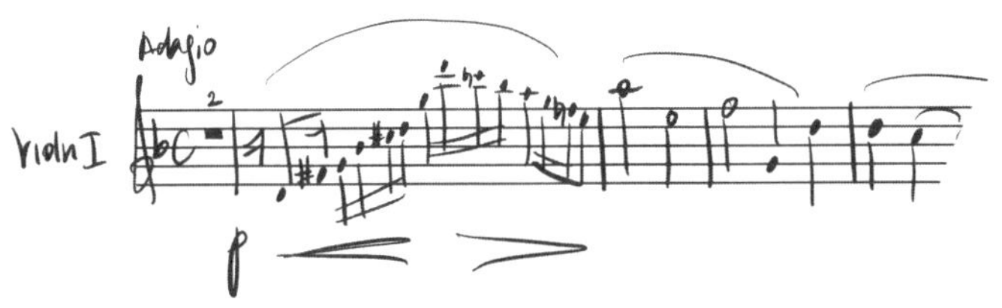

R. Schumann, String Quartet Op. 41 No. 1, iii

> To send light into the darkness of men's hearts, such is the duty of the artist.
>
> —Robert Schumann

Robert Schumann: String Quartet in A Minor, Op. 41 No. 1

{i. Andante espressivo}

[Wells Fargo Stage, Walt Disney Concert Hall]

Standing backstage, the guys and I couldn't see the crowd. We could hear them, though—throbbing, swelling, chatting with ease. Then the lights dimmed and the hall fell into a prickly quiet. I used to take comfort knowing that somewhere out there, Dad was watching. *Make them cry, Potka.* He'd never seen me play at Disney Hall.

I plucked the strings on my new, very old violin. A few months earlier, the LA Phil's concertmaster had handed me one of the orchestra's treasures: a 1731 Montagnana from Venice, high-bellied, its burnished red lacquer worn down to bare golden wood. In the daylight of my practice rooms, I'd stare at it for hours. The violin seemed to drink in the sun, glowing from within. For decades it had belonged to a senior colleague, who often left it in her locker rather than taking it home to practice.

After she retired, the orchestra's concertmaster decided I'd be a good match for the violin. At first the violin resisted my efforts to learn it, especially on the lower strings, where the sound was flubby at first. I had to dig to find the core of sound, and in the rare moments I struck paydirt, the tone was both penetrating and sweet, but it required me to play with more force and control than I'd ever had. The Montagnana made me hold my body in shapes that tied me in knots, as if I had to bend myself to its will. I could fill a hall with its voice, but it never felt like the sound was resonating inside me. When I tried to put my full strength into the upper strings, the tone thinned, as if asking me to hold myself back. I felt like I would always be an outsider inside its sound, a visitor never truly at home. It had always been my dream to play on a precious eighteenth-century Italian instrument: I had no business being dissatisfied.

Backstage, Shawn warmed up with a twisting, chromatic passage. Matt tuned, and David rosined his bow. There weren't the usual hundred-plus musicians and crew milling about backstage. Our quartet was about to walk out to perform a quartet by Robert Schumann for the Philharmonic's chamber music series: Tonight, instead of an orchestra, it would be the four of us onstage—each voice exposed, facing the music of Robert Schumann together.

A stage manager nodded to us. I checked the fine Swiss watch on my wrist: 8:57 p.m. Maggie was already asleep at home. We didn't see each other much. Maybe we were trying to avoid each other. I slept late when I could, and she woke as early as possible. She'd take weeks-long backpacking trips, and I'd go on tour.

We lined up, cello first, violins last. The stage manager opened the door, and I saw four chairs and four music stands in a ten-foot spotlight of searing-white light, shaded by a soft blue ring. My stomach did a somersault. Nerves. The stage can be a place of triumph and terror. Our primeval wiring makes us see the lit, exposed surface of the stage as a clearing in a dark forest, surrounded by the watchful eyes of predators. Adrenaline that sends blood rushing back toward the heart is helpful when outrunning a tiger. But it's a terrible way to make music.

In our last moment backstage, I put on a show of machismo I didn't feel. "Okay guys, let's kill it!"

We walked out to the sound of a thousand people applauding, but, blinded by the spotlights, I couldn't see a single person in the hall. While the quartet checked the tuning of taut strings and the tightness of bow hair, I held out my right hand. It was shaking. A man coughed in the front row.

Trying to control my bow, I raised the violin, which still felt so foreign in my hands. I had to play the first eight notes by myself. Even as a soloist, I rarely had to start a piece all alone. *Andante, espressivo.* A simple, snaking line in A minor, almost chantlike, answered by the other instruments. After a turn, soft stabs of anxiety building to a pronouncement, an off-beat prophecy. A return to quietness. *Pianissimo.* The chant's shadow.

My bow still shook.

[Allegro]

[Ensemble Room 3, Walt Disney Concert Hall]

As we entered the first theme, the music shaped itself into a sweet, impetuous song—a quick rise and three descending exclamations. Each time the melody returned it was somehow both the same and different at once: now a dance, now a hymn, now an intricate fugue—voices echoing and evolving into one another, searching for something truer—a melody that wanted to become more itself.

In 1842, Robert Schumann, at age thirty-two, was in crisis. His wife, Clara, nine years younger, was already one of the most famous musicians in Europe. She had been introduced to the concert stage at age fourteen by none other than Felix Mendelssohn himself. Robert, meanwhile, had destroyed his hand with a misguided contraption to strengthen his fingers, ending his hopes of a career at the piano. As Clara dazzled on tour, Robert stayed behind, depressed and uncertain, calling himself a "scribbler."

So he scribbled. When Robert composed, it often came in bursts of frenzy. We often think of Mozart as the fastest composer, but Robert Schumann worked with a different urgency, attempting to outrun his own mind, pushing to finish his thoughts before the waves of depression returned to drag him under, leaving him drained and silent.

Onstage, we struggled to keep pace with Robert's searing mind. We had rehearsed for weeks, parsing every accent, dot, and *fortepiano,* but our quartet still stumbled in the dark. I was embarrassed. We should have been playing way better than this. Critics were out there, colleagues too, maybe even our conductor, an unseen panel of judges hidden in the dark. But even after all our rehearsing, all the anxious control, I felt as if I were sight-reading. And we were still on the first page.

A few weeks earlier, when we had started learning the quartet, I'd had a torrent of questions, and we'd needed to rehearse our way to the answers: What was the best way to play an offbeat accent embedded in a slur, with exactly the right kind of crescendo? Should a *sforzando* be different in *piano* than it was in *forte,* and what about when it was on a diminished chord, or on a half cadence? What kind of sound should the other strings make when we were all supposed to be playing softly, but I had the melody? Wait, did I even *have* the melody? No! *Shit.* Now it was in the cello. Was this a fugue now? And then there were the notes themselves. Sometimes, our violist would stop in the middle of a phrase.

"God*damn* it, I keep fucking up letter Q!"

For hours upon hours in a soundproof studio overlooking Hope Street, we'd curse ourselves or fall into the language of diplomatic euphemism of chamber music rehearsals:

"This passage isn't clean yet." (*"You don't know the notes."*)

"I feel like it's pushing here, don't you?" (*"You're rushing."*)

"I'm just not matching your bow stroke yet." (*"It's not together, and probably your fault."*)

"Can we find a different color there?" (*"I don't like your sound."*)

Shawn, thankfully, could cut through the bullshit.

"Dude. It's out of tune. Let's fix it."

I suggested we do a mock concert, a trial run of Street Symphony's new program at the LA County jails.

"Who knows, man?" I said. "We sound pretty bad. They might make a break for it."

Matt laughed, but Shawn didn't.

When LA Phil management asked if our quartet would come to Bel Air to serenade the orchestra's donors, I didn't hesitate. Bel Air seemed like the place for this music. One of the patrons owned a Napa vineyard, and we were promised a three-course meal and a world-class wine flight.

Maybe they'd crack open a 1990 Cheval Blanc.

{ii. Scherzo: Presto}

[Stradella Road, Bel Air, Los Angeles]

As LA's power brokers worked the room, our quartet played in a tense, controlled *piano*, bows bouncing at blistering speed, striking our strings in sync, several times a second, swelling to *forte*, then—*subito!*—back to *piano*. Then I broke off, my notes fleeing the others, rising, trying to find the light. For a moment, I won: The music careened into explosive happiness, nearly heroic. But I'd inevitably fall off the edge, returning to stuttering dread: *bakadum, bakadum*.

Salons like this were the initial "chambers" of chamber music—house parties for the wealthy, places to eat well, show off, and be seen. But those rooms were also musical laboratories. In 1842, Robert Schumann abandoned Clara's concert tour, sunk in envy and debt. She was the one performing, supporting the family, exactly as her father had warned. Robert retreated to what he called his "quartetish thoughts," burying himself in counterpoint, studying Beethoven, Mozart, Mendelssohn, desperate to prove he still mattered. The music came in a torrent. He was manic that summer, skipping meals, scribbling through the night, hearing voices. When Clara returned, she found him unshaven, pacing, muttering to himself, still composing. On her twenty-third birthday, they premiered the quartets in their home for friends gathered in their parlor. The real music wasn't just the notes on the page, but the trust between Robert and Clara, two people holding the world together through love and madness.

But trust wasn't exactly the first course on the menu in Bel Air. Some attendees were people who gave both their money and their warmth, like the kind couple from Beverly Hills who had adopted me like a surrogate nephew. But many in that room were power brokers: real estate developers, CEOs and moguls, and even an organizer for the upcoming 2028 LA Olympics. Millions had already flowed from their pockets into the Philharmonic, and some had endowed chairs: the "so-and-so" Principal Flute, the "wife-and-husband" Assistant Horn. The goal tonight was to ask for more, with me and Shawn and the guys—and Robert Schumann—as the amuse-bouche. Maybe if I put on a good enough show, someone would endow my chair, too.

But I wasn't playing well. I was distracted, not really listening for Shawn, not matching my bow stroke on the crescendos the way our violist had asked in rehearsal. My eyes kept drifting to the dozens of fresh-cut, pale-pink peonies and the matching chairs and tablecloths. The room was softly lit, and the air was warm with polite clinking of glasses. An heiress of a sneaker fortune bobbed a massive diamond ring against her knee, tapping out of time. Behind them, a row of orchestra executives checked their phones. Would anyone really notice if we made a mistake? Would anyone care?

Earlier that week, I'd attended a community organizing meeting in a cramped South LA office to protest the 2028 Olympics. One sign read, "Down with the evil, capitalist, gentrifier pigs!" Another: "Homes Not Games!" We'd just seen the preparations for the Rio Olympics and how they had forcibly removed people who lived in the favelas, razing their homes to build highways. In LA, some developers were already buying up tracts of land to create housing for the athletes and hipster condos. Many Angelenos, meanwhile, some of them real American heroes—veterans—were sleeping on the streets. Some of the other activists looked to me to be a voice for social justice. Seated at a plastic folding table in a Skid Row conference room, sipping acrid instant coffee, I nodded but said nothing. I knew that a few days later I'd be drinking pinot with "the pigs."

But I'd learned a long time ago how to bury dissonance. I never admitted what I really felt, because who would care, and who would listen. Professionals kept their opinions to themselves.

[Intermezzo]

Los Angeles is a masterclass in structural violence. Zoning laws keep wealthy enclaves like Bel Air, Pasadena, and Beverly Hills sealed off, while poor neighborhoods are boxed in by freeways and concrete or bulldozed to make way for the next development. To most residents, these are neighborhoods to drive past, or through, and quickly. It's a city of borders—drawn not only on city plans but in the psyche of its residents. When the rich do cross over, it's not to connect. It's to "improve." Gentrification sounds noble, but the word's root—"gentry"—is to make things proper, refined. It's a language that so often rewards erasure, dressed up as progress.

In his book *The History of Forgetting,* Norman Klein called Los Angeles a city of facades, one that "has long thrived on the continual recreation of its own myth." Bunker Hill's Grand Avenue, once known as Charity Street, was a hilltop of ornate Victorian homes. By the 1950s, those homes had become rooming houses for immigrants and retirees. County officials called the hill a slum. They cleared it. Block by block, people were displaced, and their houses bulldozed, to make room for the financial district skyline: glass towers, marble banks. In 1964, a young Zubin Mehta opened the Dorothy Chandler Pavilion with the Los Angeles Philharmonic. Then, nearly forty years later, the Walt Disney Concert Hall—Frank Gehry's "living room of the city"—rose from a gaping hole in the same soil.

But as Steve Lopez once asked in the *LA Times*—whose living room was it, exactly? Most people looking for a place to sleep in Los Angeles would find no charity on Charity Street—or Grand Avenue. For decades, the wanderers of America ended up in the missions and shelters of Skid Row. By 1981, President Reagan had slashed federal mental-health funding and folded it into block grants, setting off large-scale deinstitutionalization. Now, the responsibility for caring for the mentally ill was handed to "communities," a word that actually meant "not us." States began practicing what they called "Greyhound Therapy": one-way bus tickets to downtown Los Angeles. The result was a quiet pipeline of the country's most vulnerable, funneled west. Over decades, zoning laws and policing strategies hardened the neighborhood into what it is today: a contained zone of poverty. What had once been a district zoned for low-rent, affordable housing became the dumping ground for a city's—and country's—unwanted. Skid Row wasn't an accident.

This problem worsened with the War on Drugs. Those dropped off by Greyhound Therapy—usually poor, usually Black or Brown—were left to manage their mental illness with the only medicine available:

alcohol, marijuana, crack cocaine, heroin—all of them a one-way ticket to County.

By 2015, the LA County jails became the largest jail system in the world, with an average daily population of over nineteen thousand inmates, and an annual budget of $1 billion. There was a revolving door between Skid Row and the Twin Towers Jail that trapped people in a cycle of poverty, neglect, and at times, brutality. The jail became the asylum, the shelter, the detox ward. But unlike those places, the jails seemed to have no mandate for true rehabilitation. No, those concrete and glass cages were built to contain, to suppress, and to disappear: to keep people in motion between institutions without any intention of addressing the root causes of suffering, and to lock that suffering away like something shameful.

[Scherzo: Presto]

I sat back as a tuxed waiter served me a plate of Scottish salmon and *haricots verts* in a *beurre blanc*. Heads nodded. Wine flowed. Across the table, the sneaker heiress asked me what I did "for fun." I swirled the cocktail in my hand. What I really did for fun was drink. Instead, I told her about playing concerts in homeless shelters and county jails. She asked if I'd ever played at Coachella. From the head of the table, a downtown LA real estate developer leaned in to interrupt me. He raised a Riedel goblet and whispered in a hot grapey hush.

"Thank God someone is doing something for those indigents."

Instinctively, I tapped my glass against his and heard it reverberate in the space between us. The rim hummed against my lips, reminding me that I'd agreed with him without saying a word.

I knew the developer's firm had recently purchased a number of buildings in downtown LA, tightening a noose around Skid Row and the housing, shelters, and vital services offered in the neighborhood. But by then, numb from three Negronis and half a bottle of pinot, I didn't have much of a self left to resist anything. It was easy to nod along. Technically, his money paid my salary. He owned the precious eighteenth-century violin I played, which meant he owned the sound that came out of me. Dad had trained me to never disagree, to never offend anyone—least of all the powerful—to stay lovable, pleasant, accommodating, unassailable, and then let others narrate my life for me. All I ever knew how to do was excel at my training.

So I let the donors tell the story in a way that made sense to them, and I let the activists tell theirs, too. To some I was a generous mensch, to others a social justice warrior.

Sometimes I caught myself wondering what I was really doing. Was I showing up because it was easy to be called *good?* Or was it because, down there, among the tents and police sirens, I remembered who I was, and why I'd ever become a musician? I'd spent so long performing—being the good son, the good student, the good colleague—that I couldn't tell where the masks ended and I began.

I knew how to wear the masks, how to win the games. I knew how to do everything I was told, as long as I never turned to face myself.

It was easier to let everyone say what they wanted, to let them believe the best or the worst. Just as I used to let Mom believe I was out of tune, even when I thought I wasn't. I knew the rules: Silence meant safety; and speaking up was dangerous.

So I did what I knew best: Freeze, fawn, swallow it all. Stay quiet, perform, and be a good boy.

{iii. Adagio}

[Twin Towers Jail, Los Angeles]

"What are you all playing today?"

The man wore a yellow jumpsuit, the same as worn by all the men here. He was in the front row, close to me, and his voice was high and clear, almost boyish, younger than the growl I had expected from his lined face. The inmate pressed his hands to his knees. The watery light of his eyes was muted but firm.

Shawn warmed up with a series of scales. The others laid out carefully taped pages of sheet music on wire music stands. A few minutes earlier, we had walked through a series of buzzing, clanking doors and traded our driver's licenses for red clip-on badges that read "VISITOR." From behind a small, barred window, an inscrutable, tan-clad deputy murmured, "If you lose these, we go into lockdown." Just a week before our performance at Disney Hall, this was supposed to be our mock concert, our trial run. I hadn't realized that for the next ninety minutes, we would be captive, too.

On our way into the inmates' concrete living quarters, we'd walked through hallways lit in a fluorescent pallor that seemed to move us out of time. In the downtown facilities, there were no windows, but no darkness either. Buzzing lights were kept on twenty-four hours a day. By disrupting natural circadian rhythms, the Twin Towers staff made the population less resistant, more docile. The deputy who led us down the halls assured me, dispassionately, that the men were sedated. "Don't worry, you'll be safe." I stared at his gleaming baton. A recent news story reported that some guards at Twin Towers were under federal investigation for human rights violations. Some had even tossed lengths of rope into the cells of inmates who said they wanted to kill themselves. Reporters documented an entire floor at the jail where inmates lay in beds, catatonic, zonked out on high doses of antipsychotic medication, primarily Haldol.

Inside the dormitory, two long rows of men lined the far wall of glass. Each man was in plain sight from the guard's tower, behind which I saw the moving shadows of deputies, the quick glare of a flashlight. A nurse, followed closely by a deputy, handed out paper cups with pills, which the men swallowed, each of them flashing a quick loll of the tongue before turning away. The room smelled like bleach and old antiseptic. Years later, a cellist would tell me the smell of Twin Towers Jail reminded him of rehab.

I turned to face the man who'd asked me about what we'd be playing. Was I allowed to talk to the inmates?

"A quartet," I mumbled.

I felt the eyes of a deputy on the back of my head. A staticky question crackled over a handheld radio. The deputy behind me responded with a string of numbers, followed by a beep.

"Yeah, I can see that. But what *music* are you playing?"

"Oh!" I felt like an idiot. "We're playing a quartet by Schumann."

He let out a hoarse laugh. "That's fitting."

His words nailed me. His face was calm, and he sat with the kind of quiet that knows too much.

"Schumann died in a place like this."

He was right. Robert Schumann's mania had become, as he aged, a pattern of auditory hallucinations: He'd heard a constant single note—A—the same note to which an orchestra tunes, and he'd wanted, more than anything, to make it stop. Robert had thrown himself off a bridge into the frigid Rhine. When he didn't die, he'd checked himself into an asylum.

There, Robert's doctors discouraged him from composing or playing, believing that music would be too stimulating. They even barred Clara from seeing him, fearing that her presence would trigger an episode. When Clara finally did visit him, he was nearly gone. She left his bedside one time, for a quick trip to the train station to retrieve their closest friends, Brahms and the violinist Joseph Joachim. When she returned, Robert had died.

As a deputy made an announcement to introduce our quartet, I leaned over to Shawn, who jerked his chin up. I wanted to try something.

"What's up?" I whispered. "Hey, let's start with the third movement today. And let's stop at Letter Q—Okay?" Shawn shrugged and passed along the message.

I'd seen the word, as if for the first time: *adagio*—"at ease." After the maze of gates and the hum of fluorescent lighting, that word felt almost absurd. Across the dormitory, the man who'd spoken to me earlier was watching closely. He sat in the front row, elbows on his knees, his gaze steady but far away, as if he were looking past us, through us, toward something only he could see.

Something in me started to unravel. We weren't in a concert hall, so why did I have to pretend like this was just another concert? What if we didn't have to perform, at all? What would it be like if the music didn't have to flow one way—from the stage down—but could move in both directions? What if we weren't just experts delivering a product, but listeners among listeners? What if music wasn't the notes at all, but the listening between them, between people, here, in a place like this?

The cello began with an arcing improvisation, pierced by a painful, soft *sforzando* chord. I responded with my own arc, turning toward a warm tune in F major, equal parts hymn and lullaby, lifted by a viola's undulating arpeggios. I stole a glance at the man in the front row. It was as if he were giving the arpeggios back to us through his eyes, a circle of music completing itself. We took it. The violins played a long, tense crescendo—the viola's waves now unsure, driving to a *forte* climax—before breaking into a heartbreaking cello solo—the hymn tune now an aria, accompanied by harp-like plucking in the violins. Then the music stopped. I heard someone let out a sigh. The room broke into applause.

Interrupting the clapping, I stood. The guard stiffened, and I could feel the guys in the quartet tense up, too. "So, what did you hear? What was this music about?"

"I heard angels," one man responded. Another hand went up, and I nodded. "Yeah, me too—it was like you were a choir. But then one of you took the lead."

"Peaceful but painful."

"Hope," another man said. "Beautiful hope."

I turned to look at the quartet. Shawn gave me a nod—curious, but wary—and the other guys wore similar looks. We were all surprised by how willing they seemed to share what they were feeling.

Most of the time in classical music, we tell audiences how to listen, like a smug waiter telling you how to eat your meal: *Sit down, shut up, find a good enough looking date, turn off your phone, and swallow "the culture."* But in that jail, I didn't want to serve another Michelin-star performance. I wanted to ask: *What are you hearing right now? What does this music say to you? Here, in a place like this?*

This was not how I'd been trained. In conservatory, I'd been taught to perfect, to blend, to comply. No one had ever taught me to ask what music meant in someone else's life—or how to listen when they answered. But now, something shifted. Our performance had become a conversation.

I placed my violin on my collarbone and continued from where we'd stopped. Now, Schumann's journey took a turn. Two abrupt, vertical strokes were answered by a short upward "hmm?"—comical, then concerning. Two more slashes, answered by a downward turn. A man in the second row recoiled as if he'd been struck by our sound. The pattern repeated until a fatal blow: Now, the undulations were as if an animal were caught in a maw. The viola's line twisted upon itself as the notes passed to the violin, back and forth, ever perverting—then slammed every few bars by violent slashes. This was where our quartet had faltered in rehearsals, but now—*now*—we were totally present with something larger than ourselves. We were playing into the deep listening of our audience, and suddenly, we weren't tallying our mistakes and bracing for errors but making as much music as we could: Now, it wasn't just the four of us in the quartet who were making music. We were playing for—and *with*—our entire audience.

I nodded for us to stop. This time, the hands were already up.

"It's like he's lost and keeps hitting a wall."

"Damn, man. That's fucking heavy."

"Trapped. Trying to escape." I looked over at Shawn. His eyes were wide, his head nodding—he had pointed out that very same element during rehearsals. The inmates were on a roll.

"It's like he's trying to set his life right, you know?"

"Yo." A young man—who hadn't spoken yet—fidgeted with his hands. Shawn called on him.

"That music sounds like the way I feel."

{iv. Presto}

[Walt Disney Concert Hall]

Back onstage, in the fiendish romp of the last movement, my bright terror had turned into a laser focus. Throughout the whole piece, I'd trembled with the cavalcade of adrenaline, and now, we all threw brutal blows and fistfuls of rabid, scampering eighth notes.

I missed the guys in the jail. I wished that I could have seen them somewhere in the hall. Part of me even wished they could sit onstage with us here and talk to the audience between movements, explaining how they heard the music, how they had felt Schumann in that dormitory. I wanted Disney Hall to give me the same kind of unguarded, living *contact* I'd felt in the jail—the way those inmates had leaned in, the way they had listened to us, the way we had listened to them, how their listening had changed the way we played. I wanted that current of awe that had moved among us all and knew that our performance would have been better for it, but I had absolutely no idea how to find—or create—that kind of connection in a concert hall.

And besides, they were still in that dormitory, because they were criminals, and I was here, because I was—what—a professional? What was it, exactly, that made me so very different than those men? I couldn't deny that my being, stretched taut against the irreconcilable poles of Los Angeles, was starting to fray.

Over the past few years in Skid Row, I'd accepted the idea I was going there to help, to heal, to be generous. Why else would a

Philharmonic musician go to a place like Skid Row? I'd been a child soloist since I was nine. By nineteen, I was in one of the best orchestras in the world. So when the donor raised a toast to the "extra" work I did, of course he thought he was right. And to be fair, nothing in his world—or mine—would've told him otherwise. I never would have entertained the notion that I was the one in need of healing: Everything in my life system told me that I was a winner playing for losers, and if I admitted that I was in any way *not* a winner, well—then I was a loser, too.

But after Twin Towers, I couldn't hide anymore. I'd convinced myself that I was bringing light into the darkness, but the truth was that I was the one living in the dark. I was the one blinded by the spotlight, playing on the stages I'd once dreamed of, only to find the music there reduced to a curio of high culture, a dead thing behind glass. *Fragile: Do not touch.*

It was the people I thought were broken who showed me the truth: At an art studio open mic on San Pedro, I once saw a rail-thin woman belt out "Jolene," taking the roof off the place. One night, as I was leaving San Julian Street, I watched an impromptu band form around an upright piano, a guitar, an upturned bucket drum. A security guard told me later that the band had played all night.

At the end of Street Symphony performances, people often came up to us and said they'd grown up singing in church, or that they could play the guitar. They wanted to join our symphony. I'd smile, stall, promise we'd figure something out someday. The truth was, I had no idea what making music together would even look like. Collaboration—sharing, improvising—wasn't something I'd learned at Juilliard. All I'd learned was how to outplay the person next to me, hoping to get ahead, sometimes even hoping that they'd falter, so that I'd remain the victor.

At Disney Hall, the scrambling Presto came to an abrupt halt and the viola held a bagpipe drone. Shawn and I played a small, folklike ditty, which rose into a hymn that we all played together. The music drew down into swells of doubt, and then detonated in a panicked, overbright blaze.

The house lights came up in the audience. They were on their feet, applauding: one ovation, then two more. I didn't know whether to believe them, but as I looked at the guys, I knew we were still performing. Now, even as the music ended, we had to believe that we were the experts, that we deserved these ovations, even though we knew that the music we had just delivered to this audience had felt dead on arrival.

I looked toward the back of the illuminated hall the way I always did, as I had done ever since I was a child, searching for Dad. And I saw him, there, where he was not: Dad's face, in every face, the face I hadn't seen in two years, the face I'd never see again.

Play from the heart, Potka.

Part 3

TeReKeTe Takadina Dha |
TeReKeTe Tirakita Dha |
TeReKeTe TeReKeTe Dha Dha Dha

[Dum Dum, Kolkata]

Bulbul sat before two drums, his hands poised: He struck the membrane of the dayan with his right index finger, and the taut goatskin let out a piercing *na*. He suspended his left hand over the bayan like a cobra's head and struck a resounding *ghe*. With four careful finger strikes, he let out a Ta Re Ki Ta. He practiced the strokes over and over, until the pattern sank deeper and deeper, beyond his conscious mind, embedding itself into his motor cortex. He could practice the notes in his sleep, and he did, his fingers itching with dream-rhythms. Ta Re Ki Ta. Ta Re Ki Ta.

All through his childhood, Bulbul had dreamed of playing the tabla. One day, he worked up the nerve to ask his father, Babu, for lessons. But Babu saw what was happening to boys in their Kolkata neighborhood—some drawn into militant Naxalite circles, others caught in the crossfire of Indira Gandhi's crackdown. One boy from a good family was shot dead at his kitchen table. Others were dragged into the street and executed. Survival mattered more than talent.

Now his son wanted to become a musician?

Bulbul was barely passing his classes, wasting time in alleys, playing cricket with other good-for-nothings, and now *this*? No Gupta became a musician. That was either the privilege of the upper castes, who could afford gurus, or the burden of the lowest, forced to perform for coins on the street. To Babu, a musician was either a pandit or a chakor. Nothing in between. Nothing worth risking a son for.

Dhur sala! Tui pagla hoigecchish?

But for the rest of his life, Bulbul would be crazy about rhythm. The pulse never stopped. Even when he came to New York, while he worked at baggage claim at JFK or peeled potatoes at the Jewel of India, his fingers itched with pulse, clattering on the bags he lifted, the boxes he carried. And once he became a successful businessman, answering the calls to send his countrymen home, he'd wedge the long-corded landline between his neck and ear and drum on the red formica kitchen counter, making goofy faces at his children as they giggled through facefuls of Cheerios. When he drove us to rehearsals and lessons in the City, willingly becoming a chakor so that his children could become pandits, he tapped and popped his fingers on the dash, the steering wheel, the console, bringing his everywhere-tabla in time with Rod Stewart, Paul Simon, Nusrat Fateh Ali Khan. Once we were back home, he drummed his unceasing, clattering rhythm on any resonant surface he could find. He tapped on boxes and bowls, even on his boys, until they'd beg him to stop.

Daa-aad!

Then he'd dig his wiggling fingers into our ribs and tender bellies, drawing out his favorite music of all. The squeals of his two precious sons.

Chapter 9

DON'T MAKE PEOPLE YOUR SPECIAL OCCASION

Thelonious Monk, "'Round Midnight"

It is cruel, you know, that music should be so beautiful. It has the beauty of loneliness, of pain.

—Benjamin Britten

Nusrat Fateh Ali Khan, "Nothing Without You"

[Echo Park, Los Angeles]

Takadhin. Takadhimidha.

I woke in a cold sweat, retching, the sound of the tabla still hanging in the air. It was true. He was gone. And I hadn't been there. Cardiac arrest. They scattered his ashes without me. Where? I didn't even know. It should have been my duty as the firstborn son—to light the fire, to speak the mantras—but Shonu had stepped in because I had refused to go.

I kept hearing Mom's voice.

"Tor baba maragache. He died in his sleep."

I started having panic attacks at Disney Hall. They would start at intermission, right after I threw up in the stage left bathroom, and would last all the way through the second half of the show, all the way through the applause, in the locker room, to the car, all the way through the parking lot, all the way through the drive-through, until I ate my grief, still wearing my tails, his tails, and no matter how much I drank when I got home—one glass, two glasses, the bottle—I'd bolt awake before 3 a.m. hearing his voice—*eyy Potku, eyyy Potkai*—and tell myself the clenched fist in my chest was stress, overwork, too much coffee, too much booze, the gram of hash, the entire-other-person's-worth-of-weight my bones carried around, the eighteen-hour days of rehearsing, touring, teaching, fundraising, flying, planning, procrastinating, performing, pretending, *fucking coward*.

I hadn't said the mantras I was supposed to say, the ones he chanted each morning. Now, I could barely remember them.

Tryambake yajamahe sugandhim…
Om namo Narayana Om namo…

"His last meal was a Whopper."

I hadn't heard Mom's voice in five years. The last time, she'd screamed at me, saying I'd made her homeless. Now, her voice was resigned, robbed of its venom. He had been sick. He'd tried calling, but I'd blocked his number. He'd sent emails, but I'd blocked those, too. In my spam folder was an invitation to Thanksgiving. *Potka, come home, we want you to come*. And when Mom asked me to perform the rites—the mukhagni—I refused. He'd told me I wasn't his son. He'd told me to leave his home.

He had never stopped being my father. And could I ever stop being his son?

I clung to justifications. He could've stopped smoking. He could've managed his diabetes better. Maybe he wanted to die. Maybe he was weak. I was the strong one. I was in therapy, breaking our long lineage of codependency, the intergenerational cycles of trauma. Boundaries.

No excuse for abuse. *He had invited me to his last Thanksgiving.* A son couldn't save a father. It was a meaningless ritual. His journey wasn't mine to complete.

"He kept a picture of you in his wallet."

So I threw myself into overdrive, which meant overwork, which meant overeating. A double rehearsal followed by a two-hour drive in rush hour to meet with a funder who gave me advice instead of dollars—*I'll get the twelve-piece and an extra biscuit*; two grant applications due the week after an international tour—*Could I please have a large sausage and peppers and a bottle of Central Coast Syrah*; managing a staff of interns, a roster of thirty musicians, and three Street Symphony programs each month—*Hey yeah can I get two double-doubles bun well done with grilled onions and an Animal Style fry and a Neapolitan shake?* I had even started smoking Dunhill Reds—his favorite cigarette—enjoying the heady toxic rush of the first drag and the crinkling unwrapping of several layers of dread: plastic wrap and aluminum foil and neat rows of deadly white cylinders that brought me closer to him in morbidity.

"He died under a picture of Maa."

I was right to cut him off, wasn't I? He'd cut me off from my ancestors. And now that he'd become an ancestor, I would cut him off. Why did I need to return for the empty ritual now that his body was gone?

But if that were true, why did I see him everywhere? Why was he haunting me? Toward the end of concerts, my body stopped obeying. The ache in my shoulder knotted through my ribs to the center of my chest and the tendons in my forearm became smoldering cables. My eyes blurred over the black dots on the page. I'd lift my head to steady my vision, and there Dad was: in Front Orchestra during *Firebird*, in the Terrace during Mahler 2, in Orchestra West at the close of Tchaik 6. Each time, I blinked, but the outline stayed, a figure of light.

Now he was the smiling man in the trucker cap at First and Grand. Or the guy in the blazer at Second and Main. The man pushing a shopping cart on Wall. Wearing a yellow jumpsuit at Twin Towers.

And I swear I saw him touching his heart before the Dodge Ram came out of nowhere and my airbags deployed, spinning my crumpled Lexus around in a harsh white haze. I walked away from the wreck unscathed, but for months I kept holding my breath, waiting for the next blow to come out of nowhere.

Thelonious Monk, "'Round Midnight"

[The Midnight Mission]

Sixth Street was cordoned off. Across two blocks, rows of plastic folding tables, covered in pastel-colored tablecloths, had been laid on the road. In the courtyard of The Midnight Mission, Georgia greeted the dozens of bleary-eyed, coffee-gulping volunteers. I didn't have my violin with me, but in a few hours, from the back of a flatbed truck, Street Symphony's jazz band would play for the guests.

"We want to make this a day of sweetness," Georgia said. Even at 7:30 a.m., she was radiant in a long, flowing dress and leather boots, an ankh pendant swinging beside her staff lanyard. "If folks want seconds or thirds, we have plenty of food, okay?" The Mission usually served a thousand meals a day, but on Thanksgiving it would be nearly double that. It wasn't just Skid Row residents who came, but people from all over LA County in need of nourishment—and yes, sweetness.

Nearby, a group of volunteers pulled on plastic aprons, gloves, and hairnets. I caught a glimpse of the tall blonde actress behind me, realized it was Charlize Theron, and looked away. Today wasn't about Hollywood sightings, though I knew Dick Van Dyke and Ed Begley Jr. would be showing up later to dish out mashed potatoes and ham. We all tried not to stare as Mr. T, in an American-flag durag, posed for a selfie with a Mission staffer.

I was ushered to my station: plucking the thorns off roses that would be laid out on pastel-covered tables in the street. No one explained why, but I figured removing the thorns had as much to do with preventing blood-borne illness as it did with "making a day of sweetness." Six other volunteers stood around the cardboard boxes full of roses. I picked up a long-stemmed pink one—its bud still closed—and pressed on a thorn until it snapped off. It was slow, quiet, careful work. One thorn pricked my thumb, drawing a drop of blood like Dad's lancet for testing his blood sugar. I cracked a few stems by accident. I thought of the flower plates at Dad's mukhagni, and had to swallow back a sob. *Get it together, man.* No one else at my station seemed to notice the voice in my head—and I was glad. I picked up the next flower and kept going.

After I laid a dozen roses on each table—sometimes handing guests a single, thornless stem—I delivered desserts to people seated in the street. Here, no one waited in line like at some Depression-era soup kitchen. Instead, meals were brought to guests by hundreds of volunteers. One family asked me for an extra helping of dessert, and from a small blue suitcase covered in Elsa-from-*Frozen* stickers, a woman pulled out a pack of birthday candles and stuck them into the slices of pumpkin pie I'd just set down. I hadn't even noticed the little girl—her head barely reached the table—who sang along with her own birthday song.

From the flatbed truck stage, Mr. T shouted a benediction, and the Street Symphony jazz band kicked off its set with a swinging number. Behind the stage, I spotted a tall Black man with an instrument case slung over his back. I recognized Christopher Mack, an outreach worker from the nearby clinic. He wore a wide-brimmed green hiking hat, lined with a ring of sweat, and even across Sixth Street, filled with thousands of people eating their Thanksgiving meal, I could see him beckon to me.

I'd met Christopher at a few Skid Row community meetings. Afterward, he'd always hung around to play his bass ukulele—that he'd named "Bob"—and sing his favorite tunes, hoping I'd join in.

At one meeting, I learned that Christopher knew these streets better than anyone else I'd met in Skid Row. He'd survived them himself, first during his own recovery from addiction, and later when he chose to return to Skid Row and walk others through the hell he had survived. In the early 2000s, Christopher became an outreach worker, asking the unaskable in tent encampments: questions about needles, sex, and survival. Sometimes he'd be told to fuck off. Other times, he'd be met with a bare, glinting muzzle. He told me that before entering a camp, the best thing he could do was sing, so people knew he was coming. Some would even sing back to him from inside their homes.

Recently, Christopher and a few organizers had founded a community choir that met in the waiting room of a Skid Row clinic. While people waited to get blood drawn or a tooth pulled, they sang the songs they loved: Cat Stevens, Sam Cooke, Bill Withers.

Christopher hugged me in a musk of patchouli and sweat, and I found myself at eye level with a heavy amethyst pendant resting against his chest. He was chewing on a stick of neem, the same kind Dad used to bring back from India.

"It's good that you're here, Vijay. This is good work. But if you really want to make a difference, come back tomorrow."

I didn't know what to say. There was no way I could come back tomorrow. I'd have a three-hour dress rehearsal, then a show at the Philharmonic. Plus, I had a year-end fundraising email to start.

"You'll see piles of rotting turkey six feet high and rats in the street. No cameras or celebs, then."

I stared at him, feeling my palms itch. I'd heard there had been a recent outbreak of bubonic plague in Skid Row. The guy who ran the Union Rescue Mission had lost a leg to flesh-eating bacteria.

As the jazz band played Thelonious Monk's "'Round Midnight," Christopher's eyes drilled into me. "Show up," he said, straightening up. "Don't make these people your special occasion."

I felt thrown off—and more than a little dismissed. The Mission staff had been working like hell, coordinating hundreds of volunteers to feed thousands of people. But something Christopher said got under my skin. What happened here on the days I didn't show up? Until then, even my concerts in Skid Row had felt like special events—occasions where I could play, feel useful, maybe even proud, and then leave. Was I doing something wrong? Or not doing enough?

"You should come sing with us sometime. I know the choir would love to jam with you."

We didn't break eye contact. My silence was already saying too much. I could play a movement of Bach, even sit in on one of their sessions as an observer, but I didn't know how to tell him that musicians from the Philharmonic didn't "jam."

Seeing the panic flicker behind my smile, Christopher threw his head back and let out a rasping, full-body laugh. A saxophone wailed somewhere behind him. Out on the street, Georgia was dancing with a guest in a faded gold tank top, her hair tied in a red bandana. The two of them rolled their hips to the hi-hat, grinning, and grinding, daring each other, laughing harder each time one tried to outdo the other.

"We're people, Vijay, just people. Learn to leave a man with his dignity, and he'll come around."

I had no idea what he meant.

Terry Riley, *In C*

[Wesley Clinic, Skid Row]

A few weeks later, I showed up at the squat concrete clinic with my violin case hanging from my shoulder. On the drive over, I'd caught myself thinking about Terry Riley's *In C*, that wild minimalist experiment I'd once played at Walt Disney Concert Hall. Riley had written it in 1964 for anyone who wanted to join in: fifty-three short musical cells, each player moving through them at their own pace while listening to everyone else. The pulse—one steady C, struck like a heartbeat—held the whole thing together.

When we'd performed it at the LA Phil, there was chaos before it began: musicians scattered across the stage, unsure when to enter, tuning anxiously while the house lights dimmed. But then someone started the pulse and the overlapping patterns shimmered into a kind of fractal order, the music deciding its own shape.

Now, walking into the clinic, I felt Skid Row's own internal pulse, something steady that moved through the streets. Even after years of coming here, my stomach still lurched when I saw a pair of feet sticking out from under a tarp, or caught the sharp smell of the heavy shit—acrid, sweet-sour, like burnt plastic—usually crack, and recently meth. But beneath the shock, I began to notice how people here looked out for one another. Someone called a name across the street. Someone steadied a neighbor's cart. Someone checked in on a man who had not been seen all morning. It was a kind of everyday wisdom I had never learned. I still moved through the neighborhood like an outsider, convinced I was deserving of special treatment just for showing up, when the truth was that I had never understood the simple dignity of being part of a community.

When I announced myself at the clinic window, the security guard behind the bulletproof glass didn't even look up from his cellphone. When I asked where the choir was meeting, he gave a half-shrug and jerked his head toward a locked door before going back to scrolling through his phone. I might as well have been at the DMV. I tried calling Christopher, but the call went straight to voicemail.

I sat down in the waiting area, which smelled like sweat and Jolly Ranchers. A guy to my left had one earbud in, tinny rap blasting from the loose wire. A man across from me scratched at the GPS monitor strapped to his ankle. Two seats over, a woman talked loudly into her phone. When she caught me staring, I looked down quickly. No one cared that I was there, and I realized that no one was supposed to. I had come expecting someone to greet me, maybe to thank me for coming, maybe to walk me back, like I was waiting in a greenroom before going onstage. But no one came.

After twenty restless minutes, I went up to the nurses' station and asked about the choir. One of the nurses simply nodded and swiped her badge against a keypad, unlocking a set of heavy doors. I followed, feeling like an idiot. The hallway smelled of antiseptic and something metallic. Passing a dentist's room, I saw an old woman slumped in the chair, the dentist's gloved hands prying at her mouth. Her tongue lolled bright red against her chin, a thread of bloody drool trailing down to the floor, pooling dark on the tile. I looked away.

Then, faint but unmistakable, I heard it: voices down the hallway, layered and warm, lifting into harmony. The choir was warming up:

"La-la-LA-la-laaa."

My heart pounded, hearing the same vocal warm-up that I'd done as a child at Juilliard, with Shonu by my side. I didn't have a reason to be nervous, but I was. *What was I doing here?* I'd said yes to Christopher, thinking I'd drop in, play a little, maybe say a few words, and leave. I assumed they'd ask me to perform and I'd get to sit back and observe. But now, walking into the middle of their rehearsal, unprepared, unannounced, unintroduced, I didn't know what to expect. I hated being late to anything, but worse than being late was being extraneous. If I wasn't there to perform, what use was I?

"La-la-LA-la-laaa—*Vijay!*"

A dozen people stood in a circle around the table, still singing, the instructor filling in chords at an electric keyboard while Christopher shouted my name. He pointed to a spot beside him, across from a man in a leather bomber jacket and trucker cap, the same getup Dad used to wear when I was a kid. The man gave me a faint smile. The mustache was the same, but gray. My chest clenched. *Is that what he would have looked like before he died?* No. The nose was sharper, the eyes closer together. No scar on his forehead from when I scratched him at four, no birthmark on his cheek. I nodded back, set my violin case on the table, and opened it, waiting for the warm-up to stop so I could play. But Christopher kept singing in the circle, and I was trapped, now expected to sing. Sweat slicked my back under my shirt.

A man on Christopher's left side sang louder and higher than everyone else. His whole body contorted as he pushed for the top note. "La-la-*LA*-la-laaaa!!!" It came out more like a scream.

The instructor cut in, reminding Billy not to force his sound. For a moment he looked sheepish, then broke into a wide, unashamed smile. He nodded, straightened his posture, and kept going. I felt envious of him. Billy didn't care that he wasn't perfect, or even that he was a beginner. Unlike me, he had never learned to feel ashamed of being himself. As the warm-up went on and his screams softened into something closer to singing, I kept sneaking glances at the man in the jacket across from me: his worn New Balance sneakers, the veins on his hands, the bony wrist.

After the warm-up, the instructor went over and sat on a box, bending over to slap the wooden surface with his hands. He played a smooth, easy pulse on the cajón.

Boom-pop! Baboom-baboom-pop!

"Okay, who wants to start?"

What the hell was happening?

A smiling woman in purple rhinestone glasses began a melody—bright, bluesy, a breathy "da-dee-dee-da-daaah." She pointed to a woman with a bandaged arm, who echoed it note for note then spun her own: slower, softer, soulful. My stomach tightened. What note had she started on? Could I match it? Was that a minor sixth, or a major? *Shit.* This is what Christopher had meant by jam: improvisation. I would rather play ten blind auditions than improvise in front of anyone.

I could sight-read anything—Mahler, Brahms, John Adams—but ask me to play without a part in front of me? Total shutdown. Improvisation was for jazz cats and pop stars, not for orchestral musicians. We had been trained to execute the notes, not invent them. Most of my colleagues at the Phil would have shared my terror, except for a handful, like the substitute bass player who gigged in jazz clubs, or the trombonist who played in a salsa band. But for most of us, the idea of making music in the moment, unscored, unscripted? No fucking way.

The beat from the cajón kept going—*boom-pop!*—like the theme from *Jaws*, stalking me, hunting me. And yet here I was, watching this group of folks groove and sway like it was the most natural thing in the world. And me? Stripped of my veneer, failed by overanalysis and perfect pitch, I stood there, frozen and dumb.

As Ms. Rhinestone finished her improv, the woman with the bandaged arm repeated it—not getting it exactly note for note, but closer than I expected—and then she sang a bar of her own, which was repeated by Billy, who listened with bulging eyes and went full Robert Plant, singing something wild, unrepeatable. My mind went blind in panic. *Fuck fuck fuck!* It was Christopher's turn, and he didn't even try to copy Billy, unleashing jazz scat instead: "Zooobah dah de diddly doo doo bah."

Soon it would be my turn, and I had no earthly idea what I could sing. No Beethoven sonata, no Mozart concerto, no Brahms symphony could live inside the pulse of that cajón. When Christopher finished, the room turned to me, waiting. My heartbeat filled my ears and I couldn't swallow. My fists closed. I stood there like a kid who'd missed the bus. No one bailed me out with a scat line or a riff, and at last the instructor lifted his hands off the cajón and the pulse slowly drifted away.

With nothing left, I reached for my violin. I had no plan, no tune in mind. But as soon as the bow touched the string, sound poured out of me:

D-1-2-2-23212-4-3-2-1-D-D-1-21-D...

My bow shook during *23212*, and my fingers were in a slick of sweat. *What was I even playing?* I didn't recognize the melody that had come welling from my memory. A dip onto the G string, a simple turn back to the D, repeating. *Wait, this?*

"Boro Asha Kore"? The song I'd played at Durga Pujo?

I kept playing.

A-1-2-3...

I moved to the A string. My bow was steadier now, but I could barely hear myself over the high, needling pitch of panic in my ear. Of all the tone poems, lieder, symphonies, cantatas, and sonatas I could play blindfolded. *Why this? Why now?* I kept playing, gripped by terror, as Tagore's anthem poured out of me. I'd never learned the words from my parents, and now it was too late. I still had no idea what the words of the song meant, and now, even the taste of Bengali had faded from my lips.

I forgot the ending of the song, so I played the beginning again, searching for any kind of cadence, before I stopped. The choir offered a kind, scattered round of applause, and Billy whooped with delight while the instructor snapped his fingers in time, as if to reassure me that I'd done something brave or impressive, but I couldn't take any of it in, because all I could see was the man in the leather jacket shifting in his seat, haunted by his neutral eyes.

I bent to pack up my violin, trying to keep my face arranged in something like gratitude or humility—maybe even charm—but all I felt was the sludgy aftertaste of shame. I turned to leave, trying to disappear with whatever dignity I could muster. But before I could get past the doorframe, Christopher stepped into my path and took my free hand. He placed a heavy chunk of black tourmaline into my palm. As my fingers closed around it, the stone was cool and smooth in its striated surfaces, but jagged at the edges.

"Keep coming back, Vijay," Christopher said. "Keep walking your steps with us."

I knew Christopher knew about Dad. I hadn't told him directly, but he'd seen the Facebook posts, the condolences pouring in. I also knew he'd recently lost his son. He wasn't trying to corner me—he was offering something he knew I needed: a place, a path, some grace. He could see that I was shattered, and he was trying to meet me there, out of his own shattering.

I almost gave in. I almost let go. I almost let the lump in my throat rise into the scream I hadn't been able to scream since the day Mom called. But if I broke now, I wasn't sure I'd ever stop breaking, and after that there would be nothing left of me at all. Looking up into Christopher's eyes, I felt so small.

I smiled, waving off Christopher's warmth, but inside, I hardened like the stone in my hand. No, I had no steps to walk. I couldn't really believe that all Christopher wanted was for me to be myself.

Who *was* that, anyway?

Benjamin Britten, *War Requiem*—"Dies Irae"

[Los Angeles, London, Worcester]

Maggie and I ended things quietly. After she left, I folded her things into boxes, keeping my hands busy so I wouldn't have to feel anything. Soon I slipped into a routine that passed for living. A cocktail while I answered emails. Two glasses of wine while I hunted for grants or let Netflix run. At some point a pizza would arrive, and I would finish the bottle and sometimes open another, watching the screen blur with the edges of my own numbness. And then, in the middle of the night, I'd wake in a panic, hearing Dad's voice, his breath, his playful nightmare rhythms hanging in the air.

Takadhin. Ta dhin.

At the LA Phil, I played four concerts and four rehearsals a week. On my days off, I crisscrossed the city—from Mount Baldy to the Pacific Ocean—pitching donors and partners, and building Street Symphony into a six-figure nonprofit. Backstage at Disney Hall, I taught myself to write grant proposals for foundations and arts councils. In the middle of it all, I practiced harder than ever, preparing for the Philharmonic's associate concertmaster audition. It didn't leave much time to think, and that was exactly the point.

I had to win that job: the job my teacher had held, the job Dad had wanted for me. I wanted to have the same authority as Mr. Dicterow, because then, maybe I could make others feel the way he made me feel: like I mattered. The job would also mean half the season off and three times the pay, and to top it all—an even better violin than the one I played: a Stradivarius. Maybe if I won that job, I would have enough time to run Street Symphony properly, enough time to build a studio at a conservatory, enough time to drop a few dozen pounds, enough time to remake myself into someone worth loving. Maybe I'd finally have enough time to be enough.

But when I came in as runner-up at the LA audition, I walked into my dressing room and slapped myself across the face, hard enough to leave welts across my cheek. I packed up my violin and told myself I'd try again. Becoming a concertmaster was Dad's dream for me, and as long as I still lived inside a world built on his dreams, failure wasn't an option.

A few months later, I was invited to play a two-week concertmaster stint with the Philharmonia Orchestra in London. At the Three Choirs Festival—where Handel's oratorios had once shaken the rafters—I led six monumental programs in as many days: Mahler's *Resurrection,* Dvořák's *Stabat Mater,* Britten's *War Requiem.*

Britten had written his *Requiem* after World War II, setting the Latin Mass for the Dead amid Wilfred Owen's battlefield poems, texts from across millennia reflecting on a world reduced to ash. The first rehearsal at the Philharmonia began with the tolling of distant bells, then the orchestra's eruptions. By the time the boys' chorus entered—pure voices floating above the wreckage—I felt utterly unconsoled by music that made violence reckon with beauty.

By the fourth night, though, every note I played felt like agony. The ache had spread from my shoulder to my ribs, each breath needling the cartilage between them. On our only day off, while the rest of the orchestra went back to London to record the score for a World War II tank movie with Brad Pitt, I stayed behind in my hotel room, curtains drawn, with an ice pack pinned between my elbow and ribs. All week, I'd barely kept it together, play-acting at being a concertmaster, and now, without the music, I could feel the fault line widening in myself.

I thought being a concertmaster would mean having a chance to shape the music. I'd played well enough that week, but one botched shift during a solo threw me off for the rest of the concert, and I relished having a reason to hate myself. Back in my room, while watching cricket highlights on SkySports, I relived the concert in my head, rewinding every missed note, every cue I gave too soon or too late. When the ice packs softened into useless goo, I peeled off my shirt and stared at the lumpy flesh sagging over my rib. I pressed into the angry ridge with my knuckles until my eyes watered, savoring the electric welt.

The moment I missed that note, I had seen him sitting in the chapel.

Dad.

~

There was no lack of talent in Skid Row. Some members of Christopher's choir had sung in church or performed in regional theaters, and some, on larger stages. Some had come to LA chasing the dream of Hollywood only to wake up in the nightmare of an addiction. Others had survived violence, incarceration, or addiction and—after recovering in Skid Row—wanted to give back to the community that had saved their lives.

After my first visit to Christopher's choir, whenever I ran into his singers at Street Symphony events at the Mission, they'd ask when I was coming back to sing with them. I didn't believe that they wanted me to be their friend or become part of their community. I couldn't believe that anyone would want to just hang out with me, so instead, I gave them what I thought they wanted: the currency of my world. A chance to perform with Street Symphony. Or to be on TV. Or featured in the *LA Times*. A chance to be famous.

When news crews started following me around Skid Row, I'd invite Christopher or a few choir members to tell their stories. I told myself that was how change happened: *Pass the mic, use your platform, lift someone else up.* And a part of me genuinely believed that Hollywood wasn't so far from Skid Row, that a good news story could build awareness, and that advocacy could lead to change.

But really, in every soundbite, every smile, every thumbs-up I gave from behind a camera, I was repeating the same message that had been drilled into me as a child: *Don't let me down.* Dad had shown me love by making me famous. Now, I was trying to offer the same thing to others—Maybe because it had been the surest form of love I had received.

One morning in early 2015, my phone buzzed with a 213 area code, a downtown LA number.

"Is this Street Symphony? I'm a singer. I lived on San Julian for ten years."

I glanced around my apartment—empty bottles, takeout boxes—the stale fog of another lost night. By now, I'd learned how to field unexpected calls, adjusting my tone as quickly as Dad changed languages while running his travel agency. In a heartbeat, I could tell if I was talking to a potential funder, or a reporter, or a musician. Recently, I'd been getting calls from community organizers across the country, asking if I could help them start something like Street Symphony in their own city.

But this one was different. A reedy tenor poured through the speaker, breathless and hard to follow. My head pounded with a particularly nasty mixed-alcohol and entire-large-sausage-and-peppers-pizza hangover. My laptop was still open to the previous night's *Black Mirror* Netflix binge, and as I closed a browser, I brought up the grant portal for the National Endowment for the Arts and a few dozen unanswered emails.

"I've been singing since I was a kid, man—but the pain down here, it's too much. It's a fucking war zone. You could get PTSD just being down here."

Frank was a Desert Storm combat veteran. He'd spent a decade in a tent on San Julian Street before finding a subsidized apartment downtown. Church choirs had been his lifeline.

A 2014 *LA Times* article had reported that 4,600 veterans were living on the streets of LA and that suicide was the leading cause of death among them. For much of the previous year, I'd been driving to Veterans Affairs in Long Beach to launch a concert series, funded by my first grant from the National Endowment for the Arts. In a cramped room with linoleum floors and flickering fluorescents, I'd played for small groups of veterans—some in wheelchairs, others silent behind crossed arms and caps stitched with their service branch. One man, whose cap read "IRAQ," asked if I knew "Danny Boy." As I played, he buried his face in his palms and sobbed. But after a few visits, the VA canceled our concerts. With a five-year patient backlog, there was no time for music. I mailed a check back to the NEA, hoping to find another reason to apply one day.

Back in my apartment, I asked Frank how I could help.

"Listen man, you gotta do *Messiah*. I need to hear it before I die. I don't know how long I've got. Can you imagine?" His voice cracked. "Handel's *Messiah* in Skid Row?"

I glanced at the laptop screen, still glowing, expectant.

I couldn't imagine what it would take to bring a full orchestra and chorus to Skid Row. I couldn't imagine what it would mean to this man, this veteran whose inner war might never end, whose home had once been a stretch of cracked pavement on San Julian Street. Before heading to rehearsal, I made myself a pot of coffee and sat down to write the beginning of the grant proposal: "Street Symphony presents Handel's *Messiah*, in Skid Row."

What was the saying? *Go big or go home?*

I might as well go big, because I knew I could never go home again.

Chapter 10

SIMPLE GIFTS

Esmail, *Take What You Need*

Attention, taken to its highest degree, is the same thing as prayer.

—Simone Weil

George Frideric Handel, *Messiah*, HWV 56—"For unto Us a Child Is Born"

[Church of the Nazarene, Skid Row]

"For unto us a child is booooooo-oooooooo-oooooooo-oooooooo-oooooooo-oooooooo-oooooooo-rn!"

Along and across the frozen Hudson River, my brother and I would sing the choruses of *Messiah*. On the way to New York City, our voices spun out in impossibly long melismas as our breath fogged the back seat windows of the Nissan Sentra. When Dad died, Shonu became the eldest son who ignited the sacrificial fire—the mukhagni—at the crematorium. For most of our childhood, I had outshone him, pulling in more than my share of Dad's attention. Now I felt like I had abandoned him. It seemed difficult to believe that there was anything

I'd ever be able to do that could ever earn my brother's affection, or forgiveness.

But I still believed in *Messiah*, not just because it had comforted me as a child or because it scored every December of my life, but because *Messiah* is the most overperformed piece in classical music. The "Hallelujah" chorus was the stuff of car commercials, cartoons, sitcom punchlines, even flash mobs. Everyone knew it, even if they didn't know they knew it. For generations, it had been the gateway drug to classical music, claimed by choir nerds, boomers, Baroque purists, and Mormon Tabernacle fans alike. Each December, concert halls across the world belted out sing-along *Messiahs*—just enough classical reverence without getting too Jesus-y. And the best part? *Messiah* came with a guaranteed payoff: No matter how jaded the room, when that chorus hit, people stood. Resurrection: guaranteed. Donations: inevitable.

I wanted people to stand up for Skid Row, in Skid Row, and in my naïveté, I believed the problem was ignorance: that people simply didn't know about Skid Row. I thought all they needed was a reason to come, hear the music, and they would be changed.

Change *would* come. Just not the way I thought.

On a November evening of 2015, I led a group of musicians out of The Midnight Mission's parking lot for our first *Messiah* rehearsal. Until then, I had known Skid Row in daylight, on my schedule and terms. At dusk, though, I felt like an intruder. People unrolled sleeping bags and zipped tents closed for the night. Others sat cross-legged against the Mission's concrete wall, wrapped in thin blankets as sirens screamed past.

I stepped into the street, skirting a quickly spreading puddle of urine. Beside me, an oboist whispered, "Is it safe for us to be here?"

I didn't answer, thinking about the people who would be sleeping outside that night. Georgia had told me that on the streets of Skid Row, women were raped in their tents almost every night.

Over the past several months, while juggling a full-time LA Phil schedule, I'd been bouncing between fundraising lunches in Beverly Hills or Pasadena and open mics in shelters and community centers, often playing a bit of Bach and then pitching the upcoming *Messiah*. Organizers in Skid Row smiled politely at my zeal, asking if they could attend the concert. When I told them that the concert was supposed to be *for them*, they seemed suspicious. "I've never been to a concert before! Can I bring my sister?" However, donors were suspicious for the same reasons as the oboist. One donor in Pasadena said they didn't feel safe driving to downtown LA, much less Skid Row, because there was "nowhere to park." Instead of a check, I drove home with their dusty Yamaha keyboard rattling in the trunk of my Prius.

I'd pulled together an orchestra of two dozen, including a few colleagues from the LA Phil. Amy, who had organized the a cappella choir at the Mission, had recruited some of the best singers in Los Angeles, most of them from the famed Los Angeles Master Chorale. I heard them before we entered the Church of the Nazarene, a ground-floor warehouse in the heart of Skid Row with brown carpet that reeked of urine and Febreze, laughing those full-throated, big-hearted singer laughs. Joy seemed to follow them wherever they went.

Inside the church, I saw several dozen plastic bags from CVS and Walgreens lining the walls. The singers had taken up a collection to assemble kits of essentials to be distributed after our concert. Now, I watched twenty world-class vocalists place travel-sized soaps, tampons, socks, toothbrushes, hand towels, and granola bars into hundreds of paper bags.

My Philharmonic colleagues were helping, too. One had appointed himself as the volunteer stage manager, setting out chairs and music stands, passing around library parts. Joanne tested the Yamaha, which let out a wheeze like a ballpark organ. Matt ran a tricky line from one of the arias. In the corner of the room, a trumpet player warmed up with something that almost sounded like *Taps*. From outside, people peered in, wondering what was happening. A few singers waved to them, inviting them to the following week's concert.

Most of these musicians were used to greenrooms, catered lunches, and private warm-up suites, and although they had none of that today, they seemed glad for the communal, self-organized chaos. As Amy called the room to order, I saw the veteran Frank step into the room, his eyes wide. In his hands he held a dog-eared score. I had invited him to sing the tenor part during the rehearsal, but he seemed cowed by the sight before him—a full choir and orchestra about to sing *Messiah*. He sat quietly in the corner, watching, until Daniel—the tenor who had brought the Mission dayroom to a halt with his rendition of "Shenandoah"—brought him into the chorus like a reluctant dance partner at a wedding.

Amy's singers had been joined by Christopher's Skid Row choir, along with local church and community choristers. Even as the wail of sirens threaded through the night outside, the music felt alive. We whooped and clapped for solos. Professionals who could sing *Messiah* from memory leaned in beside vocalists from Skid Row, some of whom had arrived in Los Angeles only recently, carrying burdens of addiction, incarceration, or trauma.

At the rehearsal break, Daniel pulled Frank aside for an impromptu, on-the-spot voice lesson. Frank's tone was bright and reedy, but his breath gave out before the end of a phrase. On one of our calls, he told me that when his PTSD nightmares got bad, he would sit up in his tent and rock back and forth, singing "Comfort Ye" until his breathing steadied. Now, Daniel was asking Frank to sing the same aria, before a room of professional musicians.

Frank threw his hands up.

"There's no way I can do it man, no way."

Daniel smiled, asking him to try. Frank refused.

"There's no way I can't hold a note that long!"

Daniel took Frank's broad hand and placed it on his own rib cage.

"Here. Feel this. Breathe from here."

Then he lifted Frank's other hand to his chest.

"And here. From here."

They breathed together, and again Frank tried: *Comfort. Comfort. Comfort.* His voice swelled, steadier each time. A few of Amy's singers stopped what they were doing to listen. One gave a whoop.

"You've got some pipes, man! Maybe *you* should be the one singing the solo."

Frank glowed.

~

Walking through Skid Row, one saw art everywhere: mosaics made from tile and bottle caps shimmering in the sun. Some murals were reverent, others furious. Sculptures rose from tent frames and shopping carts: mannequin heads with feather boas, reclaimed tinsel, crucifixes of crutches and duct tape. Loudspeakers strapped to bicycles carried R&B, gospel, Sade, and cumbia, all in counterpoint with each other.

Here, reinventing oneself was an art form. On Sixth Street, someone once turned the bare wall over a tent into a four-poster bed, flanked by spray-painted dressers and a high canopy, set before a mountain moonscape. Above it, in a cartoon thought bubble, hovered a single plea: "SAVE HUMANITY." Weeks later, the mattress was gone, but the mural remained for a few weeks, before it was whitewashed back into a blank canvas, ready for the next artist to arrive.

In December 2015, in the gym of The Midnight Mission, Daniel stood in a beam of sunlight, singing the very words on which Frank's life had once depended.

Comfort ye. Comfort ye, my people.

I sat in the orchestra behind him, playing a tender, pulsing *accompagnato,* staring past him into the crowd of hundreds that had come to hear our *Messiah.* Under the basketball hoop at the back of the gym, a knot of police officers leaned against the wall. Frank—wearing a tuxedo shirt under a windbreaker—watched Daniel, mouthing every word. The room was packed with residents, volunteers, and Mission staff, but still, I was disappointed. In the weeks leading up to the event, I'd run myself ragged—photocopying and binding booklets of sheet music, wrangling musicians, sending blind, hopeful emails to every county supervisor, the mayor, and any other powerful person I could think of. At the Little Tokyo Kinko's, I gnawed my cuticles bloody as I watched the print-job price jump left another decimal place. I had already ordered chairs, printed T-shirts, designed the flyers myself, begged a church to loan us enough music stands, and rented a battered PA system from a hole-in-the-wall shop in Echo Park. But even after weeks of emailing and self-composed press releases, of in-person meetings and countless phone calls, not a single official or news crew had shown up. No mayor, or county supervisors. No power brokers. No donors with clout.

In my mind, I had already failed, and we weren't even five measures into the first recitative.

And cry unto her, that her warfare is accomplished.

A voice cut through the crowd. I looked up. In the front row, Brother Jubilee, wearing his bowler hat, pointed a single finger at the ceiling, shouting "YES!" Around him, others murmured their assent. I glanced at my colleagues, unsure what to think, still stuck in my own funk. Some in the orchestra seemed stunned, but Amy and the others in the choir smiled broadly, encouraging the man.

When Daniel launched into "Ev'ry Valley Shall Be Exalted," a woman wrapped in a blanket leapt to her feet, spinning down the aisle, her cape flaring with each turn. By the time Daniel finished, the room had erupted in ovation. He bowed, then slipped back to the chorus, where Amy rubbed the space between his shoulders.

I knew music would bring joy to Skid Row. But in my naïveté, I also believed that this bright afternoon performance of *Messiah* might draw in the power brokers of Los Angeles—developers, donors, lawmakers—and that if they experienced that same joy, they might feel moved, or even shamed, into doing something for Skid Row. Hollywood moguls and serial philanthropists were donating hundreds of millions of dollars to museums and concert halls all over LA. I convinced myself that if I could just get the people who mattered—or who I thought mattered—into that room, my work would be done. The music would take care of the rest.

In the "Hallelujah" chorus, Daniel waved to Frank, who had been singing softly in the front row. The gesture was unmistakable: *Come up and join us!* Frank's eyes went wide. He rose. And as he stepped onto the stage, three hundred people rose with him.

And He shall reign forever and ever!

But the shift wasn't in the audience. It was in us.

A few weeks into the new year, Amy emailed asking what our plans were for next year's *Messiah*. Next year? I stared at the screen, unsure how to respond. I thought this would be a one-and-done sort of thing. She wanted singing workshops so Skid Row residents could get to know us better. One of the singers, an occupational therapist, offered to work with women in shelters. Another suggested a writing workshop, so residents could share their own stories.

I had counted on philanthropists, not musicians. I had thought the people who would be moved to make a difference would be the ones with money, not the ones with voices. But it was the musicians who actually wanted to show up. They didn't see any of it as extra, or as charity: to them, showing up was the point.

I hadn't expected musicians to care this much after the music stopped. At the Philharmonic, once a concert was over, we were already preparing for whatever concert came next. We had little time to process the music we played, even while we played it. But even though the singers were just as busy as I was, they seemed to care what happened next at Street Symphony, maybe even more than I did.

I wanted to be more like them, especially the singers, who laughed loudly, cried in public, and didn't hide how much they loved their work. They didn't hide how much they loved me, either. Throughout the months following *Messiah*, they pulled me into bear hugs at Disney Hall and the Bowl, treating me like one of their own.

Amy told me Daniel was already giving Frank regular lessons—getting him ready to sing the "Comfort Ye" solo by next year. I *mhmmed* on the phone, holding back what I really thought. That aria was exposed, demanding, and it had to be perfect. *Would Frank really be ready?*

But Daniel had his own reasons, that he kept to himself. I knew that Amy and several other singers wanted to do whatever they could to help out in Skid Row. One soprano, who had trained as an occupational therapist, wanted to see if she could work with older adults in SROs. An alto volunteered to become a teaching assistant in Christopher's choir. A tenor started going to the Mission to serve meals and took his daughters with him. And after a concert in a county jail, one bass admitted to me that he really wanted to sing at reentry centers, because he had himself been incarcerated for a time. Everyone seemed to have their own motivations for being part of Street Symphony, and not a single one of these artists seemed to expect me to pay them. In fact, they insisted that they were the ones getting the gift.

Eighteen months later, I learned that Daniel's leukemia—once in remission—had returned, and this time, it was devastating. That December, we performed our Skid Row *Messiah* in his memory, before a posterboard photo of him gazing into the beyond he had become.

Reena Esmail, *Ragamala*

[Twin Towers Jail, Los Angeles]

"We've just played music written by two very dead Austrian guys."

The dorm cracked with sudden, defiant laughter. Our violist had made a joke about powdered wigs and tights after we played Haydn and Mozart for a group of women inside Twin Towers Jail. In the front row, one woman had kept her eyes closed throughout the music, her head tilted back as if she was letting the sound restore her. Others had quietly wiped their faces. By then I'd learned to expect that—laughter, tears, or some uneasy mix—when we played in the county jails. Like the men at the facility across the street, most of the women here were dark-skinned. Fluorescent lights hummed above us. I raised my hand and the room quietened.

"But we actually have a composer with us today." I turned to the caramel-skinned, almond-eyed woman seated at the edge of the dormitory pod. Reena Esmail rose with quiet confidence and stepped forward.

She introduced a string quartet based on ragas, which she called "scales with personality." The women straightened, suddenly alert to the person who, until a moment ago, had simply been sitting among them in one of the same, strangely molded plastic chairs that were impossible to use as weapons. Reena explained that the word "raga" comes from Sanskrit for "color" or "passion," each one a mood, a story. Some belong to a time of day: Ahir Bhairav at dawn, Puriya at sunset. Others summon elemental forces: Basant invokes the season of spring, Deepak lights a fire, and Malhaar brings rain. She had woven a garland of them into this quartet—*Ragamala*—each movement shaped by a different raga.

Before each section, I asked her to sing a phrase so the women could hear the voice behind the music. She didn't call herself a singer, but she closed her eyes, lifted her hand, fingers pinched in air, and let a soft, nasal "aaahhh" float over the drone I played on open strings. The jail's edges seemed to blur, concrete and steel giving way into a shimmering haze. In her voice, I felt a tug deep in my gut, as if I were hearing someone I'd known in another life. For a moment, we all forgot where we were.

Like me, Reena was the child of South Asian immigrants—the daughter of a Goan Catholic mother and a Shia Muslim father from Gujarat who had met, improbably, in Orlando, Florida. Music had poured out of Reena first through a three-quarter-sized guitar, later the piano. Her father's work in marketing had brought the family west, and she'd grown up a middle-class kid down the street from the Hollywood Bowl—classmates with the children of Hollywood A-listers. Years later, she studied composition at Juilliard. My mother once spotted a recital poster with her name on it and pointed, delighted: "Dekecho? Another Desi!"

When I first met Reena in India, she was there on a Fulbright, trying to find ways to integrate *do-re-mi-fa* with *sa-re-ga-ma*. "I want to introduce these systems to each other in a way where they're not just playing past each other, but talking to each other, where they can show their best selves to one another, you know?"

Each time the quartet finished a movement of *Ragamala* at the Towers, there was a cheerful howl of applause—followed by total attention, as they awaited the next flower on Reena's garland. The intimate Bihag came first, then contemplative Malkauns, springtime Basant, and the lilting, elfin Jog, halfway between "major" and "minor"—the music like an inscrutable *commedia dell'arte* mask. The second movement was a complicated dance—off-kilter mixed meters that kept us on our toes, counting like fiends: 5/16, 10/16, 7/16, 3/16, 13/16, 9/16, 4/16. The inmates tried clapping along, but laughed when they lost time, slapping knees or shoulders. We, on the other hand, turned red with each of our errors, embarrassed to be screwing up in front of the composer.

Reena and I had gone to all the same schools, but at different times—Juilliard, Yale—and we'd each gotten the usual questions: "You must know..." But instead of meeting in a conservatory hallway or at some industry gala, we'd met in Jaipur, during a festival in the old city. I was launching Street Symphony, and she was there on a Fulbright between graduate degrees, developing a musical language that bridged Hindustani improvisation and Western notation—ragas written out on staff paper. I could have talked to her for seven lifetimes.

Playing Reena's music felt natural to my ear but awkward in my hands. Her lyrical, expressive, unpredictable music moved like quicksilver. In rehearsal, my colleagues kept looking at me as if I were the authority on Indian classical music, but I'd never trained in it. Even though I had chanted in Sanskrit and learned Robindroshongit songs like "Boro Asha Kore" by ear and by heart, I hadn't grown up improvising or thinking in ragas. I knew what a raga was, but I couldn't have told you which one summoned fire, or rain, or twilight. But Reena could, and the miracle of her work wasn't in writing down an improvised tradition, but rather, in preserving an instance of a raga's expression into a form that could be grasped by Western classical musicians. Playing her *Ragamala*, I could hear both sides of myself—the arias I knew, and the ragas I wished I did—finally in conversation with each other, within me.

On our way out of the jail, the musicians stumbled over themselves in the elevator, apologizing to Reena for the mistakes we'd made in the performance. It wasn't often we played for a living composer. But I wondered if what we were sorry for wasn't the missed notes, but that we were leaving our audience behind.

The women hadn't wanted the concert to end. They'd asked for an encore, and Reena obliged, singing an improvisation in Jog while I played a drone on my D and A strings. It was a farewell in half-shade, half-sorrow, for women we'd probably never see again, women we would never forget.

Igor Stravinsky, *The Rite of Spring*—"Danse Sacrale"

[Echo Park, Los Angeles]

WHAM! WHAM! WHAM! WHAM! WHAM! WHAM! WHAM! WHAM! WHAM! WHAM! WHAM!

The timpanist raised his mallets high over the kettledrum's vibrating membrane of goatskin—*bom-bom ba-bom, bomba-bom-bambabom!*—while strings shrieked and cackled their *ka-ka-ka*. Muted trombones sliced the air with a stuttering *yatatatata-tam!*, and between terrifying silences, the whole orchestra growled and screamed and slashed, tightening the circle, closing in on the final, necessary, required sacrifice: a young girl dancing herself to death.

The 1913 premiere of Stravinsky's ballet, the choreography of a pagan fertility ritual, had sparked hostility from the Parisian audience, but had changed music forever. Stravinsky's music pushed every boundary of what an orchestra could do: This was no traipsing waltz of the old world, no genteel inner romanticism for well-heeled pearl-clutchers. No, Stravinsky's orchestra was an elemental rage that would make death metal look like child's play. Ninety years later, Esa-Pekka Salonen would choose to open Walt Disney Concert Hall with *The Rite of Spring*, and even though the LA Phil badasses could play this music as easily as we played Beethoven or Mozart, I was still frantically hissing a mantra of pulse to myself as if my life depended on it: 2/16, 3/16, 5/16, 2/8. One misplaced slash, one missed sixteenth-note rest, and everyone would know: I was just another human being, holding on for dear life.

I lived as if an attack could come from anywhere, as if everyone were the enemy, especially myself. I couldn't fix grief or guilt, but I could master every room I entered. I knew I couldn't soothe any of it, but I could control auditions, rehearsals, committees, the machinery of excellence. I knew that if I wanted to stay in the room, I had to be at the front of it. So, I kept trying to win: every excerpt, every grant, every award. I was still performing the son Dad had told me I had to be, long after he was gone.

First, I tackled the world of nonprofits. I joined one board of directors, then another. Then, conservatories. I joined one faculty, and then started to guest lecture at another. I learned strategic planning from consultants, accounting from CFOs, and board development from executive directors. After a year, I could pitch a vision, refine a mission, and write a five-year plan. I learned to write six-figure grant proposals that I was told made panelists cry. I built budgets, tracked KPIs, and crafted timelines that spelled out exactly what would happen, what it would cost, and how we'd prove it worked. Soon, I spoke fluent nonprofit.

And most of all, I learned how to keep funders happy, especially the ones who would never set foot in Skid Row. They seemed the most concerned with where their money was going, even though they didn't want to see their dollars at work. So I sent quarterly reports, handwritten notes, and end-of-year reports and had long meetings to recount, and often justify, what Street Symphony was doing.

But all of this was a performance. I did it all so I could keep playing music in the only places where I never had to pretend: Skid Row and the county jail. Those were the rooms where I didn't have to be extraordinary, but could simply be. And though I didn't realize it, going there was healing me.

Once, a therapist asked if I'd noticed how the places I chose to play—jails, shelters—mirrored my childhood home: places filled with rupture and chaos, where I played to make others—and myself—feel safe. It wouldn't even have occurred to me that I was never in physical pain when I played in Skid Row.

Over time, I realized that what I felt in those rooms was not courage but a new kind of self-knowing, a re-cognition: The people I played for were not "the least among us," but people whose lives had been ruptured by forces they'd never chosen. Some part of me understood what it meant to feel cast out of the places that were supposed to love you.

The Canadian physician Dr. Gabor Maté writes that trauma is not the broken story of what happened to you, but the broken story you come to believe about yourself. Without knowing it, every time I walked into a shelter or a clinic with my violin, I was loosening the grip of my own story, rewiring my relationship to my instrument, to music, and to myself.

In Skid Row, I did not have to pretend that everything was fine or that I'd earned my way into some gleaming, enviable life. I could stand with my violin and feel the truth of my own fractures, and no one turned away. Gradually it became the one place where my whole body unclenched. The tension I carried through Disney Hall—the tight jaw, the rigid posture, the careful mask I wore without thinking—dropped the moment I stepped into a clinic waiting room or the courtyard of the Mission, where I didn't have to impress anyone, or outplay anyone. People listened, or they slept, or they drifted in and out, and nothing collapsed.

Looking back, I can see that all that machinery, all that mastery, was simply survival, my way to keep the world from seeing how fragile I really was. Skid Row never required me to be a maestro, but for a while longer, I felt like I needed to continue justifying my presence there.

In truth, music—and Skid Row—were teaching me how to start over.

Reena Esmail, *Take What You Need*

[Skid Row / Hollywood Bowl]

Over coffee one afternoon, Reena Esmail told me how much she missed the constant music of India: the aarti and adhan drifting from temples and minarets, the women singing from verandas as they struck dust from carpets, their Bollywood tunes spilling into the street. In the Hollywood Hills, her parents' neighborhood was too quiet, too guarded. Security cameras peered from behind topiary hedges. No one said hello. No one had to. The Hollywood sign, a canyon away, might as well have read "KEEP OUT."

The only place in Los Angeles that eased her homesickness was Skid Row. She wanted to get more involved with Street Symphony. I assumed she meant composing something, but when she asked to join Christopher's choir, I judged her. *That* choir? Maybe her career was stalling. I couldn't have known that, at the same time, she was writing *This Love Between Us*, an oratorio for Juilliard and Yale setting sacred texts from seven religions alongside sitar and tabla.

Thinking she needed something to do, I offered her a commission: an anthem for Skid Row. Short, simple, easy enough for Christopher's choir to learn, easy enough to wedge into the next Messiah Project like a musical appetizer. Maybe it would save face with Christopher's choir after my humiliating improv session. Or maybe it was my first genuine attempt to follow through on what Amy and her singers had already shown me—that having the community singers join us at *Messiah* wasn't extra—it was the point.

Either way, I wouldn't be around to see it. That spring I was on tour with the LA Phil—London, Paris, Lucerne, Luxembourg, Amsterdam—while Reena led the workshops without me. The truth was, I was too busy to get in her way, and not invested enough to worry about how it would all unfold. For better or worse, I wasn't expecting much beyond a brief new piece, a small amuse-bouche before the main course, which, of course, was *Messiah*.

When Christopher's improvisation game—the same one that had sent me into a blind panic—came around, Reena jumped in without hesitation. She answered the call with a quick Hindustani phrase, fluid and sure. The choir lit up and begged for more. At the next session, they asked her to teach them a raga. Reena sat at the table and began with a simple melody, tracing its curve in the air with her thumb and forefinger. She nodded for them to echo. At first, the men barely changed pitch, some voices too soft to hear. Reena only smiled, simplified, and kept going.

She started with the basses: *na na na hummm, na na na hummm.* Then gave the rest a rhythmic pulse: *dha tarekita, dhum tarekita, nom tarekita.* Small gestures on small gestures. Above it, she began to improvise—bittersweet phrases in Jog, a raga of enchantment and union, hovering between worlds: neither major nor minor, rooted yet open, ancient yet alive.

But after the warm-up, Reena turned to her new composition—a call-and-response built on lyrics she'd found in the most unlikely place: a yoga studio. For months, she'd been taking a class where students could choose a Post-it from a board, each with a small phrase to guide their practice. One could "Take Hope" for their backbend, "Take Pride" in Warrior II, or "Take Time" in Savasana. Each word gave the practice direction, a way to meet whatever they were holding. Reena set those words into a call-and-response, patterned like the "*la-la-LA-la-laaa*" warm-ups Christopher's choir always began with:

Take a moment... Take a moment.
Take a breath... Take a breath.

Like a vocal vinyasa, the phrases unfolded into invitations to *take care* and *take hope* in their own voices; to *take a step, take a chance* into new sonorities; to *take pride* and *take joy* in everything they had accomplished.

After a few rounds, the singing gave way to sharing. Sharon said she needed the courage to call her estranged daughter. Christopher said he needed hope. Brian, Christopher's sponsee—who had come to Skid Row with a few months clean after a seven-year-long heroin addiction—was ready to take the next step in sobriety. Some spoke, while others listened. Then someone asked if they could sing the whole song over again.

Reena realized that the real music was what was happening in the space between verses. The next week, she wrote a short loop of harmonies to play underneath the speaking, a kind of musical meditation to facilitate not just the singing, but the storytelling, too.

After their sessions at the clinic, Christopher and Brian walked Reena back to her car, guiding her through the streets they knew so well—streets where a woman walking alone could be a target. Reena had looked after them musically. Now, it was their turn to look after her.

When I returned from the orchestra tour, Reena gave me an update, laying out a plan for summer workshops at a nearby school, and then, in the fall, another round of sessions at the clinic. To me, the whole process was taking far too long. I'd assumed she'd dash off something in a few weeks and we'd teach it to the choir, the same way they were learning covers of their favorite pop or gospel tunes.

And when she told me the title of her piece—*Take What You Need*—I cringed. I'd wanted something punchier. Had I made a mistake asking her to write this piece? When the process dragged on, I dropped hints, light pressure. I mentioned that a local news crew might be coming to the next workshop. I said it like it was no big deal, my voice bright and breezy, assuming she'd respond the way I would: with urgency.

But after my needling, Reena finally sent me a demo recording she'd made during the summer workshop at a nearby conservatory—Amy and three singers with a classroom of elementary-school kids. Reena's message came in as I was driving to the Hollywood Bowl, a few minutes from the downbeat for that morning's LA Phil rehearsal. I was already running late, but I hit play anyway, thinking I'd skip through.

At first, the song felt too slow. *Take a moment, take a breath.* I bristled. This was going to drag. Was I going to have to rein her in?

Take time, take care.

But then, as I listened more closely, I realized that the children were singing back to the adults. They were hearing the young voices tell *them* to take what they needed, like they were singing into some kind of mirror. As a performer, I knew I'd always have to deliver, to give, but *never* expected to *receive* anything from a performance—especially one that I thought was supposed to heal my audience.

Take heart, take hope.

A lump rose in my throat. And now, those young voices were singing the song I never got to sing—the song no one ever told me I was allowed to sing. I had spent my whole life proving, performing—trying to be good enough. But *joy?* I'd never given myself a moment to feel joy, much less take it. To *take pause* was dangerous. *Care* was indulgent.

Courage was for people who didn't know better. And yet for them, it seemed so easy. It was the quiet insistence that joy was their birthright.

Take a step, take a chance.

What would it be like to sing for someone—only to have them mirrored back to me? What would it feel like to encourage someone to take courage, or to take heart, or to take a stand, only to have them tell me—*sing* me—into doing the same for myself?

Underneath the sweetness of those simple, repeated melodic fragments, I finally heard Reena's intention: *Take What You Need* could be sung by anyone. Professionals, community members, even children. Like the words, Reena's music was an invitation: Anyone, anywhere, was welcome. And everyone could take what they needed.

Already late for rehearsal, I replayed the whole recording. Then again. And again. The dash read 9:33 a.m.

All I could think of was Dad. I knew he had been proud of me, but I wished I had told him to take pride in himself—or to take joy—or to take hope. Or pause. Or care.

And I wished he had taught me how to do the same.

But now, I sat there, late for rehearsal, sobbing behind the steering wheel, hoping no one could see me parked under a sign that read "No Smoking."

Aaron Copland, "Appalachian Spring"

[Echo Park, Los Angeles]

On Sundays, a small crew of musicians gathered in my apartment, including Amy, Reena, an expanding circle of interns, and musicians from other Street Symphony groups. I began to understand the world of mariachi and jazz musicians, of traditions built on lineages of memory and communal organizing, and how their art was no less rigorous than mine because they improvised—as opposed to recreated—the notes they played. Later, I'd realize that a lot of the composers whose music I had learned by rote had themselves been masterful improvisers and had come from similarly communal and shared traditions of creativity: Isolated genius was a myth.

As plates and glasses made their rounds, I thought of "Simple Gifts"—that Shaker tune Aaron Copland had folded into *Appalachian Spring*. I'd played it a dozen times with the Philharmonic, all sweep and brass and reverence, but I'd never understood it until now. Here, in this cramped living room filled with laughter and food and wine, I finally heard the song for what it was: a hymn to shared hands and common hunger. *'Tis the gift to be simple, 'tis the gift to be free.* The gift was not the music itself—it was the table, the company, the turning toward one another. Generosity creates the space in which we feel safe enough to begin listening to one another.

While hosting friends in my living room, West African musicians spoke about the djembe drum as a union of three spirits: the tree it came from, the animal whose skin stretched across the head, and the hands that played it. We talked about the ancient dance forms of Yankadi and Makadu, the meaning of the word *Ashé*—"Power, so it shall be, amen"—and how a community could be carried through rhythm. A reggae DJ taught us how to emancipate ourselves "from mental slavery." We read books on nonprofit strategy, debated the pitfalls of top-down leadership, and asked what it would take to build an arts organization that didn't replicate the same old hierarchies, rooted in patronage, performance, and prestige.

I'd order a pile of cheap Indian takeout, and we'd sprawl across the living room, buzzing with ideas and conversation. As Reena sketched a stage plot for the next *Messiah*, Amy suggested a program, and a couple of my Phil colleagues drifted in from a Sunday matinee, still in their suits, eager for a glass of wine. Having people in my home felt good, especially because it gave me an excuse to clear out the clanking, swollen bags of empty bottles and pizza boxes that haunted my most shameful moments. I loved the choreography of hosting—the quiet attentiveness, scanning a room to see who needed what before they asked. It felt like the best kind of performance: a quiet smile as I topped up a glass of chardonnay, the look of delight when I served a third, or fourth, samosa, or laid out a plate of jalebis. Feeding others made me feel full in a way that a private binge never could. It took me years to realize that this was the purest form of love I had received from my parents. Meals were the only time their love was abundant and unconditional: "Ai shona, kha."

After a couple glasses of chardonnay, I'd make a pivot to business. I laid out plans for the next *Messiah* like a general marshaling his captains, framing the project in the big, polished language of my new nonprofit fluency. Usually, the people in the room stared back at me, unimpressed. Amy teased me for slipping into "TED Talk mode," and though it stung, I learned to laugh with them.

Every time I stood at the whiteboard, I reached for the language that won money—impact metrics, deliverables, grant reports—still trying to frame human connection as a key performance indicator. At one meeting, I suggested we hand out surveys to Skid Row audiences after performances. "Maybe a few questions," I said. "Something simple—like, 'Did you feel inspired?'"

Reena didn't even look up from her plate of jalebis. "That's just idiotic," she said, still chewing. "How do you measure inspiration?"

She was right. A few months earlier, we'd workshopped *Take What You Need* at the women's jail in Compton. After one verse, Amy asked the women what kept them going. As they answered, I played the looping vamp—soft, steady chords under their voices. "My dad," one said. "My sister." A few women in the back called out names of loved ones. Then a young woman, no older than twenty-five, pointed to her belly. "My baby," she said.

By the end of the performance, the women were singing back to us—returning the hope and care Reena had written into the piece. In that moment, there were no performers and no audience, no "us" and no "them."

As the singers packed up, one woman waved at Reena, who'd been in the back scribbling notes on how to improve the score.

"Hey girl, aren't you gonna sing for us today? We had the whole choir, but we didn't hear you."

Reena blinked, startled, and took the woman's hands.

"Oh, I'm not really a singer," she said. "I just write the notes."

"Bullshit, honey! You sang for us at Towers, with that quartet—we remember!"

A few others nodded, smiling. As we left, one of Amy's singers leaned in to hug the pregnant woman. A nearby deputy looked down at the floor. Even there—in a place designed for disconnection, for punitive control—music had, even for a short time, closed the gap between jumpsuit and uniform.

Back in my apartment, others seemed to agree with Reena, nodding quietly. We didn't need to measure impact for funders who would never come to Skid Row. We were beginning to understand: In Skid Row, music wasn't a form of entertainment; it was a lifeline. Skid Row was a creative ecosystem, where people practiced reinvention the way I practiced scales. People came to the Mission, the clinics, and rehabs in Skid Row—those crucibles of transformation—shattered. And it was only after hitting rock bottom that they began the long, slow work of making themselves whole again. Art, as the German painter Gerhard Richter said, is the highest expression of hope, and in Skid Row, one always needed hope in order to begin again.

On another Samosa Sunday, Reena pitched an idea: We'd premiere a new, concert-length version of *Take What You Need* at that year's Messiah Project, with community members as narrators. The members of Christopher's choir would tell their story between the verses, and in response, everyone—the entire audience—would sing *Take*

What You Need. On my whiteboard, Reena drew circles and arrows between each group, sketching out a diagram of reciprocity: professional musicians, the Skid Row community, burned-out case managers, security guards, foundation reps in tailored blazers, and even the donors themselves.

Everyone in my living room understood the quiet distortion that happened when donors hovered over a project. They meant well, or said they did, yet they always seemed to stand just far enough away to keep their hands clean. But we had all visited the homes of wealthy patrons who seemed unhappier, for all their riches, than people who lived in Skid Row. We had experienced how the presence of money—and the control it bought—could drain the life out of a room before a single note was played.

But what if the invitation came from the other end? What if the people the world had discarded were the ones to lead the healing? After all, they were the ones who had led their own healing, together. Reena, Amy, and the musicians gathered around the meal at my home agreed. Skid Row had shown us how to take what we needed.

Who was to say Pasadena didn't need to take care?

Or that Beverly Hills didn't need to take joy?

Skid Row would show us the way.

~

After the next Street Symphony workshop for *Take What You Need* at the Midnight Mission, I wrapped the LA Phil's violin in a silk scarf and told my friends I'd have to skip the next Samosa Sunday. Another chair had opened at the front of the section, and I needed to practice. The next audition was just a few weeks away, and every night I wasn't playing an LA Phil concert, I made myself practice several hours of excerpts, even though the notes I played felt rote.

As I turned to leave the dayroom at the Mission, Reena looked up, gathering loose sheets into a folder.

"Vijay," she said, "I think you should let someone else have that job. You're going to leave the LA Phil someday."

I told myself she didn't—couldn't—understand. It would be reckless, irresponsible to not take the move-up audition. After all, wasn't Street Symphony just a charity outreach thing? Wouldn't my main job, my real job, always be the one of prestige, the one onstage?

Maybe Reena saw what I was unwilling to see: that I was being driven by a ghost, or the regret I thought that ghost deserved. When I played in the orchestra, my entire body burned with pain, and still, I hadn't taken a single sick day in my career. And now, I wanted *more*: I wasn't chasing excellence. I was outrunning grief. I needed a brighter spotlight to hide the dark places in myself.

Without Dad, I had no home. And without the LA Phil, I had no purpose. In the spotlight, I knew the rules. As long as I kept showing up and playing right on cue, no one would see how lost I really was.

Chapter 11

HALLELUJAHS

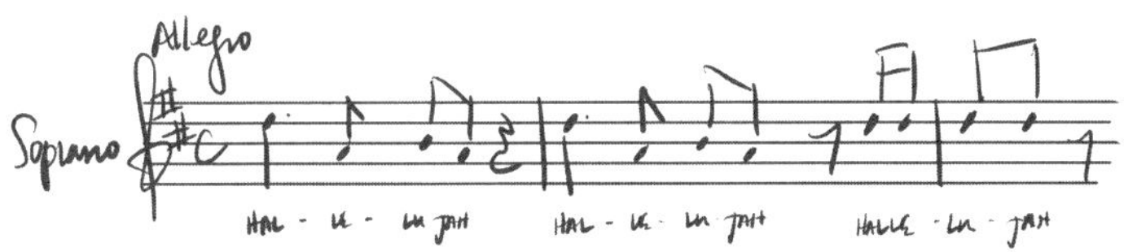

Handel, *Messiah*

My Lord, I'd be sorry if I only entertained them. I wanted to make them better.

—George Frideric Handel to Lord Kinnoull, c. 1750

George Frideric Handel, *Messiah*, HWV 56— "Hallelujah" / Leonard Cohen, "Hallelujah"

[The Midnight Mission]

That November, as Street Symphony prepared for our second Messiah Project, the news arrived that Leonard Cohen had died. Amy floated an idea: What if we sang his famous "Hallelujah" alongside Handel's?

Although Cohen had written more than eighty verses over five years, the final version was whittled down to a lean, secular benediction; its power came from everything he left unsaid. For Cohen, "Hallelujah" wasn't just an empty cheer but a promise to praise life, even through despair and loss. Gratitude is the quality of attention that makes this cracked world glow.

A few weeks later, outside The Midnight Mission, a circle of drummers blessed the sidewalk in Yoruba, their hands making goatskin sing.

"Ashé! Ashé!"

I wanted this year's *Messiah* to be a performance not just for Skid Row but *with* Skid Row. We'd invited musicians from all over the neighborhood to attend and sing, and some had even written their own songs. A small group, including Georgia, was dancing in the courtyard of The Midnight Mission, which had, just a few hours earlier, been an emergency shelter filled with cots and blankets.

And among the dancers was a woman from Beverly Hills, an LA Philharmonic patron I used to visit during intermission at the Hollywood Bowl, who had hosted my first ever Seder. Over the last several weeks, she'd gone door to door in her neighborhood demanding extra toiletries from friends fresh off tropical vacations. She knitted so many beanies for Skid Row that she gave herself tendinitis. Some gifts were more precious than dollars.

But for all the brightness and joy that surrounded me that day, I was still carrying a dread knot in my gut. Apparently a prominent music critic would be attending. What if Frank bailed, or Christopher's choir missed a cue? What if no one sang along with Reena's anthem, or Cohen's "Hallelujah" felt too cheesy beside Handel's? Part of me still cared so very much about what people thought, what people would say. After all, I had been raised that way.

That day, before I had even played a single note of music, my chest and ribcage had already seized with a burning, searing sensation. Upstairs in the gym, after Georgia's introduction, Frank stepped to the front of the room, unsmiling and wary. He was about to sing the opening aria of *Messiah*—"Comfort Ye." After this concert, I would only see him a few more times, and then we'd fall out of touch. In Skid Row, that happened often. Some found apartments or new lives and didn't look back. Others slipped into older, deadlier patterns.

The orchestra began a soft, pulsing line in E major, and Frank pressed his palm to his ribs and drew a deep, deliberate breath—the same way Daniel had taught him. His first notes wavered, his breath catching on a gulp of air, but the words were clear.

Comfort ye, my people.

He lingered on "my," and a smile spread across his weathered face, aimed straight at the crowd—his people. The ones who'd seen him through addiction, who'd sat with him through withdrawal, who'd held his name when he couldn't remember it himself. The ones who loved him when the rest of the world said he wasn't worth loving. Now he was singing for them, offering back the hymn that had guarded his nights.

"Yes, Frank," came a soft voice from a man in a brown jacket.

"Sing, brother. Sing!" an elder shouted from the back.

The voice of Him that crieth in the wilderness:
Prepare ye the way of the Lord, make straight
in the desert a highway for our God.

When Frank reached "Ev'ry Valley Shall Be Exalted," people were on their feet, dancing. Someone let out a holler so loud it startled a bass player. One woman swayed in place with her eyes closed. As Frank sang, several of the sopranos in Amy's choir gasped, and one tenor—who had been close to Daniel—wept into his score. A small pang tightened through me: Even though Daniel was gone, Frank's voice was moving through the world Daniel had opened for him.

When Frank finished his aria, the professional singers were the first to give him a standing ovation. When he turned to me, I rose to meet him, and he buried his giant, bushy head into my shoulder, sobbed once, then turned to face the audience. He didn't smile, but bowed deep, one hand behind his back and another across his front.

Reena Esmail stood up in a slant of sunlight, smiling gently. She pushed her bangs across her forehead and spoke into the glow left by Frank's performance.

"When people hear the word 'composer,' they think it means writing notes on a page. But the word really means 'to put things together.' Sometimes that's notes. And sometimes—it's people," she said.

"The text you'll hear is two things at once. It's a meditation, for yourself. A reminder to take a moment, take heart, take care. But it's also a wish for the people around you to do the same."

The music lifted with a hush, first sung by Amy's choir, and then Christopher's. The conductor turned to the audience, her arms opening like a bridge, inviting the room to join in. At first, only the people from Skid Row joined in. I saw a number of the donor-types—and the critic—sitting stone-faced, unsinging. I gulped, knowing that we were violating a cardinal rule of classical music: *Don't spook the money.*

We had printed the music into the program, so that people could follow along if they wanted, but none of the singers from Skid Row were using the music. Instead, they were each looking at someone in Christopher's choir—someone they *knew*. They were doing exactly what Reena had asked them to do: Send their song to someone they loved.

As the first verse ended, Christopher stepped up to the microphone. My mind raced—What would he say, and for how long? Behind him, Reena's harmonies looped in a soothing but poignant vamp. He looked out across the gym and spoke into a long-corded microphone.

"I started doing outreach in 2003," he said. "My first job was walking up and down these streets doing HIV surveys. I had to ask people really difficult questions. And I learned early on: No matter what you ask, you always leave a man with his dignity."

He paused. In the front row, Georgia nodded, and I caught the eyes of other staff from the Mission and nearby shelters. Many of them, like Christopher, had walked through their own addictions and had returned to Skid Row to help others.

"I cried for two years. Every day. Walking those streets, seeing what people were going through—it broke me. I used to think I was walking through the elephant graveyard. Like these big, beautiful souls were coming here to lay down and die."

He looked up, steady now. "But I also learned something else. People don't become homeless when they run out of money—they become homeless when they run out of relationships. When there's no one left to call. No one left who'll take the call."

Underneath his voice, Reena's music swelled. "But maybe homelessness isn't the end. Maybe it's the place where hope begins. Skid Row is not a graveyard but a place of the phoenix. Down here, I've seen people rise. They get jobs. They go back to school. They give back. They sing."

He turned back to his choir, cheeks wet with tears. As I had listened to Christopher tell his story, something had shifted in me. My ribs still ached, but the pain in my chest was moving up within me toward my throat, and my eyes watered. I wanted to cry so badly. I kept playing.

Take a moment…

The conductor lifted her arms. More of the room answered this time.

Take a moment.

Take a breath…

Take a breath.

I saw a cellist nod toward a man in the front row, urging him to take heart. A singer near Reena wiped his eyes and waved at someone in the audience. I learned later it was his mother, who had come to see her son perform after years of leaving him to grapple with his addictions in Skid Row. Now, she was part of celebrating her son's renewal.

Take a chance…

Take a chance.

The words surged through the gym—not from the stage, but from the ground itself, rising from people, into people, spilling outward across the vinyl tarp and folding chairs, up into the rafters and fluorescent lights, dissolving the line between audience and performer.

Take joy. Take pause. Take what you need.

And I remembered the words of a swami, written years ago in the margin of my Gita: "What you give, you get. What you never give, you never get." In my blurred vision, the room seemed to waver on the edge of something—an overbrightness, like noon light on fast water. Somehow, I wasn't in pain anymore.

After *Take What You Need,* Handel's "Hallelujah" rang out into the vast, connected field: Everyone was warmed up now, ready to sing, ready to celebrate, and as the choirs surged—*King of Kings*—I heard something else breaking through, woven between and through the music: bells, gongs, the shattering ululation of mashis, a piercing shonkho. For a moment, in that infinite in-between, I was hearing my first music again, like an arati of Handel, a pujo of music—*Lord of Lords.* The shelter rocked and it felt as if the earth opened, and *I* opened. And for a fraction of a measure, I saw what Handel must have seen when he wrote the "Hallelujah" chorus in 1741.

"I think I did see heaven open, and the very face of God."

It struck me then: I was making music in a sacred place. God wasn't just in a concert hall or a cathedral. God was the space within people, between people, brought alive by resonance. We were all part of an infinite Song—and that Song could be sung by anyone, anywhere.

Now, in a cradle of harmony, the gentle voices of men sang:

I heard there was a secret chord, that David
played and it pleased the Lord...

I listened, hearing Cohen's words as if for the first time, looking into the room of faces singing another "Hallelujah."

In trying to create belonging for others—for Skid Row and the musicians surrounding me—I hadn't yet figured out how to belong to myself. I could orchestrate an entire symphony for the streets of LA, but I hadn't yet taken a single honest step toward my own healing—toward taking what *I* needed. And somewhere inside, I knew why: It was simpler to save the world than it was to tell myself I deserved saving too.

And yet, Cohen's anthem revolved through the room like a koan.

I'll stand before the Lord of Song, with
nothing on my lips but Hallelujah.

What would be my answer for the Lord of Song?

George Frideric Handel, *Il trionfo del tempo e del disinganno*, HWV 46a

[Foundling Hospital, London]

In 1737, George Frideric Handel was a broken man. His music had once crowned a king, but London had lost its taste for Italian opera from this short, temperamental, corpulent German. His posters were ripped down. Creditors circled, threatening lawsuits—or worse, debtor's prison on Fleet Street. After a stroke left his right side paralyzed, his doctor pronounced, "We may be able to save the man, but we have lost the musician."

Even his friends turned on him. At his lowest point, his set designer, Joseph Goupy, published a cruel caricature: Handel slumped at the organ, belly distended, a ham draped across the keys, a pig's head grinning from the table. It was a public execution—meant to confirm what many already believed: that Handel was a grotesque foreign relic, out of touch and finished.

On April 8, 1741, he presented a farewell concert—including selections from *Il trionfo del tempo e del disinganno* (The triumph of time and disillusionment)—and billed it as "Mr. Handel's last performance for the benefit of his creditors." That summer, he left for Dublin, invited to stage benefit concerts for hospitals and prisons. Many saw it as a retreat. One account put it bluntly: "A great career had come to a tattered end."

But one person stayed by his side. Handel's librettist, Charles Jennens—a devout Anglican—had assembled a setting of the King James Bible, weaving psalms and prophecies from Isaiah, Job, and Revelation into a libretto that argued for the divinity of Christ at a time when Enlightenment skepticism was gaining ground. Jennens urged him to "lay out his whole Genius and Skill upon it, that the Composition may excel all his former Compositions."

Handel composed *Messiah* like a man possessed. In twenty-four days, he wrote more than one hundred pages. He barely slept or ate, and worked alone, as usual. When he completed the score, he signed it *Soli Deo Gloria*—"to God alone be the glory."

Exactly 370 days after his farewell concert, a few days before Easter, *Messiah* premiered at the Fishamble Street Music Hall. Operas were banned during Lent, but this oratorio—staged to benefit three charities, including one for debtors—drew a wide crowd. Advertisements asked ladies not to wear hoop skirts and gentlemen to leave their swords behind, so more people could be crammed into the hall. Some 700 people attended. During the performance, when Susannah Cibber—Handel's contralto, still mired in scandal—sang "He was despised and rejected of men," a chancellor of St. Patrick's Cathedral cried out from his seat in the audience, "Woman, for this be all thy sins forgiven thee!"

The concert raised the equivalent of $100,000: enough to pay off the debts of 142 men. Well, 143, counting Handel himself. The next year he staged *Messiah* at London's Covent Garden, billing it as "a New Sacred Oratorio." Audiences didn't quite know what to make of this work that was neither opera nor church service, but something in between. In one of the concerts, as the legend goes, King George II stood during the "Hallelujah" chorus—whether from devotion or simply to stretch his legs, no one knows—but the audience rose with him, and nearly three centuries later, audiences still rise for the "King of Kings."

But *Messiah* remained too unruly for London, so Handel kept revising. In a break from custom, he insisted it be performed annually. Before then, most music was only performed once, for a specific occasion, and then forgotten. In 1750, *Messiah* found its home: the Foundling Hospital, a refuge for abandoned children. Each year before Easter, Handel conducted benefit performances there with a professional chorus and London's top soloists. *Messiah* became the first Live Aid: Over a decade, the concerts raised more than £7,000—over $1.5 million in today's currency. It restored Handel's reputation, transforming him from a composer to a public figure of moral force.

In April 1759, days before his death, Handel conducted *Messiah* one final time. He collapsed soon after the concert and never recovered. In his will, he left the Foundling Hospital a handwritten score of *Messiah* and a portion of his estate. He was buried in Westminster Abbey, resting among kings and poets.

Within a generation, England forgot it had ever cast Handel out. Like the composer himself, *Messiah* became an institution. It stayed a fixture at the Foundling Hospital, raising money for the children, as Handel had intended. An oratorio born of failure and rejection had become his final act of grace.

After the Dublin premiere, Handel is said to have remarked, "I was sick, and now I am cured. I was in prison, and now I am free. I was in darkness, and now I am in light."

~

Messiah became a cultural phenomenon.

In 1775, Abigail Adams called a Boston performance "sublime," though she noted with irritation that a woman nearby chattered through the entire piece. In 1789, Mozart reorchestrated it for Viennese tastes, adding clarinets, horns, and trombones. By the Victorian era, attending an annual performance of *Messiah* marked one as properly pious, an edifying ritual that signaled membership in the moral middle class.

Around then, "classical music" was rebranded as eternal and refined, abandoning its improvisational, volatile origins. *Messiah* became a display of uprightness: Christian, choral, respectable, impeccably dressed. It was no longer performed to comfort the desperate, as in Handel's day, but to reassure the proper. Obsessed with decorum and national pride, the Victorians turned the oratorio into a spectacle of order.

By the mid-nineteenth century, *Messiah* had crossed oceans and denominations, echoing in cathedrals, colonial parlors, and civic halls. It gave amateur choirs something sacred to do, and concert halls a respectable anchor guaranteed to draw a public. By the 1880s, it was the most widely performed classical composition in the world.

In North America, it became a civic rite. In Toronto, Boston, Philadelphia, and New York, performances drew thousands, the soundtrack of a society craving transcendence but fearing transformation. As *Messiah* became absorbed into the bloated machinery of prestige, scale replaced spirit: the Crystal Palace performance of 1859 featured a chorus of 2,000. As one of my teachers at Juilliard used to say, "loud is beautiful."

At some point, *Messiah* migrated from Easter to Christmas. Presenters favored the Nativity—which was easier to market and celebrate—over the Passion, the occasion for which the work was intended. The "Hallelujah" chorus, torn from context—following the aria "Thou shalt break them with a rod of iron"—became a bombastic carol announcing the birth of a baby king.

By the time I reached conservatory, singing *Messiah* as a boy soprano at Juilliard Pre-College, the piece had become a rote, pedagogical tool—used to teach melismas, passaggio, word painting, orchestration. Later, as a violinist in historical performance seminars, I learned how to play without vibrato, how to use a baroque bow, and how to use the appropriate gauge of gut string. But for all we did to re-create Handel's musical intentions, we never once considered his human ones.

~

There is no such thing as classical music.

Not, at least, in the way we've been taught to believe it exists: a sealed-off canon, a universal language, a luxury good. "Classical music" is a branding strategy, a Victorian invention marketed like haute cuisine, haute couture, or haute horlogerie: precise, expensive, and European. But the music we now call "classical" wasn't written in airy, well-lit ateliers and ivory towers, but rather, by aching, bleeding, passionate, and flawed human beings—beings in grief, debt, exile, and love.

Take Bach—the most-streamed classical composer on Spotify today. Born the same year as Handel, he never reached any real fame as a musician during his lifetime, and he was better known as an organ mechanic and a midlevel church bureaucrat than as a musician, or even a composer. His superiors sometimes scolded him for writing music that was "too complicated." He spent his life juggling choirs, teaching unruly students, and absorbing grief after grief. Near the end, he went blind after botched eye surgeries (incidentally carried out by the same quack eye surgeon that made Handel blind), scribbling out what he could. When he died, his music was forgotten and largely unperformed, until Mendelssohn revived the *St. Matthew Passion*.

Mendelssohn was born Jewish, and his family changed its name in an effort to live and work within a society that limited Jewish participation. His parents gave him a new identity to enter society—and he spent his life never fully accepted. A prodigy, a polymath, a composer, painter, and conductor, he gave everything to his art. But when his sister Fanny—his musical twin—died suddenly, he broke. He followed her into death barely six months later. He was thirty-eight. Later, prompted by the composer Richard Wagner, the Nazis would attempt to erase Mendelssohn, banning his music and even tearing down his statues.

This list goes on.

Beethoven died estranged from his brothers, hated by his nephew, drunk, deaf, and alone. He wrote "Ode to Joy" after thirty years of obsessive sketching—an anthem to a brotherhood he never found. At the Ninth's premiere, he stood onstage, still conducting long after the music had ended, unable to hear the ovation until a soprano turned him to see the crowd waving handkerchiefs. On his deathbed, he asked to see Handel's scores again. "There is the truth," he said.

In Italy, Verdi buried his wife and both children before he was thirty. He vowed never to compose again. Then, out of that devastation, he wrote *Nabucco*. Its chorus, "Va, pensiero," became the anthem of a nation's longing for freedom. When he died, he asked to be buried not in state but among the elderly musicians he had supported, and even housed, with his wealth, who he called his "children of sorrow."

Bartók was a refugee in New York. He had fled fascism and left behind his home, his friends, his archive. Poor and dying of leukemia, he copied folk melodies in a threadbare apartment and collected butterflies for solace. He wrote his Third Piano Concerto as a gift for his wife, Ditta, so she could have a career after he was gone. The final bars were unfinished when he died.

For all my training, I had never been taught to connect, or even consider, the human lives of composers as I learned their music. In a sense, I wasn't even trained to think of them as human beings at all. But when I brought the music of Bach and Brahms, Bartók and Beethoven, Clara and Robert Schumann, Mendelssohn and Handel into Skid Row, I wasn't presenting some lifeless canon. I was playing for people living through the chaos of withdrawal, court dates, psychosis, fresh grief, and the daily strain of staying alive. In those shelters, clinics, and jail wards, my colleagues and I played without the usual armor, because the people listening had none. Their responses were immediate and unvarnished, and in that clarity, we recognized the original spark—the feeling that made us want to be musicians in the first place.

And whereas it's not always true that a composer's music reflects the circumstances of their lives, something about playing music in Skid Row made us think about the humanity of composers and their art—in ways we never had. In Skid Row, or in the jails, the stories of the composers—their imperfect, wholly human lives—shifted into focus. Schumann's visions made sense beside men fighting their own minds. Bartók hit like heavy metal inside concrete walls. Brahms's melodies became the unfulfilled longing of lost love. Handel sounded less like ceremony and more like someone reaching for his own redemption song. Beethoven's anger felt familiar to people who knew something about abandonment. And Reena Esmail's work bridged cultures and continents, and the impossible, irreconcilable worlds of Bunker Hill and Skid Row.

Once, at The Midnight Mission, a man in our audience came up to me and said, "Thank you for playing fucked-up music for fucked-up people." I laughed and gave him a fist bump. What I should have said to him was that we played music because we were trying to understand something, *anything*, about ourselves, our place in the cosmos, and what to do with our short time here on earth. And perhaps we could only understand questions that vast through small, fleeting, and uniquely precious interactions—like smiling at someone on the street, or offering a friend a second helping of samosas, or playing a concert for people in Skid Row.

I should have told him how fucked up I was, too.

George Frideric Handel, *Messiah*, HWV 56—"The People That Walked in Darkness"

[The Midnight Mission]

Before our third Messiah Project, Christopher, Reena, and I distributed T-shirts printed with the words from the song "Beautiful City" to people outside a mobile hygiene center. Beside us, a cellist played a Bach prelude. When one man asked for a shirt, I invited him to the concert, and he scraped a grime-caked hand across his forehead, considering the cellist, and then exploded in a thick Spanish accent.

"No! I don't want to listen you, no *gringo música*!"

Even after years in Skid Row—where yelling men were a constant presence—I still felt a flicker of panic. This one stood rigid, raving in rapid Spanish I couldn't follow, arms slashing the air. I turned away, prickling with regret. If my Spanish had been better, I would've told him that upstairs, in the second-floor gym, a troupe of women mariachis were about to sing.

When the time came, Georgia—glowing in a red skirt and blue blouse—welcomed the crowd. Then, the mariachis played a bright burst of strings, letting out *gritos*—shouts that carried grief and joy at once. I'd seen the mariachis perform at Men's Central Jail, where they'd worn brightly colored skirts and blouses, almost in defiance of the drab brown and concrete of the jail. At the end of one concert there, they'd sung an anthem by Juan Gabriel, Mexico's beloved gay pop icon, and a group of inmates in light blue jumpsuits leapt up to sing along. Deputies told us afterward that they were gay and transgender inmates, rarely allowed amid general-population inmates for their own safety.

The only time they were included at events was for Street Symphony, because the deputies felt the music lowered tensions within the jail.

The mariachis launched into "Guantanamera," and the man I'd seen outside, the one raging at me in Spanish, stood at the back of the gym. He had raised his fist high above his head, and tears were streaming down his cheeks. He was singing every word.

After a few numbers of *Messiah,* a tall, strapping man named Brian, a member of Christopher's choir, as well as his sponsee, stepped up to the mic, ready to sing. A few weeks earlier in the dining hall of the Mission, he had been nervous, gulping air like a weightlifter about to attempt a personal record. His teacher, Scott—a professional vocalist in Amy's choir—had been working with him for months. Before Brian sang, Scott told him not to worry and to "focus on the words."

"You know these words. You've lived them. Just sing your story. We're just walking each other home, right?"

Brian nodded, steadying himself. And then he sang.

The strings entered behind him with a slow, slurred gesture, opening into a wide vista of light:

The people that walked in darkness have seen a great light:
They that dwell in the land of the shadow of death,
Upon them hath the light shined.

Before leaving the stage, Brian turned to the crowd.

"One act of love," he said, "I know for sure, is to listen."

~

Two weeks later, I picked Brian up from his apartment so that we could attend the Los Angeles Master Chorale's annual singalong of *Messiah* at Disney Hall. We shared his score, the one he used for his solos, and I kept my finger glued to the bass part we sang together. From the terrace, he hummed through "The People That Walked in Darkness," proud to recount his triumph. Outside the hall we posed for a selfie, which I would caption "From Skid Row to Disney Hall."

But there was no redemption story for Brian, the same way that there wouldn't be one for many of the people I'd meet in Skid Row. Often, "success" in Skid Row—recovering from homelessness and addiction—involved returning to family dynamics or circumstances which could send people reeling back into old, deadly patterns.

Even after singing a solo in Skid Row—or, in Brian's case, being featured in *The New Yorker* and Dateline NBC—there was no white-picket fence American Dream, no easy redemption story. That was stuff for Hollywood, not real life. Often, the best that folks could hope for was a tiny one-bedroom Section 8 unit and a general relief check, maybe some food stamps, and, for Brian, a construction job that probably didn't include health insurance. And even then, nothing was guaranteed: Stability could vanish overnight. Injuries happened on jobsites and, after a prescription of opioids ran out, a relapse could happen any time.

A few months after the singalong, Christopher would call to tell me that Brian's "big heart had stopped." I told myself that it was impossible. I had been telling his story all over the country: He was proof, he was my impact metric, and most importantly, he was my friend. Denial was easier than accepting how hard the climb had been for him every single day. And denial was easier than admitting that there was nothing I could have done to save Brian, or to save anyone at all.

But as I sat at his memorial, weeping, all I could think of was the tattoo he'd commissioned with the money I gave him for his *Messiah* solo: a phoenix, to honor Christopher. The last time he'd shown it to me, I'd marveled at the red-gold sheen of the bird's beak and head, but the wings were still outlines, to be filled in another time.

Brian's phoenix would be forever incomplete, only ever rising—climbing higher, *higher*.

Richard Rodgers and Oscar Hammerstein II,
***Carousel*—"You'll Never Walk Alone"**

[The Midnight Mission]

In December 2018, eleven-and-a-half years since my audition, I played my final performance with the Los Angeles Philharmonic. The program—which featured Brahms's Second Symphony—was conducted by Zubin Mehta. My buddy Shawn, who had played with me at Street Symphony in jails, shelters, and on tours, had asked Mark, our personnel manager, if he could sit with me. Together, we listened to a turn from the cellos, a lift of horns answered by a flute. In Brahms's music, written during a rare, happy moment in the composer's life, the sun rose through clouds tinged with shadow, like morning light on a wharf with the sharp tang of sea air.

Then Shawn and I played, entering the light with a single, soft high "E," suspended and singing. We held it steady, then descended, step by step, down the A string, down the D string, until we reached the bottom of our instruments and had nowhere else to go. For a moment, the music turned dark. The timpani gave a low rumbling warning and a bass plunked once—a single drop of rain—but then, the horns began their melody, and the sun broke through, and the doubt was gone.

In the audience somewhere was my teacher, Glenn Dicterow, who had retired to Los Angeles, the city where he'd grown up. Even though I couldn't see him, I played for him, remembering the sound. And I played for—and with—Shawn, my friend who had become like a brother. For us, Brahms was all the joy we would ever need. I would miss him. I would never stop loving this music. But it was time for me to move on.

A week earlier, at Street Symphony's fourth annual *Messiah*, we were joined by two singers from Skid Row: Linda and Patrick. I'd first seen Patrick during Christopher's clinic improvisation game a few years earlier. He was slight and wore a black pleather jacket and trucker cap, and his hands shook with a parkinsonian tremor. Charles—an elegant tenor from Amy's choir—had coached him through "You'll Never Walk Alone" from the musical *Carousel*. Linda had joined Chris's choir the year that Reena composed *Take What You Need*. Inspired by Hindustani music, Linda had requested to learn how to sing in a raga. One of Reena's collaborators, a vocalist named Saili Oak, taught Linda the ornamented phrasing and curlicue hand gestures of Hindustani vocal technique. Linda, whose right arm was swollen with edema and wrapped in gauze, found the motions painful, but she said she sang better when she could "see the music" in her hands.

Like Patrick and Linda, many older folks in Skid Row were "permanently" housed in Section 8 or subsidized units, but barely—trapped in a web of red tape where one misfiled form could mean the loss of food stamps, therapy, and their hard-won apartment. Patrick even told us not to pay him; if his income ticked a few dollars too high, he'd no longer qualify for benefits and could even lose his apartment.

Two weeks before the concert, he had a bad case of nerves. After more than a decade living alone in single-room occupancy housing, he carried the dread that getting recognized or even seen for his talent could jeopardize the fragile stability he'd built for years. After years of homelessness, he had learned to survive by staying invisible.

Charles, Patrick's coach, had spent months helping him feel safe enough to sing, coaxing out confidence little by little. He even asked if Street Symphony could cover massage therapy to loosen the tension trapped in Patrick's body. Patrick was having trouble projecting his voice. He had grown up under an abusive father who had frequently yelled at him, and since then, he'd spoken in a hushed near-whisper. He never wanted to sound like the man who had hurt him.

At the performance, the drummers opened the afternoon with Yoruba chants, and the mariachis followed with an exuberant prelude. Their lead singer—draped in embroidered lace and flowers—spun across the gym floor with a man in a red T-shirt who looked stunned to find himself dancing with a radiant woman crowned in blossoms.

I slipped into my seat in the back of the second violin section. To my left sat Shawn. To my right was a Persian violinist who had once been homeless, who'd come through the Mission's recovery program, and to whom I'd given a few *Messiah* lessons backstage at Disney Hall. Soon, he'd land a steady job driving soloists and guest conductors for the Philharmonic.

After a few movements of *Messiah*, Patrick stepped up to the mic, shoulders curled in their familiar hunch. Across the gym, Charles walked into the center aisle, placing himself directly in Patrick's line of sight. During rehearsal he'd told him, "Forget the crowd. Just sing to me. Hold your head high—like the song says."

Patrick took a breath, rolled his shoulders back, and lifted his chest. His voice emerged, reedy, and I noticed that his hands, for once, were not trembling.

When you walk through a storm, hold your head up high,
And don't be afraid of the dark.

Patrick's eyes stayed fixed on Charles, who stood in the aisle mouthing the words, his hand pressed to his chest. And then the room seemed to shear away—clean, sudden—like a glacier breaking from its ridge. My vision swam.

Dad. Dad would have done the exact same thing.

Like Patrick, I had sworn I would be nothing like my father, the chirping Bulbul. But over the past few months I'd started to realize how much of him lived in me. At home, notebooks piled across my dining table, scrawled with codes and acronyms for grant portals. I thought of Dad's desks when I was growing up, littered with airline locator numbers scribbled on the backs of envelopes. Then, on my resignation letter to the Philharmonic—the same hard, slanted block capitals—we had the same handwriting.

I ran Street Symphony the way he ran his business—constantly codeswitching. In an instant, I could shift from TED Talk to earnest organizer, from orchestra pro to clinical metrics, from fundraiser to roadie. I could charm and cajole and people-please the same way he did. On donor calls I wanted to avoid, I rolled my eyes and flipped the phone the same way Dad had flipped his while Shonu and I giggled. The fidgeting, the nail-biting, the late-night binges—the hope to love and be loved. The ache for legitimacy. Behind the extroversion, we shared the same restless anxiety, the same search for purpose, for home.

If he was Charon, ferrying people across continents, then I was the boatman's son, building a bridge of music between Skid Row and Bunker Hill: Patrick and Charles, Brian and Scott, Frank and Daniel, Linda and Saili. Reena, Amy, and all those singers in her choir, creating music with Christopher and the Skid Row singers. The mariachis in the jails, the drummers in the parks. Mr. Ayers and me—playing symphonies on the streets of Los Angeles.

Walk on, walk on,
with hope in your heart,
And you'll never walk alone.

And I couldn't deny it anymore: I was him, both because of him and in spite of him. He was there all along—in my charm, my grit, my anxiety, my addictions.

As Patrick took his bow, hugging Charles, I saw what I had avoided since Dad's death: my father, myself—a fractured reflection of one. And that the only way to keep loving him was to love the only part of him I had left.

Me.

And when the "Hallelujah" chorus began and the shelter rose to its feet in jubilation, I broke down. I buried my face in my hands, and the two violinists on either side of me—one from Skid Row, the other from Disney Hall—held my shoulders.

Chapter 12

BEGINNING AGAIN

Tagore, "Boro Asha Kore"

> How do you end homelessness for sixty-nine thousand people? One person at a time. With love. And trust. And patience. And hope.
>
> —Georgia Berkovich

Heinrich Ignaz Franz von Biber, Passacaglia in G Minor

[Benning Violins, Studio City, Los Angeles]

Grief is a strange restringing.

Even after loss, the person we love remains alive as braids of connections within us, active circuits of neurons firing into a void, like a severed string trying to sing. Our brain predicts their voice, their touch, their smell. We have rehearsed this connection—this love—trillions of times, and our brain keeps practicing that connection, even if its recipient only exists as the tangled loop of our memory. Neuroscientists call this disorientation of grief a prediction error: Our brain is just too good at remembering.

But as old circuits become quieter, one learns to live a different self, weaving that neural wiring into new connections, new routines, and new relationships.

So we begin again. We restring ourselves into new patterns. We retune and rewire our brains and bodies and beings. And perhaps, in that way, grief is a sacred gift, one that reminds us that we are out of tune, just practicing at life.

~

After my last concert at the Phil, I walked into the backstage office and handed Mark the orchestra's million-dollar violin. Before I let it go, I took one long last look. The back of the Montagnana was a book-matched two-piece of tiger maple from the Dolomites, its stripes worn down by centuries of hands, the deep red varnish fading in places to pale gold. I'd only played it for four years—a blink in its long life—but it had shaped me around itself. Perhaps I was more its instrument than the other way around.

Being a steward of anything precious is knowing how, and when, to say goodbye. The violin would pass to another member of the orchestra. A few years later, I'd hear about the accident at Disney Hall: the missed step onstage after rehearsal, the fall backward, and the violin flying out of the musician's hands, hitting the stage with a *crack* and shattering into dozens of splinters across the stage. Even a priceless instrument, I learned, is still a thing. And no thing lasts forever.

But as I closed the case that day, I realized I wasn't only returning an instrument: I was giving back someone else's dream. That violin belonged to a life I no longer wanted, a version of myself trained to vanish, to be a perfect part of a perfect organism. I didn't want to disappear anymore. I wanted to find an instrument that would help me find my way to my own voice. And I wanted to be part of helping an instrument find a voice that could, with luck, outlast me.

A few months later, I walked into Benning Violins, the LA luthier's shop I had first visited with Dad twelve years earlier. Eric Benning was the third generation in a family of master makers, and the shop had become a regular stop for me during my time in the Phil. That day, the light from Ventura Boulevard glanced off the wood of instruments hanging from the walls of the shop, and the sharp tang of pine pitch and turpentine made me feel as though I were stepping into the body of the instrument I'd come to find. Eric's son Nathan greeted me, followed by his father, Hans, who had worked on instruments for 1950s superstar soloists like Jascha Heifetz. At the front desk, Nancy, Eric's mom, looked up from a neat stack of receipts and asked me about an upcoming concert. They made me feel welcome, and I could have spent hours playing the violins and bows in that shop—or just watching Eric bring a new violin to life.

He used the same techniques Antonio Stradivari had used centuries ago: hand-carving a scroll with a small gouge, attaching the thin resonating plates of the instrument with hide glue, letting an instrument cure in the sun before applying coats of varnish. Then, Eric would brush the Benning family's own recipe of bright-golden varnish, made from a mix of amber and resin, crushed cochineal, and iron oxide.

Once Eric's violin was in my hands, I didn't want to stop playing it. For five or six hours a day, I practiced concertos and sonatas and études, living into its silver-sheen, moonlit sound. I felt like I was playing light itself.

I returned to music I hadn't touched since childhood—Biber's Passacaglia for solo violin, written in 1676 as a hymn to the Guardian Angel. Four notes toll like footsteps, steady beneath a melody that rises and returns, each variation a prayer offered in motion. As I practiced, I began to hear the music showing me how to live inside repetition—how to begin again without starting over, how to let the same notes open into something new.

After a few weeks of this kind of practice, the strings began to fray. The metal windings around the nylon cores loosened, and small shards of coil caught on my fingers. I ordered replacements: synthetic cores with nickel winding, aluminum A strings, silver Gs, chrome and tungsten blends. But they weren't the right match for Eric's violin. Some were too bright and tinny, and others felt hollow, choking the instrument's voice. On a whim, I ordered a set of strings made from wound gut—sheep intestines washed, scraped, stretched, and dried. For centuries, surgeons used the same material as sutures, threads strong enough to close a wound and then be absorbed back into the body. I lifted one string up to the light, and then another. Each was dense and faintly luminous with striations running through a narrow column of amber light. They warmed quickly in my hand, as if a different kind of life was still ready to move through them.

At first, I didn't know how to secure them to my instrument, so I looked up "how to tie a clove hitch" on YouTube. My fingers trembling with excitement, I threaded the string through the tailpiece and drew it taut. Then, I threaded the other end of the string through the peg and pulled it through, tightening and plucking the string. The knot at the tailpiece broke with a snap, biting into my hand. I cursed, trimmed the end, and tried again.

I plucked and twisted and listened. I rubbed the taut string with my palm to warm it, and tightened the peg again, hearing the *crick-crick-click-ik-ik* as the string settled into its pitch.

Just like the strings, I would learn how to live in the tension.

"La Caña"—Traditional Son Jarocho

[Downtown Women's Center, Skid Row]

Mi padre fue cultivando
la tierra a cada minuto,

Y la tierra le fue dando
cariño calor y fruto. . . .
Que yo soy como la caña
que crece en la inmensidad.

My father kept tending
the land, minute by minute,
And the land kept giving him
affection, warmth, and fruit. . . .
For I am like the sugarcane
that grows in the vastness.

—"La Caña" (traditional son jarocho, made popular through Patricio Hidalgo and El Chuchumbé)

Four centuries ago, in the port of Veracruz, a new music was born. The sounds of conqueror and slave, Native and migrant, braided together into what became son jarocho. Spanish and Portuguese vihuelas—tuned like Arabic ouds and strummed with indigenous horn plectrums—turned into the jarana and requinto, their rhythms drawn from Africa and the Caribbean. At first, *jarocho* was a slur, aimed at mestizos and mulatas who danced *el chuchumbé,* a dance the Church tried to ban for being too lascivious.

Like the ingredients of the Americas that changed global cuisine forever, the dances of the New World—fandangos, passacaglias, and chaconnes—became popular in European courts, woven into Renaissance and Baroque suites. But the roots of that music, which later went on to inspire Bach, and Brahms, stayed in Veracruz, in the street, in the people who refused to stop singing.

When the son jarocho group called Son California began playing with Street Symphony—in prison yards and Skid Row parking lots—I stood back and watched in awe. Their music was elastic but often settled into a rollicking 6/8 groove that switched between pulses of two and three—exactly like in the Baroque dances I'd played since I was a child, like the gigue and courante. The rhythms were tight, the harmonies simple, but the glory was in the *décimas*: improvised ten-line poems, sung in Spanish, launched with a long, wailing *ayyyyyy*—part call to prayer, part invitation to party.

They sang of laborers cutting cane under a punishing sun ("La Caña"). They praised the love of a dark-skinned woman ("La Morena"). They sent firecrackers snapping at dancers' heels ("El Buscapiés"). Even "La Bamba"—long before Ritchie Valens—was faster, rawer, improvised on requintos and jaranas, calling for *una poca de gracia* for anyone boarding the ship of life. The fandango—the communal gathering at the center of *son jarocho*—was a shared stage where musicians and dancers built the music together, answering one another in real time, much the way a life is built: step by step, phrase by phrase, shaped by whoever shows up.

And no one could hide from life. At a community center in South LA, Son California's lead singer, Marisol—who went by the stage name La Marisoul—handed handmade maracas to kids and welcomed them into the circle. I stood mute, holding my violin, struggling to follow the décimas with my 8th grade Spanish, when someone called out, "Vijay! Come play!" Panic rose—my old improvisiphobia—and I demurred, trying to act humble. I didn't know their songs, and the last thing I wanted to do was trip them up, or more honestly, embarrass myself. The jaraneros laughed. "Then what good is all that super-violin training?"

I gave in. At first I fumbled, relying on perfect pitch to pick out the chords to play. Sometimes, I kept playing a full measure after the song had already ended. Then, in "La Morena," Jorge—who sported an LA Dodgers cap and switched effortlessly between jarana, requinto, and accordion all while singing harmony—cued my solo: "Okay, time for

Vijay! GO VIJAY! SOLO!" My bow shook, so I leaned into it and began to tremolo, playing rapid, jagged notes with my bow, while my left hand climbed higher until I ran out of fingerboard, then slid back down in a screeching glissando to cheers. I had blown through Marisol's solo and lost the pulse completely, but the band forgave me. When they asked me to join them again—this time at a Mexican restaurant in a hipster neighborhood—I said yes without even checking my calendar.

I was catching on: *Se necesita una poca de gracia*. I needed a little grace. And this is how I would learn the way.

At a women's prison in Chino, I watched grandmothers grow young again, belting Aaron Neville with Marisol. At the Downtown Women's Center, a security guard with bright blue eyes asked if he could sing a mariachi tune at the end of our set. I tried to brush him off, but the jaraneros completely ignored me and extended their set, learning the guard's song on the spot. They had a rule: If anyone wanted to make music with them, they never said no. Jorge told me that this was the essence of their tradition: not just to sing, but to help everyone *else* sing, too.

The jaraneros were teaching me the concept of *compromiso*—meaning "shared promise"—the artist's promise to a community, which granted the artist solitude to work, and a reprieve from the obligations of daily communal life. In return, the artist committed to return to them to tell the truth: the truth they had discovered in their practice, the truth they'd found in the world, even the uncompromising truth that could hurt, or offend. The community knew to invest in—and trust—their artists, because the artists weren't just entertainers, but *curanderos*, healers and culture-bearers, stewarding the medicine meant to restore their community and themselves.

When the guard finished, flushed and proud, he turned to the women in the shelter and said, "I know I'm here to keep you safe. But now you know what I really do."

Johann Sebastian Bach, Cantata BWV 82, *Ich habe genug*

[Union Rescue Mission, Skid Row]

A clerical error brought Linda Leigh to Skid Row.

In her sixties, after a breast cancer diagnosis, she turned to painting as her medicine. Between chemo sessions she'd made up her mind: It was time to chase a lifelong dream. She packed up her things in Los Angeles, moved out of her apartment, and put down a nonrefundable deposit at the School of the Art Institute of Chicago. She wanted to be in "a snappy place with snappy food and snappy people."

Then came the paperwork. A missing graduation date on her high school transcript made her ineligible to enroll, even though she already had a college degree. When she asked the registrar if he'd consider a "hardship case," he looked at her blankly.

"What's that?"

She pointed to herself. "That's me."

The answer was no, and overnight, her savings vanished with the deposit. The next day, Linda boarded a train back to Los Angeles. She stepped off at Sixth and San Pedro, and managed to find emergency shelter at the Union Rescue Mission. For months, she survived on essentials: a bag of toiletries, a threadbare square of cloth for a towel, a hard cot lined up beside 150 other women. From the dormitory windows, looking out over San Pedro Street, she saw faces like her own.

"My God," she thought. "Are we broken?"

After what felt like years of red tape, Linda finally qualified for a room at the Russ Hotel: her own room, with a bed, a door, and a vase holding two lonely flowers. She had never realized how precious a door could be. When she sat on the bed—her bed—she wept. On the blanket lay two wrapped chocolates, a small sweetness to welcome her home. It was enough to make her feel human again.

Linda chose to stay in Skid Row, where she'd always have plenty of work to do. She volunteered at the Downtown Women's Center, making lunches. She comforted the women like they were her daughters.

She created tile mosaics, acted in plays, and held exhibitions of her paintings, donating the proceeds to her new family.

The first time I met her—a few years after launching Street Symphony—she was in a Skid Row art studio, brush in hand, working on a dark canvas depicting her mother's wedding. The lace of the dress blurred like fragments of cloud over the blocky outline of her father's World War II army uniform. In her mother's hand were six blossoms: a bouquet foreshadowing the six children she would bear.

She calls herself "Hari Deva"—the joined names of two Hindu gods. But across Skid Row, as Linda walks through the streets, people call out to her, telling her to be careful. "Look out, Ms. Lady," they say. She is treated with the same respect and dignity she gives to others.

Some call her "Mother Linda."

~

During the first weeks of the pandemic, I started to listen to a particular piece of music, over and over: gentle waves of paired thirds, a pulsating, descending line that was half dirge, half dance—an upward wail of an oboe in a motif of grief, echoed by a voice that sang a lullaby of departure. This was music of grief and praise, life and death united in harmony—the unsayable contradictions of life which can only be sung: *Ich habe genug,* a beloved cantata of Johann Sebastian Bach.

Meaning "I have enough," the cantata was written for one singer, an oboe, and a small orchestra—celebrating the early February feast of Candlemas, the purification of the Virgin Mary, and the presentation of Jesus at the steps of the Temple. The music depicts the biblical scene of the old man Simeon, who cradles the infant in his arms and realizes that his life is fulfilled:

Ich habe genug,
Ich habe den Heiland, das Hoffen der Frommen,
Auf meine begierigen Arme genommen;

Ich habe genug!
Ich hab ihn erblickt,
Mein Glaube hat Jesum ans Herze gedrückt;
Nun wünsch ich, noch heute mit Freuden
Von hinnen zu scheiden.

I have enough,
I have taken the Savior, the hope of the righteous,
Into my eager arms;
I have enough!
I have beheld him,
My faith has pressed Jesus to my heart;
Now I wish, even today with joy
To depart from here.

Even though I had never played this piece of music before, I knew it, and had *craved* it ever since I was a student, the same way I had loved Brahms. I was unsure of when or why I'd ever get a chance to learn the music, or ever perform it, but during the looping days of the pandemic, when life had been stripped bare, there was little else I wanted to hear.

And the more I listened, the cantata morphed into new forms, knocking on the doors of my mind, like the myriad forms of a trickster deity: *I have enough. I am enough. I've had enough.*

And Life played along. On long walks near the Huntington Gardens, I'd find myself singing the opening aria into the shining sun, astonished as a Cooper's hawk dove in sync with a plunging oboe. The second movement lullaby would come unbidden during repetitive, monotonous worldly tasks, chopping vegetables or stirring a large pot of chili. The eager, dancing third movement—a joyful minor that united life and death in one—was the soundtrack of a fierce rescue puppy who nipped at my old LA Phil tour T-shirts, literally ripping past identities off my body.

Ich freue mich auf meinen Tod,
Ach, hätt' er sich schon eingefunden.
Da entkomm ich aller Not,
Die mich noch auf der Welt gebunden.

I delight in my death,
Ah, if it were only present already.
Then I will emerge from all the suffering
That still binds me to the world.

But as much as I wanted to put on the cantata for Street Symphony, I couldn't find a good enough reason. How could I make Bach—this jowly, Lutheran, Saxon—relevant to an audience in Skid Row? I imagined the groups sitting in shelters, wheezing in dorms; those who wished nothing more than to depart the crowded shelters, to be quarantined with whatever family would accept them. How might the story of Simeon on the steps of a temple be offered to them with the same soul-nourishment it offered me?

One pandemic morning, I called Linda. Her niece—barely out of her twenties—had recently died. Linda was spending the pandemic with her daughter in Dallas, calling in for Zoom voice lessons on "Deep River" and "God Bless the Child." On the phone, Linda told me that singing had helped her find the path of her mourning, and she wanted to help others find some encouragement, to help them find what they needed. She wanted people to feel like no matter who they were, they'd *have enough.*

I froze on a patch of lawn, under an avocado tree heavy with hard unripe fruits. What did it mean to have enough? The first notes of the opening aria hung in the air, like cradling comfort. *Genug.* I recounted the story of *Ich habe genug,* and halfway through my recitation of the text of the first movement, Linda interrupted me.

"Vijay, *Vijay.* Honey. Can I tell *you* something?"

She spoke to me in a gentle, thick accent, dropping her r's and g's, her vowels round.

"Do you know what my niece said as she was dying? She kept ripping off her ventilator and saying 'God, *enough*, I've had *enough*. I want to go. I'm *done*.'"

The words of Bach's cantata flooded me:

Mein Gott! wenn kömmt das schöne: Nun!

My God, when will the lovely "now" come?

The realization was like a bolt of lightning: Linda was my key to how we could present the cantata in Skid Row. She'd tell the story of her life like a sermon between the movements, weaving the story of her life in Skid Row and what it meant to make art, to have purpose—to have enough. It would be like the original purpose of the cantatas: to intertwine the sacred lessons of music and humanity.

I hesitated for a moment. But would the story of Linda's niece be too raw for Linda to recount in front of an audience?

"No, Vijay, we have to tell her story. It would honor her life, her memory. She's a part of me now."

Her niece was named *Simone*.

~

A few months later, we workshopped *Ich habe genug* with Linda in Skid Row, first playing at the Downtown Women's Center—where Linda had volunteered for lunch services even though she was still homeless—and then at The Midnight Mission. Between the movements of the Cantata, she told us more of Simone's story.

After she ripped off her ventilator and begged to be released, Simone had fallen into a coma. Soon, a doctor pronounced her "brain dead."

The family reeled. Linda's sister would have to make the impossible decision to turn off her own daughter's ventilator. Linda suggested they sing Simone an "Ave Maria," since she was Catholic. When they finished singing, Simone had died.

As Linda spoke, at the center of a semicircle of musicians, I noticed that people in our audience were hanging on to every word she said. Linda had always held herself in a posture of power and grace, but now, I felt like she had become a kind of mother—not only to people in Skid Row—but to me, too.

Between movements at the Mission, a Black woman in the audience raised her hand. By her side was a small stroller with a panting, slightly mangled Chihuahua. Linda called on her.

"I just want to thank you for telling us your story, Ms. Lady. I'm in the same place you were—sleeping in that crowded dorm downstairs—and I've been asking questions about who I am, and what I can give the world. You're giving me hope right now, mama. You're showing me I have a way out. Thank you."

Linda nodded slowly, nearly regal. "You know, I've been thinking recently about *mothers*." My stomach dropped and something in me went cold. This wasn't part of the script we had rehearsed. Linda was going off-book.

"We need to forgive our mothers. The first thing I did when I became a mother was to forgive my own. It helped me move on and become a better mother myself. I just couldn't carry her any more..."

Whenever I thought about my mother, which was more often than I wanted to admit, I felt a gut-wrenching bitterness. I wasn't ready to forgive her, but I saw her everywhere. Every time I came to Skid Row and saw a stocky figure with short, curly black hair, I did a double take, wondering if Mom had finally taken me up on my invitation for her to come see me play in Skid Row. The last time I had spoken to her, I told her how heartbroken I was that she had never acknowledged Street Symphony.

"Why are you going to places like that?" she asked. "You're a Brahmin. Our people don't go to the smashan," referring to the cremation grounds, forbidden and unholy for people of our caste.

"You may as well become a Suzuki teacher."

And yet, I knew that she was the flesh that had made me. If my outgoing personality was wrought from Dad's chameleon charm, my grit was all her: the determination, the self-inflicted harshness. The fear and the strength. The tightness in my gut that I carried around like a child I was protecting from the world. Her body had become my being, and that was a debt I could never repay.

I wish I had told Mom that in the myths I had read as a child, the smashan is also the place where Shiva, the God of change, awaits his rebirth.

After the performance with Linda, in a room overlooking the corner of Sixth and San Pedro, I talked to my friend Georgia Berkovich from the Mission about how hard it was to forgive our mothers. She said, "I spent my whole life looking for love from my mother, but what if my mother never *got* the love I was looking for? Once I realized that, I started *giving* her the love I wanted."

During a break in one of our rehearsals, I walked up to Linda, my heart pounding. I wanted to share some exciting news, but I was nervous. In my pocket was a key to a new home in the mountains, north of LA, with three century-old citrus trees in the backyard. I hadn't breathed a word of it yet, even to my closest friends. At first, I felt trepidation. Would it be boastful—arrogant, even—to tell Linda, a woman who had once been homeless, that after years of saving, and looking, and trying, that I finally had a house, a home to call my own?

I knelt by Linda and whispered into her ear. I wanted someone to be happy for me. I wanted a mother's blessing.

"Oh Vijay, that's *wonderful*. I'm so happy for you."

She laid a gentle, puffy hand on my cheek.

"You will make such beautiful music there."

Franz Schubert, "Ave Maria"

[Twin Towers Jail, Los Angeles]

When we were children, Shonu and I were companions in our parents' world of expectations. The Gupta brothers, a duo in bunk beds and matching flannel pajamas, twins in music, violence, and love.

When Shonu turned thirty, I sent him a watch, one with cathedral hands and a compass bezel. The dial was a deep green, a color I hoped he still loved, the way he had when we were boys. I wear a matching watch on my wrist, hoping that one day, we'll find our way back to each other.

~

After Mom told me to become a Suzuki teacher, we didn't talk for a while. But during the second year of the pandemic, I finally read Shinichi Suzuki's book *Nurtured by Love*, wondering if I could still learn something from the musical system that had raised me.

Suzuki had been born in Nagoya, Japan, and was the son of a violin maker. His father had built instruments but never played them. Suzuki himself didn't start until he was seventeen, when he heard Mischa Elman play Schubert's "Ave Maria," which Suzuki described as "soul-shaking sweetness."

Later, in Berlin, he met Albert Einstein, who reached for the violin whenever thinking grew difficult, letting music clear a path while the math simmered. Einstein's simplicity stayed with Suzuki, how music was inseparable from the scientist's inner life. "The real essence of art turned out to be not something high up and far off. It was right inside my ordinary daily self," Suzuki wrote.

In 2022, a week before Christmas, I played a Street Symphony event at Twin Towers Jail. Beside me, Shawn stood, not holding a violin, but a viola. He was working on his own restringing, too. As I gave him the cue that would begin a duo by Mozart, bending my knees as if to launch into a dance, I smiled, realizing who I was reminding myself of: Ms.

Behrend. I had been thinking of her, as I read Suzuki's writing. She had always danced when she played, even in the chemotherapy ward at the Rusk Institute, where Shonu and I had once asked Dad why the children were bald.

Dad had told us that one day we'd understand—and now, I think I did. Ms. Behrend had made music come alive for dying children. She had made the children and the parents see that music didn't need to be a special occasion reserved only for special places, but that music was for everyone. And she had made music come alive in me. Seeing her in myself at Twin Towers, I realized that Street Symphony hadn't originated from me at all: from any desire to do good to others, to bring them, or myself, any kind of healing. It had been Ms. Behrend's idea all along. And now, if I was lucky, I would just continue her work.

Before we left, an inmate asked if I could play an "Ave Maria" for him. I played, and he leaned his head back and closed his eyes. When I finished, he asked if I could play it for him again. I did, and this time, he sang along with me.

I was glad to accompany him.

Rabindranath Tagore, "Boro Asha Kore"

[Altadena, Los Angeles—Montgomery, New York]

After a decade of being a hundred pounds overweight, I started to see a nutritionist. He told me to start "by putting the good things in." Shame could no longer be a staple in my diet. Maybe discipline didn't have to feel like punishment, or deprivation. Maybe self-care was just the end of self-harm.

My diet would be simple: fish, greens, and lentils. Maybe a bit of rice. His smile was gentle. "I bet you ate something like this as a kid, right?"

Macher jhol, thorkari, and daal.

I had. They were the dishes Mom had cooked while I practiced. Now, I realized, all the while, I had been hungry for Mom's love.

When I emailed her, asking for her recipes for daal and puishaak, she also sent a translation of Tagore's "Boro Asha Kore," in her handwriting. It was the first song I'd learned from my family, and somehow it had become my life's prayer—its themes and variations.

I have come to you, filled with great hope—
Please do not send me away, Life-Giver.
No one cares for the poor and downtrodden,
yet I know you will shelter me.
I ask for nothing but this: Let me sit at your feet.
I ask for nothing but this: Let me call you mother.
If you refuse to keep me, where will I live?
Weeping, weeping, where will I wander?
I see it—the deep, thick night of darkness,
dense, overwhelming, Life-Taker.

~

It took me a few years to settle into the small blue house in the Altadena foothills. The days there felt different. Quieter. The old citrus trees were heavy with fruit, and the green parrots screeched across the ridge as if announcing a life I was still learning how to live. At night, a pack of coyotes called from a nearby golf course. The neighborhood itself seemed to impart a kind of steadiness I had never known. For the first time in my adult life, I was home.

Each day revealed a chance to practice the spiritual hygiene of attention: the way light played on the brown canyons, turning gold at one hour and purple at the next, the kestrel calling after a rare storm, and the will of wildflowers. Love was a kind of attention tuned to twin poles, equally outward and inward: toward the outer world I loved, and toward myself—the person I was now learning required the same kind of attention.

On my daily walks near Eaton Canyon, I'd listen to Dad's favorites. Nusrat Fateh Ali Khan. Paul Simon's *Graceland*. In the evenings, around dusk, a small bird would come sit on the telephone wire outside my studio. It had a dark body with a spot of red under the tail. Pointed crown. After a minute, he twitched away, but he'd stayed long enough to sing a sharp, chattering song. I used an app called Merlin to figure out what kind of bird it was. When I saw the answer, I gasped.

A red-vented bulbul.

~

In January 2025, a ridge ignited in the Pacific Palisades and wild Santa Ana winds engulfed one thousand homes in twenty-four hours. A day later, along the course of my daily walk, a failed power line exploded and the hurricane-wind turned the air into the color of rust. A line of flame worked its way down the slope. Houses crumpled, wrapped in smoke. Embers drifted at random. The sky reddened and dimmed and the mountain grew even brighter.

Two days later, when I returned to the house—which had miraculously survived—I shoveled the ash of my neighborhood into a Ziploc bag. I kept it in my studio, under a picture of Dad.

Months later, on the banks of the Hudson, I released the ashes into the river.

I still don't know where Dad's ashes are scattered, but every day, I will try to sing him home.

~

Later that summer, I performed at a music festival in the Berkshires, two hours away from where I grew up. On a day off, I rented a car in Albany and drove south down the Thruway until it met Interstate 84, and got off at Exit 17K toward Montgomery. I had been avoiding going home for thirteen years.

When I pulled up to the gate, the picket fence had rotted through, and the tall Norway spruces had grown into a thick, foreboding wall. The yard was swallowed in shadow. A plastic lawn chair lay overturned. The ornamental pear tree, the one that had given me my first violin bow, had split down the trunk and collapsed across the deck. Even the air felt neglected. I knew Mom was living somewhere else now, but she had kept this house. She'd listed it on Zillow a bunch of times, and I assumed I'd be coming back one last time to say goodbye to a home that would no longer be in our family, a home that would become someone else's dream.

The moment I heaved my shoulder against the basement door, the smell overwhelmed me. Rot. Mold. Piles of refuse rose in every room, some several feet high. Every window was covered with black plastic bags and the light inside was dim and stale. Upstairs, in a closet, Dad's suits were stippled with a green bloom.

Dad used to joke about how Mom would never throw anything away, how she reused cooking oil until it turned rancid, how she saved every piece of our childhood clothing. Every bag, bowl, and shirt had to be kept for reasons that only made sense to her.

But now, after so many years in Skid Row, I thought I knew what I was seeing: the heaviness of despair, the terror of letting go of an old life. Mom had kept telling me to return, to come home, that everything would be okay when I did, but now I could see that she had been living in the ruins of a life she hoped I would put back together.

My whole life, I had lived according to Mom's fear: that the world was out to get me, that if I got too big or ran too fast or fell in love—or became myself in any way—I'd be ruined. The truth was that without me, my mother couldn't be the only thing that had ever mattered to her: my mother. And now she couldn't see the shape of a fear that had shaped her world, a fear now—given the state of my childhood home—impossible to ignore. What she saw instead was my distance, my refusal to reenter her version of being her son: my betrayal.

After a few hours of walking through the house, I became overwhelmed, and I had to leave. I drove to Torino's in Newburgh, my favorite childhood bakery, where the small, worn, linoleum-tile kitchen smelled of fresh buttercream. I bought a chocolate cake—the one I had always asked for on my birthday—and a box of Italian wedding cookies. Downtown Newburgh felt hollowed out in a way I recognized from other towns where the factories had shut their doors and the center never knit itself back together. The old mills stood quiet and rusting along the Hudson, their brickwork fading toward the same color of murky, faded earth as the river. A few storefronts clung on, lit by whatever hope kept them open. People moved with fatigue. The sense of neglect felt different from Skid Row, quieter and somehow more desperate. Part of me wondered where the local shelter was.

Back in my car, as I was about to bite into a cookie, a man and a woman waved me down. They looked to be in their sixties, their faces worn in ways that would have frightened me when I was young; now I recognized the lines of hardship, the earnest veneer of a story told many times. Somehow, I already knew the story I was about to hear would be devastating, and that the storytellers were already expecting to walk away empty-handed. But I listened.

Their house in New Windsor had burned down, and now they were sleeping by the river. The man told me that the manager at the Super 8 on Route 300 had promised him a job folding sheets and a place to stay if he could pay a fifty-dollar room fee for the first night.

I knew that motel. The Patels who ran it had once bought their tickets from Dad. Without really knowing what I was doing, without planning it, I reached into my wallet, took out the fifty I kept for emergencies, and handed it to them with the cookies. Maybe some part of me was moved by their story and so grateful that my home had survived a fire. Maybe it was because I wished that I could have given them the keys to my own childhood home.

Homelessness is not only an epidemic of poverty and isolation, but of apathy. We ostracize the people we call "the marginalized" because we fear our own spiritual poverty, the dispossessed parts of ourselves we have pushed into the margins of our minds. The cost of this inner banishment is that we miss learning from what—and who—we so mistakenly call broken and irredeemable: In rejecting the people we call the least among us, we reject ourselves, too.

What I learned in the neighborhood of Skid Row confirmed something Jung intuited: Whatever we avoid in ourselves returns at the edges of our lives, often in the face of the person we least want to see. Jung also said "in sterquilinis invenitur"—"in shit it shall be found": that what we most need to find will be in the place we least want to look. Perhaps the creative act is so transformative because it requires us to bring light to the dark places inside ourselves. Perhaps the act of going to Skid Row to make music had been me bringing light to another's darkness. And now I might try to bring light to my own.

Before I left the house, I went down to the basement, the place of my first song, and now a heaping warehouse of decaying memory. Beneath newspapers and warped lids, I found two VHS tapes from 1992: my first Suzuki recital, my first "Twinkle." The shelves still held Dad's travel notebooks and binders filled with my notes for Chem 202. In a closet still filled with Dad's molding clothes, I found a red Mickey Mouse tie, preknotted for a child's neck. From a shelf layered with books on justice and spirituality, I pulled beloved novels off the shelves, and placed two books—my old copies of *The Namesake* and *The Iliad*, the pages thick with notes I had left in the margins as a teenager—in my suitcase. I packed one of Dad's old shirts, which would fit me now, and one of his notebooks, filled with old reservation codes and the names of Bengalis written last name first.

Upstairs, in a cupboard buried behind towers of garbage bags and cardboard boxes, I tried looking for the white stone from Jerusalem. As I cleared a path toward the cupboard, wading through pounds of bundled trash, I opened the cabinet door. On the bottom shelf was a black leather case. I pulled it out and opened it.

Inside was a 1/16-size violin. Even though the bridge had collapsed, the strings were still attached. I closed the case, descended the stairs back down to the car, and carefully placed my first violin in the back seat, ready for its journey home.

CODA

Bob Dylan, "Knockin' on Heaven's Door"

[The Midnight Mission]

I've recently joined a guitar class. The instructor, Philip, is gentle, soft-spoken, and for the past several years, he has been running Midnight Strings, which takes place in the library of The Midnight Mission. Classes last twelve weeks. In the first few sessions, beginning guitarists learn basic chords and strumming patterns. Then they start writing their own songs. Once, Linda helped them write a song titled "Grateful Power," which has since become their anthem. Philip often guides the group through "Worried Man Blues" and "Amazing Grace." Sometimes the son jarocho musicians come by. Other times, the mariachis.

During one of the sessions, we were learning Bob Dylan's "Knockin' on Heaven's Door." Seven chords: G–D–Am–G, then G–D–C. The strings cut into my fingertips, the neck was too wide, and my thumb began to cramp because I was trying to press down a clean D chord. I'd fumble the G—index finger too low, ring finger sliding off the string in a loud twang. How did they make it look so easy? I was bad at this, and that was good.

In the corner of the room, I watched a man open a violin case. Inside was a bright green instrument with its bridge set backward, strings slack. He asked if I could help, and I nodded. He sat beside me, and I guided his fingers, showing him how to tune the strings, winding them into coils around the pegs. While the rest of the circle played Dylan, we tuned his violin string by string. I showed him how to place the instrument on his collarbone. When he was ready, we joined in—him on his violin, me on guitar—both of us out of place, accompanying the circle's steady chords. I improvised something simple he could play on his violin, and wrote it on a piece of paper.

G–D–A–G
G–D–E

He looked up at me, holding his bow, searching my face for what to do next.

"Hey, man," I said. "Just play the open strings."

ACKNOWLEDGMENTS

The stories in this book may be astonishing—even miraculous—but what has made them so are the exceptional people I have been fortunate to surround myself with, a symphony of guides and challengers who pushed me toward a truer self.

I'm indebted beyond measure to Pico Iyer, who read several barely ready drafts of this book, and whose mentorship guided me into the life of stillness required to listen to the space between thoughts. Rebecca Gayle Howell applied her exacting insight to the structural and developmental edits to this book, and I am grateful for her many lessons.

The team at the Lavin Agency—David Lavin, Charles Yao, Tom Gagnon, and many others—have brought this work into rooms I could not have reached on my own. Through their advocacy, I have shared the story of Street Symphony with countless campuses, companies, and communities across North America, and the resonance of how music can be medicine has been a constant wellspring of encouragement.

I'm grateful to Alex Ross for introducing me to Farley Chase, who helped steer this project to Brant Rumble. My thanks to the team at Da Capo and Grand Central Publishing, who shaped this book into its final form.

This book could not exist without the many people who live and work in Skid Row, the largest reentry zone in America. Over the past fifteen years, I have met tens of thousands of people in clinics, shelters, prisons, jails, hospitals, and reentry centers whose names I never learned, but who raised their hands and asked questions, or shared stories, or sang back to me when I was dumbstruck and scared, or showed their vulnerability, and their humanity, when I was too afraid to show mine. In the face of despair, they sang *Hallelujah*, and encouraged me to do the same.

I'm grateful to Nathaniel Ayers and Steve Lopez, whose friendship taught me how to become an accompanist, as well as to my many teachers in Skid Row, including Linda Leigh, Christopher Mack, and Georgia Berkovich Hawley, and to Black Lincoln Kennedy, Don Garza, Duane Garcia, and the late Brian Palmer and his family. My deepest thanks to the tens of thousands of people I have met at The Midnight Mission, the Downtown Women's Center, the Weingart Center, and the Skid Row Arts Alliance for carving an altar in my heart. Deep thanks to Urban Voices Project, Los Angeles Poverty Department, and Piece by Piece, among many other Skid Row arts organizations.

The musicians I met at the Los Angeles Philharmonic said yes to me when I didn't know how to say yes to myself, and taught me how to listen better: Camille Avellano, Jin-Shan Dai, Zach Dellinger, Carrie Dennis, Barry Gold, Jonathan Karoly, Marion Kuszyk, Teng Li, Kazue McGregor, Oscar Meza, Jeff Neville, Mitchell Newman, Tao Ni, Ellie Nishi, Joanne Pearce-Martin, Danny Rothmuller, Esa-Pekka Salonen, Lyndon Johnston Taylor, Ben Ullery, and Jim Wilt.

I'm forever indebted to Amy Fogerson, who has tolerated my inability to respond to emails for twelve years and counting while assembling one of the most soulful vocal ensembles I have ever known. I'm immensely grateful for the life lessons I learned from Tamara Bevard, Scott Graff, Charles Lane, Alice Kirwan Murray, Dr. Zanaida Robles, and Kristen Toedtman. And Daniel Chaney, for bringing exultation to the valley.

I learned jazz standards from Brandon Bernstein and Putter Smith, reggae from Sir Oliver, mariachi anthems from Las Colibrí and Las Chorizeras, and dances of the Yoruba tradition from the Ashé Ashé Drummers. Philip Graulty taught me how to hold a guitar. Federico Zuñiga, Jr., La Marisol Hernandez, and the jaraneros of Son California taught me *una poca de gracia* and welcomed me into the deeper practice of *compromiso*. Valerie Bischoff and Louis Ng helped tell our story.

I am immensely grateful to the countless musicians, staff, board members, advisers, and supporters of Street Symphony, and to Rebecca Mlenar and Carina Whaley.

I'm grateful for the generous mentorship of Maureen Markel, Toni Saldivar, John Pagano, Joan Panetti, Markus Rathey, Bob Lynch, and Liz Lerman and to this book's readers across countless rewrites: Eve Claxton, Ryan Davis, Eliana Estrada, Toni Jensen, Yumi Kendall, Madison Marshall, Laurie Niles, and Joe Williams. Special thanks to Erik Elmgren, who exchanged years of weekly essays.

A nomoshkar to Naren Schreiner, my karmic soul-swap brother, and to my collaborators, Yamini Kalluri, Ian Pritchard, and my Darshan Trio brothers, Dominic Cheli and Yoshika Masuda. I am also grateful to my friends and collaborators at the Strings Festival in Steamboat Springs, Music Worcester, and Emmanuel Church (and special thanks to Pamela Dellal for her lyrical translation of *Ich habe genug*) and to the countless presenters across the country who have invited me to play, speak, and share my work. My deep thanks to Dan Visconti.

I am grateful for the hospitality of Alda and Ozair Esmail and Sandy and Barry Pressman, who have always made me feel welcome.

I have been myself restrung by the guidance of Debi Fries, Teya Wolvington, Harvey Slater, Eric Shah, and Daniel Hernandez, who stood with me at the edge of exhaustion and helped me find my way home.

I am grateful to my mother, to my brother, and to Dad; to Rusty, who kept watch through every page and every mile; and to Reena, for more than everything.

SUGGESTED READING

Alexander, Michelle. *The New Jim Crow: Mass Incarceration in the Age of Colorblindness*. New Press, 2010.

Davis, Mike. *City of Quartz: Excavating the Future in Los Angeles*. Verso, 1990.

Day, Dorothy. *The Long Loneliness*. Harper and Brothers, 1952.

Frankl, Viktor E. *Man's Search for Meaning*. Beacon Press, 1959.

Gioia, Ted. *Music: A Subversive History*. Basic Books, 2019.

Hernández, Kelly Lytle. *City of Inmates: Conquest, Rebellion, and the Rise of Human Caging in Los Angeles*. University of North Carolina Press, 2017.

Hogwood, Christopher. *Handel*. Thames and Hudson, 1984.

Hyde, Lewis. *The Gift: Creativity and the Artist in the Modern World*. Vintage, 1983.

Jourdain, Robert. *Music, the Brain, and Ecstasy: How Music Captures Our Imagination*. HarperCollins, 1997.

Kidder, Tracy. *Mountains Beyond Mountains: The Quest of Dr. Paul Farmer, a Man Who Would Cure the World*. Random House, 2003.

Kidder, Tracy. *Rough Sleepers: Dr. Jim O'Connell's Urgent Mission to Bring Healing to Homeless People*. Random House, 2023.

Klein, Norman M. *The History of Forgetting: Los Angeles and the Erasure of Memory*. Verso, 1997.

Lopez, Steve. *The Soloist: A Lost Dream, an Unlikely Friendship, and the Redemptive Power of Music*. Putnam, 2008.

McGilchrist, Iain. *The Master and His Emissary: The Divided Brain and the Making of the Western World*. Yale University Press, 2009.

Ross, Alex. *The Rest Is Noise: Listening to the Twentieth Century*. Farrar, Straus and Giroux, 2007.

Sacks, Oliver. *Musicophilia: Tales of Music and the Brain*. Knopf, 2007.
Suzuki, Shinichi. *Nurtured by Love: The Classic Approach to Talent Education*. Alfred Music, 1983.
Taruskin, Richard. *The End of Early Music: A Period Performer's History of Music for the Twenty-First Century*. Oxford University Press, 2009.
Whitaker, Robert. *Mad in America: Bad Science, Bad Medicine, and the Enduring Mistreatment of the Mentally Ill*. Basic Books, 2001.